Readers are invited to view and download
five worksheets that are designed to accompany
Building Donor Loyalty and help you to build the outline
of a donor retention plan for your organization.

The worksheets are available FREE on-line.

If you would like to download electronic copies
of the worksheets so you can print them out
or fill them out on your computer, please visit
www.josseybass.com/go/buildingdonorloyalty

Thank you,

Adrian Sargeant and Elaine Jay

BUILDING DONOR LOYALTY

The Fundraiser's Guide to Increasing Lifetime Value

Adrian Sargeant
Elaine Jay

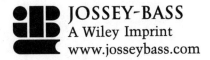

JOSSEY-BASS
A Wiley Imprint
www.josseybass.com

Published by Jossey-Bass
A Wiley Imprint
989 Market Street, San Francisco, CA 94103-1741   www.josseybass.com

Jossey-Bass books and products are available through most bookstores. To contact Jossey-Bass directly call our Customer Care Department within the U.S. at 800-956-7739, outside the U.S. at 317-572-3993, or fax 317-572-4002.

Jossey-Bass also publishes its books in a variety of electronic formats. Some content that appears in print may not be available in electronic books.

Readers should be aware that Internet Websites listed in this work may have changed or disappeared between when this work was written and when it is read.

Library of Congress Cataloging-in-Publication Data

Sargeant, Adrian.
  Building donor loyalty : the fundraiser's guide to increasing lifetime value / Adrian Sargeant, Elaine Jay.
      p. cm.
  Includes bibliographical references and index.
  ISBN 0-7879-6834-X (alk. paper)
  1. Fund raising—United States. 2. Philanthropists—United States—Attitudes. 3. Nonprofit organizations—United States—Marketing. I. Jay, Elaine. II. Title.
  HV41.9.U5S27 2004
  658.15'224—dc22

                                                                                           2004015678

Printed in the United States of America
FIRST EDITION
HB Printing   10 9 8 7 6 5 4 3 2 1

CONTENTS

TABLES, FIGURES, AND EXHIBITS

Tables

Figures

Exhibits

PREFACE

"Loyalty—we need to build the loyalty of our donors!" Both the academic and the fundraising literature are currently full of such demands to develop a focus on retention and to build long-term and productive relationships with donors. Almost every book in the field these days contains a call to action or a demonstration of how donor loyalty can be fostered and engendered.

Why all the sudden interest in retention? The obvious answer is cost. The days of high-volume–low-cost donor acquisition are long gone. Mail programs no longer routinely yield response rates of between 10 and 20 percent; the economics of fundraising and in particular direct-marketing fundraising have changed. In addition, public interest in and scrutiny of the costs of fundraising have increased. As a result, sensible fundraisers concentrate their efforts and resources on "watching the door"—keeping their attrition rates low—rather than striving to recruit ever greater numbers of new donors.

Work conducted at the Indiana University Center on Philanthropy suggests that fundraisers are relatively optimistic about the fundraising climate and their ability to fundraise—and with good reason. In the United States total giving to the nonprofit sector in 2002 stood at $240.92 billion, a 1 percent increase over the previous year. A staggering 90 percent of Americans now give donations to non-profits, with people giving on average 2 percent of their income and contributing nearly 85 percent of the total income the sector generates (American Association of Fundraising Counsel (AAFRC) Trust, 2003). Participation in giving has never been higher, and the public appears to be as generous as ever.

These figures suggest that it should be relatively easy to find new donors. But the headline figures represent only a fraction of the total giving equation. Along with these buoyant levels of giving, the number of nonprofits has grown, and the percentage of certain segments of society that are willing to support good causes has declined, particularly families in which the head of the household is under thirty. The figures are also misleading. Although almost 90 percent of Americans give to nonprofits, much of this giving is low-value and spontaneous. In fact approximately 80 percent of the funds coming into the sector are coming from only about 20 percent of the donating public. As a consequence when nonprofits talk about soliciting funds from their donors, only a comparatively small percentage of American society constitutes the audience for this endeavor.

The combination of these factors has led to a fundraising environment that is increasingly competitive and hostile. Many more organizations are working ever harder to solicit charitable dollars from a donor pool that is at best static and in some cases declining. Individuals who actively support nonprofits find themselves being asked more frequently, being asked in a wider variety of ways, and being asked by a plethora of different of organizations.

Therefore, if nonprofits are to succeed, they need to stand out from the crowd and to develop fundraising practices that reflect the genuine needs of donors, inspire commitment to the cause, and build loyalty over time. In this book we identify exactly how these tasks can be accomplished, drawing on the best of both academic research and professional practice. We explore here how donors pick organizations to support, what keeps them loyal to their choices, and the strategies nonprofits can adopt to foster and develop this loyalty.

This book is not an academic summary of the available research or a comprehensive guide to individual fundraising. Instead, it offers a series of practical recommendations that are designed specifically to increase donor loyalty to nonprofit organizations. It is directed toward professional fundraisers working at all levels within nonprofits and with all categories of donors. Some of the lessons are specific to a particular area of professional practice, but many are applicable across the board.

The book is not designed to be read from cover to cover, although if you are unfamiliar with donor retention you may find it useful to do so. The first two chapters provide an overview of the topic, with the chapters that follow dealing with specific aspects of donor loyalty and how it can be fostered. In these chapters we summarize the findings from a major research project we have been involved with; the study surveyed by mail and in focus groups some twenty thousand individual donors. It identified both the reasons that donors give for lapsing and the factors that underlie their decision to do so.

As we show, individuals lapse for a variety of reasons; each of the chapters that follows addresses one or more of these dimensions. In Chapter Three we explain how knowledge of why people give can foster retention. Although many nonprofits are successful in their fundraising, few understand the psychology and sociology of giving, and few can therefore be definitive about why people choose to support their organizations. Such an understanding is important because donors give in response to a particular set of stimuli and to a particular set of circumstances and events. Although some organizations may just be lucky in the design of their fundraising appeals, those that understand why individuals support them are much better placed to design programs that genuinely reflect donor needs and aspirations and therefore to design programs that actively seek to foster donor loyalty.

Many donors lapse because of the way they are treated by the fundraising department. Many resent the transaction approach to fundraising, which still pervades many nonprofits. Donors frequently prefer a relationship with the organization that can be fostered and developed over time. They like organizations that interact with them, listen to them, and respond to their needs. In Chapter Four we discuss relationship fundraising and how the traditional tools and techniques of fundraising can be used to foster long-term relationships with donors.

The development of a relationship fundraising strategy is entirely dependent on an organization's developing a fundamental understanding of the needs and preferences of its donors. In Chapter Five we outline the research tools and techniques that fundraisers can use to acquire this knowledge. We explore some of the more common pitfalls in undertaking this research and explain the errors that can occur in the interpretation of data, errors that can lead to the development of poor fundraising strategies.

In Chapter Six we describe how knowledge of donor needs can be used to segment the donor base and to develop an appropriate standard of care and pattern of communication for each distinct group. We explore how demographic, lifestyle, and behavioral variables can be used to structure the approach to an organization's donors. We also address segmentation by examining the needs of specific groups of donors, such as direct-mail donors, major donors, and bequest pledgers. We illustrate how each category of donors can be appropriately retained and developed.

In the United Kingdom, fundraising activity has been moving away from the solicitation of single gifts to the development of regular, or committed, monthly giving. This switch has radically changed the economics of fundraising and has facilitated the development of loyalty, typically improving retention rates by as much as 100 percent. Monthly giving has also been used for some time in Canada and is beginning to make inroads into the United States. We discuss the lessons for loyalty that emerge from this form of giving in Chapter Seven and provide an overview of the factors that organizations have learned from experience affect retention in this context. We examine the needs of monthly givers, the best routes to developing these individuals, and how donor loyalty can be maintained.

Alongside the growth in committed, or regular, giving has been an increasing emphasis of late on the design and creation of fundraising products (such as adoption and sponsorship schemes). As we show in Chapter Eight, these too can be powerful tools in developing donor loyalty. Successful fundraising products effectively package the needs the organization tries to meet and make it immediately clear how a particular donor's contribution will be used to meet those needs. We provide a number of examples of successful fundraising products and illustrate how they foster donor retention.

As we show in Chapter Two one of the key factors driving donor loyalty is how satisfied donors are with the quality of service the organization provides them with. Although donors are understandably concerned about the quality of service provided to the beneficiary group, many also have concerns about how they are treated by the organization. In Chapter Nine we explore the impact of service quality on donor retention and discuss how a nonprofit can measure the quality of service it provides and how it can improve its level of service.

In Chapter Ten we consider the critical role that donor recognition and feedback can play in retention and provide a guide to good recognition practice. We discuss the mechanics of recognition and the various forms that recognition takes, and we provide a number of illustrations of successful professional practice. We also explore how patterns of recognition can and should vary for different segments of the donor database.

Loyalty does not come cheap. No book about donor loyalty would therefore be complete without a detailed examination of the leading metric in this field— donor lifetime value. A strategy is worth pursuing only if it is economical in the sense of enhancing how much a donor will be worth to the organization over the full duration of his or her relationship with it. In Chapter Eleven we explain what we mean by lifetime value, illustrate how it can be calculated, and show how it can be profitably used to inform fundraising strategy.

The final chapter of the book draws together all the disparate strands. In Chapter Twelve we provide a framework for retention planning that will allow readers to consolidate previous learning and to begin the process of developing retention plans for their own organizations. The chapter provides a step-by-step guide to the preparation of such plans as well as a number of analytical models that can be used to inform fundraising practice at every stage in the retention-planning process.

In this book we provide a great deal of information that is relevant to direct-marketing media. We have therefore used the language of the direct-marketing industry to express our ideas but are aware that some readers (perhaps, for example, fundraisers working with major donors) may find this terminology strange or even offensive. In particular direct marketers have adopted (from commercial enterprise) military analogies, employing terms such as *targeting* and *acquisition*. We believe that the use of such terms is unfortunate because they do not reflect what fundraisers are striving to do. We are certainly not at war with our donors! Because their use reflects current professional practice, we are simply being pragmatic when we occasionally use them here. We hope that before long the profession develops terminology that is more appropriate to nonprofit-donor relations and look forward to the day when we can switch to employing these new terms in our work.

If you can forgive us for an occasional inappropriate use of language, we think you will find this book of value. We recognize that not all our suggestions are relevant to all organizations or all fundraisers, but as we demonstrate, making just a few small changes to fundraising strategy can greatly enhance the loyalty of your donors. We are confident that this book will provide you with at least some ideas for realizing that goal.

Devon, U.K.   Adrian Sargeant
July 2004   Elaine Jay

THE AUTHORS

*A*drian Sargeant is professor of nonprofit marketing at Bristol Business School, University of the West of England, and an adjunct professor of philanthropy at the Indiana University Center on Philanthropy. He is the editor of the *International Journal of Nonprofit and Voluntary Sector Marketing* and is the author of *Marketing Management for Nonprofit Organisations,* published by Oxford University Press.

Elaine Jay has over fourteen years of experience as a fundraiser; she has worked for a number of charities, including the Royal Society for the Prevention of Cruelty to Animals, where she was head of individual fundraising for six years. She has also held several agency positions, at Amherst Direct Marketing, WWAV Rapp Collins, and Personal Fundraising Partnership. She is now a director of the consultancy firm Sargeant Associates Ltd.

CHAPTER ONE

WHY DOES LOYALTY MATTER?

Does loyalty really matter? As long as we can keep recruiting new donors, does it matter how many of them will offer a second and subsequent gift? After all, if we are always able to find new supporters, we will still be hitting our income targets, won't we? Loyalty does matter, however, because organizations have to spend a lot of time and effort to find new major donors, and even in the realm of direct marketing, where expenses (per donor) are lower than in major donor development work, it still costs up to ten times more to reach a new donor than to successfully communicate with an existing one. So although new donors can certainly be attracted, the costs of fundraising in an organization with poor donor-retention rates can quickly begin to climb dramatically.

Low levels of donor retention can also have an effect in other, more subtle, ways. In this chapter we explore the impact that even a small increase in donor-retention rates can have on your fundraising performance. We look both at the immediate impact and at the longer-term results, introducing the concept of donor lifetime value. As we shall see, lifetime value is a critical concept to grasp because it can turn the traditional economics of fundraising on its head and open up a whole new way of looking at the value inherent in your fundraising database.

The Scale of the Retention Problem

Nonprofits typically lose a high proportion of their supporter base each year, particularly if they use direct-marketing fundraising. Figure 1.1 illustrates the pattern of retention achieved by most nonprofits involved in annual campaigns or the solicitation of single gifts, the type of fundraising where an organization solicits a number of separate gifts over time. Most organizations find that they lose a high proportion of their donors between the first and second gift. Typically as many as 50 percent of those recruited never give a second gift. After that, organizations tend to lose 30 percent of the remaining donors each year.

In recognition of these figures many nonprofits are now moving to regular giving or (in U.K. fundraising terms) committed giving. Here donors are asked to offer a regular and often low-value gift. The gift is typically collected each month (or quarterly) from the donor's bank account or, as is more prevalent in the United States, from the donor's credit card. Regular giving changes the economics of the exchange as a much lower percentage of individuals who agree to give in this way

FIGURE 1.1. DONOR-RETENTION CHART.

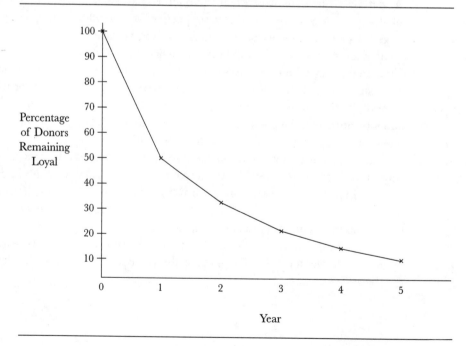

will choose to terminate their support, and the attrition rate will be closer to 20 percent per year. Although this pattern of performance is a dramatic improvement, it is still far from ideal. Imagine losing 20 percent of your friends each year!

The Real Cost of Attrition

Our experience with benchmarking fundraising costs tells us that donor acquisition is expensive. Bringing new major donors into the organization can take months, if not years, of research and cultivation. At the lower end of the spectrum most direct-marketing fundraisers lose money on their donor-acquisition activity. Although donor performance varies by media (see Table 1.1), it can typically be up to eighteen months before newly acquired donors have given enough to an organization to justify the costs of their recruitment. Comparing these returns with those from donor-development activity (that is, taking care of a donor following acquisition) shows us that it can cost up to ten times as much to reach a new donor as it does to communicate with an existing one. Donor acquisition is indeed an expensive activity.

Thus, it makes sense to focus on donor retention to ensure that the number of donors who stop giving is held to a minimum and to reduce the need for the organization to continually seek new donors. There will always be a need to make up for natural attrition (for example, when someone dies or moves away), and some organizations do look to expand their base of support in line with their need for resources, but the key here is that unnecessary recruitment activity should be avoided.

TABLE 1.1. INITIAL DOLLARS GENERATED BY ONE DOLLAR OF INVESTMENT.

	Mean	Standard Deviation	Median
Recruitment media			
Direct mail—cold recruitment	$0.39	$0.21	$0.47
Direct-response television	2.27	0.56	2.77
Direct-response press advertising	0.61	0.58	0.58
Press/magazine inserts	0.87	1.01	0.26
Unaddressed mail	0.56	0.46	0.35
Face-to-face solicitation—on-street recruitment	0.66	0.33	0.71
Development media			
Direct mail	2.88	1.45	3.00

Source: Sargeant and Lee, 2003.

Although the figures in Table 1.1 remind us of the different economics of acquisition and development activity, the impact of minimizing donor attrition can be more profound. Reducing the number of donors that terminate their support reduces the need for an organization to find replacement givers. It also, however, heightens the lifetime value of the organization's supporter base. As individuals stay longer, the amounts that they give over the duration of their relationship with the organization grow. Although this correlation seems intuitive and is perhaps no great revelation, many fundraisers fail to realize that the impact of enhancing retention compounds with the passage of time. In other words, even a comparatively small annual increase in loyalty can result in a major increase in lifetime value and in the efficiency of an organization's fundraising activity.

Figure 1.2 illustrates how compounding works. In this example we have mapped out the direct-marketing performance of two nonprofits. To keep the math simple we have chosen one with an annual attrition rate of 10 percent (that

FIGURE 1.2. IMPACT ON TOTAL ANNUAL REVENUE OF REDUCING THE ATTRITION RATE.

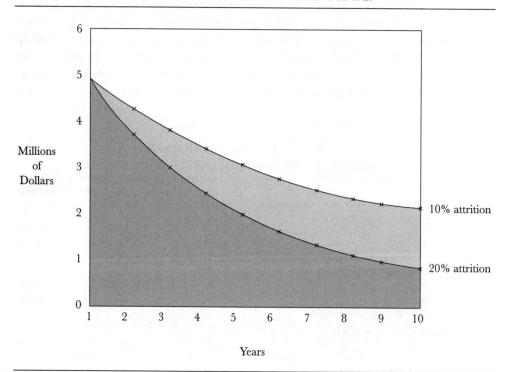

is, it loses 10 percent of its donors each year) and one with an annual attrition rate of 20 percent. In all other respects these two organizations are identical. They each start with one hundred thousand donors in their database, and they each attract average annual gifts of $50. Figure 1.2 illustrates the total revenue each organization generates each year for ten years, including the year of recruitment. At the end of year 1 both organizations have achieved revenue of $5 million. Thereafter, with every year that passes, the attrition rate has an increasing impact on the total revenue generated. When we add up the revenue generated in each case, the organization with a 10 percent attrition rate will have generated a sum of $33 million in ten years; the organization with a 20 percent attrition rate, a mere $22 million. In other words, the impact of cutting the attrition rate from 20 percent to 10 percent will have equated to an improvement in profitability of 50 percent.

The graph shows the additional revenue that would accrue from a decrease in donor attrition. But this decrease is only part of the equation; few organizations would not engage in donor acquisition over the period in order to make up the balance of support. If both organizations wish to maintain the size of their donor base over the period, or even expand it, the organization with a 20 percent attrition rate will have to work twice as hard as the organization with a 10 percent attrition rate to attract new donors to fill the gap. As we noted earlier, this activity is undertaken at significant cost, and so, if we were to factor this into the equation, for a typical nonprofit we would find that decreasing the attrition rate from 20 percent to 10 percent would increase the lifetime value of donors by over 100 percent. In a nutshell, this is why loyalty matters.

Impressive though the effect on revenue is, it does not indicate the full impact of enhancing donor loyalty. Donors who remain loyal are also much more likely to engage with the organization in other ways. Long-term donors are significantly more likely than single-gift donors to offer additional gifts in response to emergency appeals, to volunteer, to upgrade their gift levels, to lobby for the organization, to actively seek out other donors on the organization's behalf, to buy from a gift catalogue, and to promote the organization to friends and acquaintances. The value of these activities will differ from one cause to another, but, in our experience, adding the impact of these variables to our example can bring a total uplift in donor value of between 150 and 200 percent.

What Is Loyalty?

What exactly do we mean by *loyalty?* Are donors who continue to give necessarily loyal? The short answer is no. Some may feel trapped into giving, perhaps because of pressure from their family, peer group, or employer. Although these individuals will appear perfectly loyal, as soon as the pressure disappears, so too will their giving.

Loyalty also can be either passive or active. Passive loyalty is the easiest for competitors to attack and therefore is the easiest to lose. Indeed, passive loyalty isn't really loyalty at all. It occurs when donors feel comfortable giving to an organization, respond to occasional solicitations, but give relatively little money. These individuals feel no real sense of commitment to the organization; perhaps they simply have not yet found the most appropriate outlet for their philanthropy. In the case of regular, monthly givers, inertia may creep into the relationship; although these donors may not feel themselves to be loyal, they are equally not especially motivated to take the time to cancel the regular payment arrangement. Clearly, if these individuals are presented with an opportunity to give that is more inspiring or more in line with their interests, they may terminate their support. They can also lapse because giving of this passive nature suffers first when pressures increase on their budgets.

Active loyalty, by contrast, occurs when donors believe passionately in the cause, identify with the values and ethos of the organization, and regard their support as an essential component of their personal or household budgets. Active loyalty is not a function of inertia, it is a function of the genuine enthusiasm and commitment an individual has for a nonprofit's mission. Try as they might, competitor nonprofits will find it difficult to break the bond that this sort of donor feels with your organization. We need to foster active loyalty because it is the key to the development of lifetime value.

Is Loyalty Always Good?

We have so far examined the merits of developing a focus on retention and explained how even a small increase in retention can have a dramatic effect on your organization's fundraising performance. Implicitly we have therefore assumed that generating loyalty is always good. This need not be the case, however, as the following discussion of donor value illustrates.

For most nonprofits the simplest way to look at value is simply to ascertain how much money each donor in the database has given to the organization. This assessment is easily accomplished by most modern fundraising software, and the total number of all gifts at various levels can then be calculated. A pyramid is the best way of presenting this information graphically (Figure 1.3 is an example) because a typical fundraising database has a large number of individuals who give comparatively small sums (the base of the pyramid) and then progressively smaller numbers of individuals who give larger sums as one works up the pyramid. At the

FIGURE 1.3. DONOR-VALUE PYRAMID.

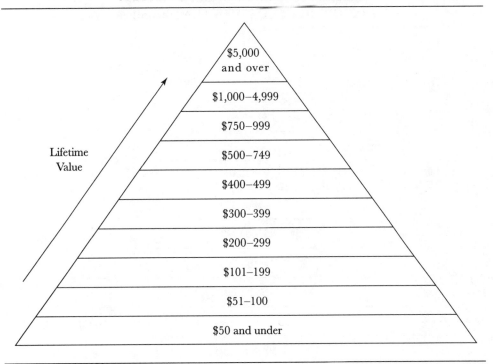

top are just a few individuals who give large sums of money. This pyramid is a representation of the Pareto principle, which (in the language of fundraising) postulates that 80 percent of an organization's funding tends to come from 20 percent of its donors. This seems to hold true even if one creams off the truly major givers for separate consideration. Even in a standard direct-marketing database a small number of individuals will always be donating most of the income.

Why is this pyramid of interest? Our simple example totals only the revenue from each donor, but if we include the costs of servicing the relationship with each of these donors and of making the solicitations themselves, a rather different picture emerges (see Figure 1.4). In this example, it is costing the organization more to look after those who give under $50 than it is receiving from them. This pyramid is fictitious, but it is typical of the pyramids many nonprofits produce when they undertake such a cost-benefit analysis.

These results present an ethical problem: the individuals giving low sums may be well intentioned, but they are in reality diverting money from the mission of the nonprofit. Deciding what to do about this group is not easy. Some would

FIGURE 1.4. DONOR-VALUE PYRAMID
FACTORING IN COSTS OF FUNDRAISING.

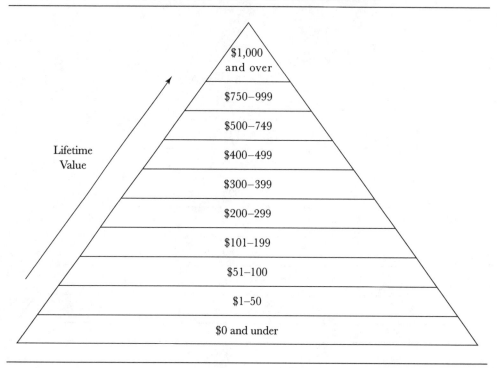

advise that you simply stop communicating with them and save your organization money. However, some of these individuals might be good bequest prospects; equally, some may have developed a personal association with the cause, and it would be harsh to deprive them of a source of pleasure. They may also help in other ways, such as through volunteering, lobbying, or advocacy. The best course is probably to develop a strategy of benign neglect and to minimize contact with these individuals, perhaps writing to them occasionally to remind them of the work undertaken and to afford them the opportunity of offering a higher-value gift or bequest.

Targeting the Top of the Pyramid

Our pyramids suggest a further strategy that may be appropriate: spending more on the retention of those individuals toward the top of the pyramid than on those toward the bottom. Losing a few donors at the bottom of your pyramid may be sad, but it will not have a dramatic effect on income. Losing donors toward the top end of your pyramid will, in contrast, have a dramatic negative effect on the money you are able to generate. The lesson here is that organizations should move away from studying their overall attrition rates and begin to look separately at the attrition rates at different levels of the pyramid and to concentrate development resources on retaining the most profitable donors.

By way of illustration, consider for a moment the case of a commercial organization whose pioneering work on lifetime value has now become part of marketing folklore. One of the first divisions of this large, diversified company to investigate the lifetime value of its customers was the division that dealt with cruise holidays on a fleet of ocean liners. To ascertain whether some customers were worth more than others, the company looked back at its records for the previous five, ten, and fifteen years. This analysis revealed that a lady by the name of Elsie Naylor took pride of place at the top of the pyramid. In fifteen years Elsie had spent 4,100 days on board the company's vessels, but not once in this time had the organization acknowledged her loyalty because she had never previously come to the company's attention!

Given the money she had spent on this organization's services, the organization should not have been marketing to her the same way it did to customers who may have taken a cruise only once every five years—particularly when one considers the revenue that the Elsie Naylors of this world would take with them were they ever to become disenchanted and defect to another supplier. Higher-value customers, or in our case donors, are critical to an organization's success, and they should be identified and treated with a differentiated standard of care to reward their loyalty and value appropriately.

In our experience, some faith-based organizations have difficulty with this approach, preferring to regard all donors as being of equal worth. They object on moral grounds to selecting individuals for special treatment because a low-value gift from one individual might be more significant for that person than a major gift is for someone else. Treating these two donors differently would therefore be wrong. We have no quarrel with this perspective, but we believe that most organizations will find it worthwhile to consider treating higher-value donors differently.

Although we are concerned primarily in this book with the issue of retention, it is appropriate to consider in passing a further use to which our pyramid might be put. In attempting to acquire new donors, many nonprofits profile their databases to ascertain the types of individuals who donate. The organization can then go out and find other individuals who match this particular profile and who therefore are statistically more likely to give. A glance at the pyramid, however, should remind us that such global profiles will be heavily dominated by individuals who give low amounts and who may even be costing the organization money. The smart approach is thus to profile particular value segments of the database and to determine whether and how the higher-value givers differ from lower-value givers. Perhaps they are older, are male, have a certain level of income, live in certain types of housing, or have certain lifestyle characteristics. This information can be used to select potential new donors for contact. To use our earlier example, the profile of Elsie and others like her would be the most fruitful tool for the cruise-ship company to use in future customer acquisition. Most organizations would prefer to recruit individuals who are likely to remain loyal over time and to donate (in aggregate) large sums.

Ascertaining Projective Value

We have been concerning ourselves here only with historic value: we have been asking how much a donor has been worth to us in the past. Many organizations determine the standard of care an individual will receive based on this form of analysis. Nevertheless it is not the ideal approach.

To understand why, it is necessary to consider newly acquired donors. These individuals are likely to have given a low amount because they have as yet given only one gift. If we manage the database as we have suggested above, they may well be assigned to a lower-value segment, and their names may even be swapped with other organizations. If, however, their potential value to the organization is recognized from the outset, they may be subject to a better standard of care. This is an estimate of likely donor lifetime value, and it is distinct from historic value.

This perspective can also help drive donor acquisition. Previously we argued for using the profile of the highest-value givers for donor acquisition. Using the example of Elsie Naylor, we would be most interested in the profile of her and those like her. When thinking about value projectively, however, we need to look back through our database and determine Elsie's profile when she first became a donor. In other words, we want to know what high-value givers looked like when they first began their support. This is the best possible profile to use for donor acquisition because the organization can then deliberately recruit individuals who are most likely to exhibit considerable loyalty and to be extremely valuable over time.

A final complication at this stage is the fact that few organizations have the time or capability to calculate the lifetime value of each donor individually or to act on this information if it is produced. Organizations are often more concerned with how certain segments or groups of donors will behave in the future and how each segment should be managed.

Combining these various approaches to the management of donor value yields the matrix in Figure 1.5. Here we can see clearly the choices open to fundraisers. They can choose to look at the value of donors historically or projectively (that is, into the future). They can also choose to look either at segments

FIGURE 1.5. APPROACHES TO MANAGING DONOR VALUE.

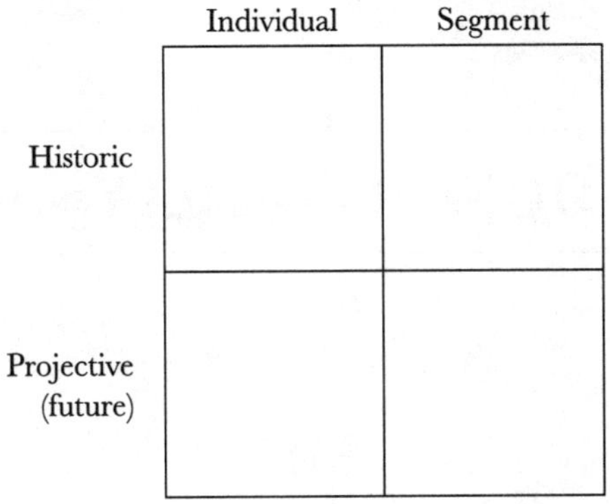

	Individual	Segment
Historic		
Projective (future)		

of donors or at specific individuals. It is impossible to predict in advance which approach will suit an organization best. As we shall see later, particular costs and benefits are associated with each approach.

Summary

In this chapter we have explained how even small increases in donor loyalty can have a marked impact on fundraising performance. We have also explained that in seeking to maximize this performance it is not enough for organizations to try to improve loyalty across the board. Nonprofits involved in direct marketing will always have some donors who are costing the organization money.

In designing the best retention strategy for your organization, you should therefore conduct a value analysis of the individuals in the fundraising database and use this information to focus retention efforts. There are two ways of looking at donor value. First, you can simply calculate how much individuals have given in the past and use this as the basis for the standard of care they will receive in the future. Second, you can take a more sophisticated approach that uses knowledge of how others have behaved in the past to predict how much similar donors may be worth in the future. This lifetime value can then be used to determine an appropriate retention strategy.

So far we have provided few clues as to the form a retention strategy might take and the factors that can persuade individuals to continue their support. We develop both these themes in the chapters to come.

CHAPTER TWO

DRIVING DONOR LOYALTY

In this chapter we map out the key reasons why donors terminate their support of nonprofits by discussing the results of a major study that we conducted of active and lapsed supporters. The study was funded in the United Kingdom by the Aspen Foundation and in the United States by the Indiana Fund through the Center on Philanthropy at Indiana University. Spanning nearly four years, it is the largest study of donor loyalty ever undertaken. It surveyed the views of over twenty thousand donors on both sides of the Atlantic through a series of focus groups and a large-scale postal survey; the donors had given to a variety of different causes. We asked lapsed supporters why they stopped giving and compared the views of active and lapsed supporters on a wide range of issues to determine underlying factors.

Because the results we obtained were remarkably similar in both countries, we speculate that they may also apply in other nonprofit contexts worldwide. Because of this similarity, we can also focus solely on the data we gathered in the United States for the sake of brevity. In only one of the sets of data are there significant differences between the United States and the United Kingdom, and these results are specifically highlighted.

In this chapter we provide an overview of our U.S. research and map out all the factors that have the potential to influence donor loyalty. Subsequent chapters then tackle specific issues, illustrating how fundraisers can manage each dimension of the solicitation process to maximize donor loyalty. Many of the factors we discuss apply equally to soliciting major gifts and to soliciting smaller sums, perhaps through the medium of direct mail, from the bulk of the fundraising database.

We consider each of the following topics: who lapses and whether lapsed supporters have any specific characteristics, the reasons people give for lapsing, and underlying relationship issues and failures in the fundraiser-donor relationship.

Who Lapses?

Can all donors be loyal? The simple answer is yes—at least in terms of demographics. When we examined the gender, occupation, income, and lifestyle characteristics of both active and lapsed supporters we could find little difference. There is thus no easy way for a nonprofit to distinguish between these two groups in advance.

The only interesting difference was that active supporters were somewhat older than lapsed supporters, with the mean age of active supporters being sixty, and the mean age of lapsed supporters, fifty-three. This difference most likely occurs because the causes we find attractive change as we move through life, and many supporters thus find that their priorities change as time goes by.

Of rather more interest was our finding that the strength of one's religious conviction is significantly related to lapsing behavior. Those expressing a strong religious conviction (irrespective of denomination) were much more likely to switch their support from one organization to another. Additional comments supplied on the returned questionnaires suggested that these individuals felt the need to spread their support around a wider pool of charities than did those with a lower degree of religious conviction. They were also driven to donate to organizations that their place of worship had decided to support in a given year. These organizations may not reflect the specific interests of the donor, and hence when a particular appeal ends, so does the support. Nonprofits have recognized for many years that a strong degree of religious conviction is a good indicator that a particular individual might give and is significantly more likely to give higher amounts than an individual with less religious conviction. Direct-mail lists identifying religious individuals have therefore always been a productive source of new donors. Sadly, however, these individuals are also significantly more likely to lapse.

Why People Lapse

The obvious starting point in examining donor retention is to simply ask individuals who have ended their support why they stopped. Table 2.1 is a summary of the results we obtained in this key facet of our survey. In interpreting these results

TABLE 2.1. REASONS FOR LAPSE.

Reason	United States	United Kingdom
I can no longer afford to offer my support	54.0%	22.3%
I feel that other causes are more deserving	36.2	26.5
Death/relocation	16.0	12.7
X did not acknowledge my support	13.2	0.9
No memory of having supported	11.1	11.4
X did not inform me how my money had been used	8.1	1.7
X no longer needs my support	5.6	1.2
The quality of support provided by X was poor	5.1	0.9
X asked for inappropriate sums	4.3	3.1
I found X's communications inappropriate	3.8	3.6
Am still supporting by other means	3.4	6.8
X did not take account of my wishes	2.6	0.7
Staff at X were unhelpful	2.1	0.5
Not reminded to give again	0.0	3.3

it is important to note that the columns will not total 100 percent because donors could offer multiple reasons, and in the United Kingdom 15 percent of respondents indicated that they could not recall the reason for their lapse.

As one might expect, many donors lapse because of a lack of discretionary income. If individuals experience a change in their financial circumstances, it is rational for them to cut back their support of nonprofits. A cynic, however, might suggest that the percentage of individuals claiming financial inability is rather high. Claiming a lack of cash is of course the easiest answer to give.

Many donors lapse because they feel that other causes are "more" or (as some donors said) "equally" deserving. This is good news for the nonprofit sector, but bad news for the particular organization because it reflects negatively on the quality of the relationship it is able to establish with its donors. It is not able to continue to make the case that its need for funding is as pressing as that of other nonprofits, and its relationship ties are as a consequence weak.

A number of donors quit because of the poor quality of service from the organization they support. It appears from our data that many nonprofits do not thank donors adequately, inform them how their money was spent, or offer them sufficient choice in communications. We are concerned here with donors' perceptions of reality. It may well be that the organization believes it is offering good service in its fundraising activity, yet this is not the perception of many of its lapsed supporters. As we show in Chapter Nine, this discrepancy emphasizes the need for an organization to measure both donor expectations and donor perceptions of performance and to ensure that expectations are being met.

A fairly high percentage of donors lapse because they cannot remember having supported the cause. Given that all these individuals have written a check to the organization at least once, this is a major cause for concern. So poor was the quality of the relationship between the donor and the nonprofit that these donors cannot even recall it existed. This finding was replicated in the focus groups we conducted: some individuals strenuously denied having supported the organization until they were shown the record of their contribution. Their faulty memory was often due to confusion with a nonprofit involved in a similar cause, but on occasion no particular explanation could be found: the donor had simply forgotten.

Further examination of the study data reveals differences between certain categories of lapsed donors. In particular donors who lapsed after only one donation were significantly more likely to cite financial inability as the primary reason they did not give again. Donors who had been giving for a period of years were significantly more likely to lapse because they felt that other organizations were more or equally deserving. Thus, it appears that many donors prefer to continue their support unless or until they encounter a similarly worthy organization. This finding has clear implications for list swaps or reciprocal mailings; by sharing their donor lists with other nonprofits, charities may well be encouraging loyal, albeit low-value, donors to quit supporting their organizations.

Relationship Issues and Failures

Simply asking donors why they decided to stop giving presumes that donors will accurately recall their reasons for terminating support and fails to take account of many other factors that perhaps had an impact on the decision, whether a donor is aware of them or not. For these reasons we also examined donor perceptions of various aspects of the relationship that they had with the fundraising department and compared these with the perceptions of individuals still giving. A number of interesting differences emerged. In our discussion here we examine perceptions of each facet of the relationship.

Acquisition: Distinguishing Donors from Responders

The starting point for retention is donor recruitment, or "acquisition." Not all who are recruited have the same perception of their relationship with the organization. Indeed many individuals do not want any relationship at all, while others have varying degrees of motivation to invest in and develop that relationship. Some individuals choose to give only once, while for others the cause is so emotive that they continue giving for many years or possibly even a lifetime.

This idea is represented diagrammatically in Figure 2.1. Here we plot how donors perceive the strength of the relationship against their potential for investing in it. In the bottom left corner are the responders: individuals with little or no perceived relationship with the organization and no potential to invest. Although most nonprofits regard everyone who contributes as a donor, some individuals are really not donors at all. Many have been motivated to respond because of the quality of the appeal. Perhaps they were asked to give by a close acquaintance or stimulated by a powerful mailing. These individuals were simply approached in the right way at the right time and with the right message. Sadly, these conditions may never be precisely replicated. Nonprofits can thus do little to manage retention among this group, and rather than persist they might do better to conserve their resources and invest them elsewhere.

In the top left corner of the matrix are the potentials: responders with a general interest in the cause who, although they have as yet responded only to a particularly striking appeal, can, if properly handled, be motivated to give again. They will, however, be persuaded only by solicitations that are similar to the one that recruited them in the first place. In a face-to-face context such a solicitation may be relatively easy: the same solicitor can be dispatched to make a similar form of ask. When direct-marketing media such as mailings have been used, the situation is more complex but still manageable. In this context developing a personalized "welcome cycle" can turn potentials into loyal donors. With this strategy newly recruited donors are sent a particular sequence of communications for the

FIGURE 2.1. A TYPOLOGY OF LOYALTY.

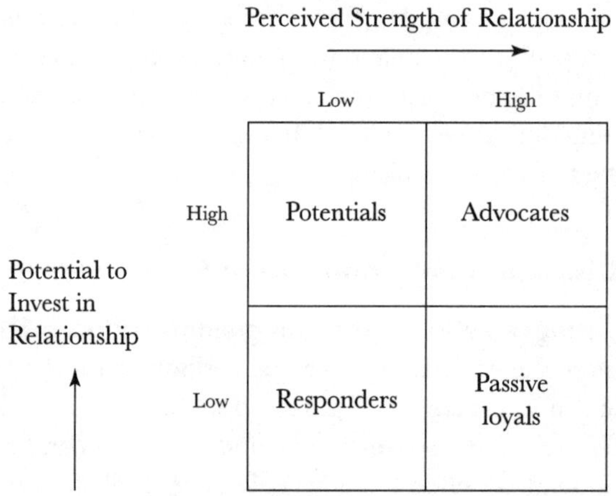

first twelve to eighteen months. During this period they aren't sent the standard development mailings but rather the set of communications that have proved most likely to engender a response. Many nonprofits use their three or four best acquisition packets for this purpose and bundle them together as the welcome cycle. If donors can be persuaded to give at least twice (and ideally three or four times), our research shows that they begin to perceive that they have a relationship with the organization and they are increasingly willing to develop it over time. The psychology literature tells us that after multiple donations donors are less able to rationalize their giving by reference to external pressures and begin instead to ascribe their giving to a genuine concern for the cause. In effect they can no longer tell themselves that they don't care about the organization because this explanation no longer fits their behavior. (See Sargeant and Wymer, 2004, for a review of this material.) If you doubt the efficacy of having a separate welcome cycle, try it with a sample of newly recruited donors. The uplift in response and hence donor-retention rates will be marked.

Individuals in the bottom right of the matrix are passive loyals: they have no interest in deepening their relationship with the nonprofit but can be fiercely loyal as they often care passionately about the cause. If a large number of these individuals have been recruited, the nonprofit likely has undertaken careful research about potential major givers or has bought particularly well-targeted mailing lists. Campaigns that generate high numbers of this category of supporter have successfully matched their cause with individuals with a genuine interest and concern. These individuals are different from advocates (in the top right of the matrix) because they are content merely to give and do not wish to engage with the organization in other ways. Advocates, by contrast, can, over time, be persuaded to engage in many different ways, perhaps assisting in raising funds or encouraging others to give or even volunteering to assist with service provision.

It would be wonderful if we were able to identify these four categories of supporters from the outset. Responders could then be left alone, and resources could be allocated to developing potentials and advocates, who, on receipt of appropriate communications, would begin to grow in value to the organization. Crucially they would also maximize the value that they in return generate from the organization as a consequence of their giving and support. With major giving, the attentive fundraiser will undoubtedly begin to get a sense of the level of interest and commitment a given individual might have and can use this knowledge to ensure that sensitive and appropriate solicitations are made in the future. With direct marketing, this is not the case. Faced with a list of newly recruited donors, the fundraiser cannot categorize them in this way. In order to maximize retention in this context, developing a welcome cycle to which all new donors are exposed will retain the interest and commitment of passive loyals and advocates, while at the same time inculcating a culture of giving among the potentials. These individuals not only become comfortable with supporting the cause but over time become more familiar with the work the organization undertakes and begin to understand its genuine value. They ultimately begin to give for these reasons rather than because they merely find the campaign materials attractive. This is a much more sustainable pattern of giving.

Recognizing Donor Motivation

As we shall see in Chapter Three, donors are motivated to give to nonprofits for a variety of reasons. One of the keys to successful retention is to recognize that this is the case and to reflect this motivation in the manner in which subsequent solicitations are made. Cancer-research donors, for example, may be motivated to give because they are themselves living with cancer or have a friend or a relative who is in this situation. They may also be motivated because they fear that they might one day contract the disease and need the services of the organization. Finally, they may be motivated to give in memory of a friend or a loved one or because they can empathize with the suffering that the condition causes.

Although there are many other potential motives, the lesson is the same: the nonprofit needs to understand what drives its donors and to shape communications and fundraising to reflect these motives. Our research showed that many nonprofits fail to take account of these motives in their fundraising strategies. As one donor noted, "I reached the conclusion that they only wanted my money. They didn't listen to me and sent me some of the most distressing communications I had ever received. It turned me right off."

The reasons donors gave for selecting organizations to support are reported in Table 2.2. Respondents were asked to rank statements about motivating factors on a scale of 1 to 5, where 1 was "strongly disagree" and 5 was "strongly agree." The table reports the mean score for each dimension. The results indicate that donors are generally motivated by a feeling that the organization has a good reputation. They also feel a high degree of affinity with the cause and believe that the organization's management is professional. Donors generally do not see themselves as being pressured into supporting organizations, either by friends or relatives or by the organizations themselves.

A few significant differences emerged between active and lapsed supporters. Lapsed supporters are significantly more likely to cite being pressured. They also feel some obligation to give, perhaps because they were approached by a friend or loved one. This sense of pressure (or perhaps duty) was also reflected in our focus groups:

TABLE 2.2. REASONS FOR SELECTING ORGANIZATIONS TO SUPPORT.

Statement of Motive	Overall Mean
I felt that X had a good reputation	4.18
I believed X's management to be professional	3.83
I felt a strong affinity with this cause	3.76*
I found X's original approach to me professional	3.71
I felt that someone I know might benefit from my support	2.61
There were tax advantages	2.27
I felt it was expected of me	2.16
I felt pressured into giving	1.76*
A friend/relative asked me to support them	1.67
My family had a strong link to this cause	1.61
I thought my family/friends would expect me to give	1.59
I wanted to give in memory of a loved one	1.57

Note: 1 = strongly disagree; 2 = disagree; 3 = neutral; 4 = agree; 5 = strongly agree.
*Significant difference between lapsed and active supporters.

I really felt obligated. One of my closest friends was volunteering for them, and it was difficult to say no. I would have felt really bad declining, but I made it clear it had to be a one off.

My daughter had got involved with [the nonprofit] and asked us all to give. I'm not really interested in [animal welfare], but you have to support your family, don't you?

[They] became a nuisance, and I ended up giving them a gift to get them off my back. When they asked again, I didn't bother returning their calls. It just wasn't professional. They shouldn't harass people into giving.

As noted, donors who feel obligated or pressured to give in this way are among the most likely to lapse. When the obligation is removed, they quickly return to their previous pattern of giving or nonsupport. No amount of creative fundraising will ever reactivate them.

The lesson for fundraising is straightforward. Pressuring donors into giving may yield an immediate return, but the subsequent attrition rate will be high. Worse still, we know that donors who have a bad experience with giving will share that experience with up to seven other people (Sargeant, 2004), and the resulting public perceptions of the organization involved will be negative. Pressuring individuals into giving can also have a negative impact on the returns the fundraising department is able to generate in the medium to long term. It can take considerable time for the donor-development team to identify individuals who will never give again, and if communications have been initiated in the interim, the nonprofit is wasting time and resources.

A further difference between donors and lapsed donors revealed in our analysis was the degree to which they felt a strong affinity with the cause, with lapsed donors expressing significantly less affinity. This finding supports our previous suggestion that many so-called donors are merely responding to a particularly creative fundraising ask and have little interest in the mission of the organization. One of the keys to a low attrition rate thus lies in successfully matching individuals with a cause that they have both an interest in and a genuine concern for and in being sensitive to their needs and preferences. On occasion this may even mean failing to solicit particular gifts and directing donors to organizations that more closely match their needs. (See the discussion about building commitment at the end of this chapter.)

Finally, in this part of our study, we examined the perceived benefits that a donor receives as a consequence of giving. In essence we wanted to know whether lapsed donors are more or less likely to seek benefits in return for their contributions. Our results indicated that lapsed donors are significantly more likely than currently active supporters to have been seeking some personal benefit or reward for their giving. Thus, individuals who are giving because they desire access to facilities, research, or communications are likely to lapse. So too are individuals who are seeking public exposure for their giving because they believe it either will enhance their career or will give them access to local or national celebrities or influential individuals.

These findings have profound implications for the solicitation of major gifts because such donors may demand many of the benefits mentioned above. We are not suggesting that it is wrong to include such initiatives in a fundraising strategy. Such approaches can be and indeed are highly profitable forms of solicitation. But, as mentioned, individuals who seek personal benefits in return for their giving tend to display little loyalty. Fundraisers need to take account of this phenomenon in their strategy in two distinct ways. First, they must adjust their expectations. Giving of this type may take place only when the rewards are offered and will cease immediately thereafter.

Second, fundraisers must distinguish between donors who are motivated by "selfish" concerns and those who are motivated by their concern for the beneficiary group. Fundraisers need to understand the difference between extrinsic and intrinsic rewards. Extrinsic rewards build loyalty to the reward, whereas intrinsic rewards build loyalty to the cause. Fundraisers need to take care not to train donors to expect extrinsic rewards. We define these rewards in the following way. *Extrinsic rewards* have no direct connection with the cause. They are the kind of rewards that any nonprofit can offer, such as access to influential people or celebrities. Many nonprofits can also offer exposure or influence in the local community. Donors seeking these rewards will tend to shop around for the best deal and may stop giving if they no longer receive the requisite return. *Intrinsic rewards,* by contrast, have a tight link to the cause. For example, organizations may offer major givers opportunities to visit a program and to meet with potential beneficiaries. UNICEF, for example, allows major donors to visit sites in the Third World to see how their money is being used, and few fail to be moved by the experience. The memories of the visit are something that money literally can't buy, and they build an intensely strong bond between the donor and the cause.

Even in direct marketing, it is possible to distinguish between these two categories of rewards. The most effective communications contain relevant and engaging involvement devices or offer rewards that are tightly tied to the cause and not the generic paraphernalia that can be supplied by any organization. Marie Curie Cancer Care, for example, sends donors a daffodil bulb. The choice of the daffodil is not arbitrary—it is the symbol of Marie Curie Cancer Care and thus provides an excellent way of engaging donors and keeping the organization in the front of their minds.

Identifying why donors support particular organizations and what their needs are is not easy, and it can be an expensive undertaking if ill conceived and ill planned. To achieve success in donor retention, organizations should thoroughly research the needs of their donors and understand all the motivations individuals might have for supporting their causes. Inevitably they will need to use a range of research techniques, and fundraisers thus need to understand the research process and the kinds of research that can be used. We provide an overview of this topic in Chapter Five.

The Role of Expectations

Focus-group data suggest that donors perceive a number of distinct components of the relationship that they have with nonprofits. These components are all closely related to the solicitation of a gift: the manner in which it takes place and the thanks and feedback donors receive afterward. The most common components of the relationship are listed in Table 2.3. Individuals were asked to rate the importance that they place on each aspect of the relationship on a five-point scale, with 1 being "very unimportant" and 5 being "very important." Again, the mean scores obtained are reported in the table.

TABLE 2.3. IMPORTANCE OF COMPONENTS OF THE NONPROFIT RELATIONSHIP.

Component	Overall Mean
Not asking me for support too often	4.30
Leaving it to me how much to donate	4.28
Being polite in all their communications	4.04
Informing me how my money is spent	3.97
Thanking me for my gift	3.77
Responding quickly when I contact them	3.68
Asking for appropriate sums	3.23
Demonstrating they care about me	3.08
Making me feel important	2.41

Note: 1 = very important; 2 = unimportant; 3 = neutral; 4 = important; 5 = very important.

We found that active and lapsed donors all have the same perception of the components that matter in a fundraising relationship. No differences could be identified between the two groups. Donors care about most aspects of the fundraising relationship, with only the dimension "making me feel important" failing to achieve a score of 3 (that is, mid-scale). Donors place the highest degree of importance on "not asking me for support too often," "being polite in all . . . communications," and "leaving it to me how much to donate." Donors thus want a degree of choice in determining their relationship with the organization they have chosen to support, and they want to be treated with respect.

Just being aware of how important each component is doesn't in itself give you much information on which to base a retention strategy. Ensuring that adequate attention is given to components toward the top of the list is clearly worthwhile, but fundraisers also need to know whether donor expectations in respect to these components have been met; in other words, they need to know how their performance measures up. Donors were thus asked to rate participating organizations on their performance against each component employing a scale ranging from 1 ("very poor") to 5 ("excellent"). The results of this analysis are reported in Table 2.4.

The most striking result is that individuals failed to rate the performance of any of these components above 4, an indication that although performance is generally acceptable, it is still short of excellent. The components that were rated highest were being thanked for the gift and politeness in communication. Lapsed donors have significantly different perceptions of performance than do active donors. For all the components marked with an asterisk in the table, lapsed donors had a significantly more negative perception than active donors did. This difference was particularly evident in three cases: lapsed donors felt that they had been asked for

TABLE 2.4. PERFORMANCE OF NONPROFITS
IN DELIVERING COMPONENTS OF A RELATIONSHIP.

Component	Overall Mean
Thanking me for my gift	3.98*
Being polite in all their communications	3.91*
Leaving it to me how much to donate	3.77*
Not asking me for support too often	3.61*
Informing me how my money is spent	3.60*
Asking for appropriate sums	3.54
Responding quickly when I contact them	3.53*
Demonstrating they care about me	3.36*
Making me feel important	3.28

Note: 1 = very poor; 2 = poor; 3 = neutral; 4 = good; 5 = excellent.

*Significant difference between lapsed and active supporters.

support too often, that they were not thanked appropriately for their gift, and that they were not given sufficient choice over how much to donate. In other words, individuals who feel they are not given enough choice over the form of their support and who believe they do not receive adequate recognition are significantly more likely to lapse than those who are more comfortable with the fundraising approach adopted and the recognition received. This difference suggests a concrete way that donor retention can be enhanced: by offering more choice and bestowing more recognition. This need not be a high-cost strategy; in fact, it may save an organization money. By offering choices and responding to donor needs, an organization makes it less likely that donors will not remember supporting the organization. We return to this topic in Chapter Four.

Service Quality

Service quality is related to the components of the relationship we described above. However, it gives a much broader perspective on how well the organization provides a holistic relationship for its donors. We found that the overall perception of the quality of the service provided by the fundraising department affects retention dramatically.

To investigate this issue, respondents were asked to indicate the extent to which they agreed or disagreed with a set of statements about their satisfaction with the components of service. The scale ranged from 1 ("strongly disagree") to 5 ("strongly agree"). Lapsed supporters were given the same set of statements, but they were phrased in the past tense. The results across the sample as a whole are reported in Table 2.5.

TABLE 2.5. SATISFACTION WITH
COMPONENTS OF FUNDRAISING SERVICE.

Component	Overall Mean
I feel confident that X is using my money appropriately	4.07*
X keeps me informed about how my money is being used	3.39*
The behavior of X's employees instills me with confidence	3.48*
X always responds promptly to requests I have for information	3.31*
X makes me feel that it is always willing to help me if I have a query	3.40*
Employees at X are never too busy to speak to me	3.36*
I feel safe in my transactions with X	3.84*
X's communications are always courteous	3.88*
X's communications are always timely	3.64*
Employees at X are always courteous	3.64*
Employees at X have the knowledge to answer my questions	3.50*
X gives me individual attention	3.24*
X has employees who give me individual attention	3.30*
Employees of X seem to understand my specific needs	3.17*
When I have a problem, X shows an interest in solving it	3.20*

Note: 1 = strongly dissatisfied; 2 = dissatisfied; 3 = neutral; 4 = satisfied; 5 = very satisfied.

*Significant difference between lapsed and active supporters.

The mean scores for each item indicate a neutral, bordering on mediocre, opinion of the quality of service provided by the organizations. Few mean scores diverge significantly from the mid-point (3), a result that suggests that nonprofit organizations are delivering a reasonable standard of service but have considerable room for improvement. The significance of this issue is highlighted by the fact that, on all the components listed, lapsed donors have significantly lower perceptions of the quality of service provided than do active supporters.

To investigate this issue further, overall individual satisfaction with the service provided was analyzed by computing the mean of all scores given by each respondent and then tallying the percentage of respondents whose mean fell on each of the five scores. (The mean varied from 1 to 5 in the same way as the original group mean did.) The results, displayed in Figure 2.2, are disappointing: almost all donors express neutrality or satisfaction, but few are "very satisfied" with the quality of service provided. Further examination of the data set indicated that those who describe themselves as "very satisfied" are twice as likely to make a further donation (to remain active) as are those who are merely satisfied. We return to this issue in detail in Chapter Nine.

We also explored donor perceptions of the quality of the recognition and feedback they received from the organizations they were supporting. We found

FIGURE 2.2. OVERALL INDIVIDUAL DONOR SATISFACTION.

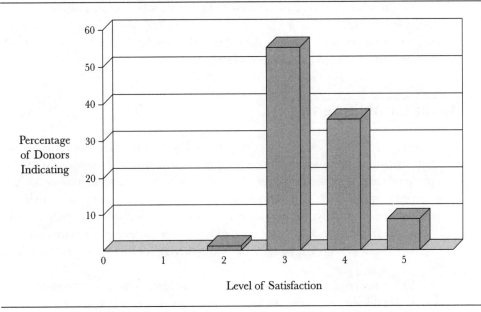

Note: 1 = strongly dissatisfied; 2 = dissatisfied; 3 = neutral; 4 = satisfied; 5 = very satisfied.

that donors are significantly more likely to terminate their support if they feel that the recognition they receive is inappropriate or insufficient given the size and nature of their gift. Particularly with major givers, fundraisers need to be careful to match donor expectations to the form of recognition they are able to deliver. One good way is to map out levels of recognition that will be provided in return for certain levels of gift. Many organizations have several distinct gift levels, each of which entitles the donor to a particular set of privileges (see Chapter Ten).

The distinction between intrinsic and extrinsic rewards that we made above also is relevant to the manner in which donors are thanked and recognized for their gift. Intrinsic rewards are far more effective than extrinsic rewards in engendering loyalty. Direct contact with the cause can be intensely powerful and can be arranged even for direct-mail donors, who may not be in a position to travel to see the work firsthand. Letters and expressions of gratitude from beneficiaries rather than from fundraisers can be particularly effective, and many sponsorship programs are designed to capitalize on this fact (see Chapter Eight).

Feedback is also key. Since the late nineteenth century professional fundraisers have been advocating the necessity of providing donors with feedback about how their gift has been used. Our study provided empirical evidence that such feedback does have an impact. Donors who believe that previous donations have brought the results the nonprofit suggested are significantly less likely to lapse than those who have not received feedback. The need is thus clear for nonprofits to provide adequate feedback when thanking donors or asking them for further resources. Our research suggests that ideally this feedback should be individually tailored and provided as soon as is practical.

Building Commitment

However good the quality of service provided, some donors will nevertheless defect and often for no apparent reason. The same is true of customers in the for-profit context. Why should this be? The short answer is that these individuals have no real commitment to the organization. They may have given once, twice, or even more frequently, but the cause is not one they feel particularly passionate about. Commitment is a complex phenomenon and is certainly in part a function of issues such as service quality, but it is also driven by other factors such as these:

- A personal connection to the cause (perhaps through being a sufferer of a particular disease or having graduated from a particular university).
- The degree of personal empowerment the organization offers. Individuals develop commitment when they believe that they can and are making a difference to the beneficiary group.
- Engagement with the organization in a variety of different ways, perhaps through lobbying or volunteering.
- The sense of the existence of a genuine relationship between the nonprofit and the donor. (See Chapter Four.)

Organizations seeking to retain donors thus need to give adequate consideration both to enhancing service quality and to building commitment.

Summary

Our results suggest a number of ways in which nonprofits can try to retain their donors. Although nonprofits may be able to do little to facilitate the retention of donors who genuinely experience a change in their financial circumstances, they can do much to deal with many of the other common causes of lapse.

A high percentage of donors who lapse do so because they perceive that other causes are more or equally deserving. If charities are to retain this category of donor, they need to find ways of improving satisfaction and deepening the bonds that exist between them and their supporters. Given that our study highlights the importance of feedback and perceived effectiveness, one way in which nonprofits can achieve this goal is by providing ongoing and specific feedback to donors about the use to which their funds have been put and in particular about results for the beneficiary group. If knowledge of their impact on the cause is strengthened, donors will be less likely to view other causes as being more deserving. The feeling of identity or association with a given cause should in general be a major cause for concern. It is particularly disturbing to note that so weak is the association between the nonprofit and donor in some cases that one in ten lapsed supporters have no memory of ever having supported the organization.

Service quality was also identified as a key issue, and it seems to be as much a prerequisite for customer retention in the nonprofit sector as it is in the for-profit sector. Lapsed donors have significantly poorer views of the quality of service they receive than active supporters and in particular tend not to regard the organization as providing them with adequate feedback about how their donation was used. We also found that donors who consider the communications they receive to be informative, courteous, timely, appealing, and convenient remain loyal for greater periods of time than donors who do not have as high an opinion of the quality of the communications they receive.

The remainder of this book considers each of the major issues that arose in our study. We combine this description with recommendations based on the best of professional practice by drawing on lessons from successful-retention case studies on both sides of the Atlantic. We begin with an assessment of what we already know about donor behavior and provide an overview of why people give and how they choose organizations to support. Although this information is relevant primarily for donor acquisition, it also suggests ways in which we can reflect these motives in development materials in order to hold donor interest and encourage loyalty.

CHAPTER THREE

UNDERSTANDING GIVING BEHAVIOR

To retain donors, fundraisers need a detailed understanding of why people give. Donors remain loyal only if the organization continues to offer them the tangible or emotional benefits that they seek in return for their giving. Many fundraisers focus on the techniques of fundraising without understanding why they work. Failure to understand the underlying rationale for giving can lead to the development of fundraising strategies that at best fail to optimize retention and at worst actively work against it.

In this chapter we review the literature on giving behavior and structure our discussion around three broad themes. First, we consider why individuals choose to support nonprofits. Several schools of thought on this question have emerged over the years, and, in addition, no two donors are exactly alike. Nevertheless, a number of fundamental motives drive an engagement with philanthropy, and they must be reflected in the form and content of donor-development communications.

Second, we examine the role of these communications. In particular we outline differences in donor response to various fundraising media and suggest communication messages that are most effective at securing second and subsequent gifts.

Third, we look at how donors select the nonprofits that they support. Donors are increasingly faced with a plethora of nonprofits to choose from. Inevitably a variety of emotional and rational factors shape their decisions, and fundraisers need to recognize that a decision will be made each time they ask for a gift. Donors are constantly assessing the value to them of association with one nonprofit as against others that may be making equally compelling solicitations. They can review their decision to offer support frequently, so it is essential to understand the factors at work.

In this chapter, we summarize the available research and interpret its meaning within the context of fundraising practice. We are eager to avoid having this book become a research text, but equally we appreciate that some readers may have an interest in following up some of the points we mention. We therefore refer to the key researchers who have contributed to our knowledge of each facet of fundraising so that interested readers can access the original material if they would like to.

Why Do People Give?

A variety of motives for giving have been identified including self-interest, sympathy, empathy, a belief in social justice, and the desire to follow social norms. Knowledge of donor motivation is essential for the development of a successful retention strategy, but comparatively few nonprofits research the motives donors have for supporting them. Instead they base their strategy on guesses. The following key motives should always be considered.

Self-Interest

Over the years there has been a great debate over whether donors ever give for truly altruistic reasons. Economists have historically argued that donors make rational decisions about which organizations to support based on an assessment of the benefit that will accrue to them. This view was frequently criticized by fundraisers who were aware of numerous occasions when no obvious benefit would ever come to the donor. This simplistic theory also failed to explain anonymous giving, where even the organization concerned might be unaware of who had made the gift.

More recently, economists have argued that the utility that derives from a gift can take an emotional as well as a material form and that donors are indeed making rational decisions based on their desire to increase their material, emotional, and spiritual well-being. Whatever stance you personally might take on this issue, you need to recognize that a variety of benefits can accrue to donors as a consequence of their giving and to be aware, perhaps through a program of research, of the benefits sought by your organization's donors. Common forms of benefit include increased self-esteem, atonement for "sins," recognition, access to services, reciprocation, memorializing or honoring friends or loved ones, and tax breaks.

Some donors can be motivated to give because it enhances their *self-esteem*. Offering a donation makes them feel better about themselves (Piliavin, Piliavin, and Rodin, 1975). This may be an entirely internal feeling of self-worth, or the recognition offered by the organization may give donors a degree of public visibility that enhances this effect.

Some gifts may be offered with the desire to *atone for past sins*, an example being the donor who gives to their church in recompense for previous nonattendance at services (Schwartz, 1967).

Donors may also be motivated by the *recognition* they receive from the organization or from their family, peers, or local society. This is particularly the case with major gifts, and so it is critical that this aspect of the solicitation process be carefully managed (Dowd, 1975).

Individuals may be motivated to support a nonprofit because of the *service* it provides to beneficiaries. Some donors may wish to benefit from these services themselves or to ensure that the work continues so that if they ever need these services, the organization will be there to provide them. Many donations to medical research, for example, are driven by this motive.

Donors may also give in return for assistance or services that have been provided in the past. Donors whose lives have been touched by the work of the organization in some way may feel obliged to *reciprocate*.

Donors frequently give *in memory or in honor* of a friend or a loved one. In such cases the gift acts as a celebration of the individual's life or allows the donor to express feelings of loss and perhaps solidarity with those left behind. Such gifts are often intensely personal and may allow the donor to find meaning in the loss of a loved one.

A number of authors (for example, Auten, Sieg, and Clotfelter, 2002) have stressed the significance of *tax breaks* in giving to nonprofits. Considerable empirical evidence indicates that the smaller the cost of making a gift, the more likely people are to contribute (Clotfelter, 1985). Nevertheless it is important not to overstate the benefits of the tax code. Whatever the rate of taxation, donors will always be better off not making a donation and keeping the money for themselves. Tax issues can, however, offer fundraisers a rationale for entering into a dialogue with donors. Particularly with major gifts, creative fundraisers seek to make the cost of offering the gift as low as possible for the donor. A working knowledge of the tax implications of giving is therefore essential.

Even with smaller-value gifts, the tax implications raise an opportunity to enter into a dialogue with donors and to enhance the quality of service provided. An annual statement to regular givers indicating how much they have donated in the previous year can greatly simplify completing tax returns, even in the United

Kingdom, where higher-rate taxpayers can now claim tax relief for their donations. There may be an added cost to providing this service, but as e-mail becomes an increasingly popular medium and ever more fundraising databases are linked to the web, the costs of providing such information are decreasing. Indeed, some websites already allow donors to access their records online to check the size of the charitable deduction they can claim.

Empathy

Many fundraising campaigns are designed to engender empathy, or "cognitive perspective taking," on the part of the donor. Shelton and Rogers (1981) define empathy as an individual's emotional arousal elicited by the expression of emotion in another. Thus donors are motivated to give because they are themselves distressed by the suffering endured by others. Numerous studies have found that the higher the level of empathy, the greater the likelihood that a donation will be made—up to a point (Eisenberg and Miller, 1987; Mount and Quirion, 1988; and Davis, Hull, Young, and Warren, 1987). To be truly effective, the arousal of empathy must be powerful enough to overcome indifference and stimulate giving but not so powerful that it becomes distressing to the donor. In such circumstances the message will be ignored (Fultz and others, 1986). Images in fundraising communications thus have to strike an appropriate balance.

Exhibit 3.1 is an example of a communication designed to foster empathy. The mailing was prepared in order to raise funds for the treatment of cataracts. The contents are standard: an appeal letter, a response form, a picture of a sufferer, and a prepaid envelope for the donation. However, the striking aspect of this appeal is the inclusion of a frosted plastic card; by looking through this card the potential donor can experience firsthand what an individual with cataracts "sees."

Sympathy

Sympathy as a motive has also received attention from fundraisers. Sympathy is a "value expressive function" that allows the donor to conform to personally held norms (Clary and Snyder, 1991). In other words, when confronted with a request to give, donors feel sympathetic if they believe it is inappropriate for the beneficiaries to be suffering in the manner shown. Again, there is a relationship between the degree of sympathy engendered and both the propensity to donate and the chosen level of support: greater sympathy leads to a higher level of gift and higher levels of loyalty (Batson, 1990; Fultz and others, 1986).

EXHIBIT 3.1. HELP THE AGED APPEAL.

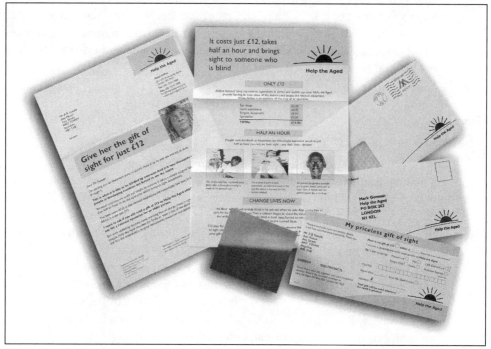

Source: Reproduced with the permission of Help the Aged.

Social Justice

A number of psychologists (for example, Miller, 1977) have suggested that some donors contribute because their belief in a just world is threatened. Proponents of this social-justice theory argue that donors give to restore their faith in a just world. Donors with this motivation have a strong sense of equity and believe that people get what they deserve. They will thus be more motivated to respond to a campaign raising funds for breast cancer victims than to one doing the same for lung cancer victims, who as probable smokers could be partially responsible for their own condition.

Conformity to Social Norms

Gifts may also be offered to a nonprofit because the donors believe that similar individuals also support the organization. Such giving is motivated by a desire to conform to social norms. Research has consistently shown that people pay a surprising amount of attention to others' contributions. In a now-famous experiment,

Reingen (1978) found that showing prospective donors a fictitious list of others who had contributed to the cause generated more gifts and higher levels of giving than were generated when prospective donors were not shown such a list. The length of the list was also an issue, with longer lists outperforming shorter ones. We can therefore conclude that some decisions about giving are made on the basis of beliefs about what is normative for the group (see also Clark and Word, 1972).

To use this knowledge, fundraisers need to understand what groups donors perceive themselves to be members of. Individuals can believe that they are members of some groups but not of others (Hogg and Abrams, 1988). The key here is to use fundraising research that determines when and under what circumstances membership in a particular group is assumed. This information can then be used to design development communications that create a powerful bond between the organization and the donor.

Sometimes charities can influence the perception of social norms by employing role models who take the lead in defining acceptable behavior. This tactic may, for example, involve obtaining endorsements from celebrities or community leaders. Role models can be provided at events (by having high-profile donors attend) and also in indirect forms of communication such as direct mail. The use of role models is particularly advantageous when encouraging behaviors that are relatively rare. An organization may be trying to solicit funds from a new audience or may be asking donors to give in a way that they previously have not considered—for example, it may be encouraging a cash donor to consider a regular gift or introducing the notion of a bequest or planned gift for the first time. In such cases, donors exhibit a degree of "social ambiguity" (Festinger, 1954) and are unsure how to behave. It can therefore be helpful to use a role model to indicate the appropriate behavior.

Strengthening the Impact of Charity Appeals

The motives of donors can thus be used to inform fundraising strategy in many ways; at the same time, other campaign-related variables, such as the style of the asker, the way the beneficiary group is portrayed, and the strength of the message, can also have an impact on giving. In this section we review the available research on these three areas.

Mode of Ask

Charities solicit funds in a variety of ways and through a variety of media. Fundraisers can solicit one-time gifts, regular or committed gifts, bequests, planned or major gifts, and they can ask for these face-to-face, through the mail, through direct-response television (DRTV), and so on. We know from both academic research and professional experience that donors' demographic, lifestyle, and behavioral characteristics vary depending on the amount they are being asked to contribute and the media that have been used (see, for example, Sargeant and McKenzie, 1998). In short, certain types of people respond to certain types of ask. As an example, a DRTV advertisement requesting single gifts will tend to attract relatively young and affluent donors and a fairly balanced mix of male and female supporters. These donors are likely to give high initial gifts but are unlikely to give again unless prompted to do so by telephone rather than through the mail.

The key to successful retention in this context is to carefully research how individuals recruited by each medium and with each form of donation behave afterward. In our experience, minimizing the attrition rates of some groups is problematic. Donors who respond to press ads and television commercials are historically difficult to reactivate following their initial gifts, and it is not unusual to experience attrition rates among this group of upward of 60 percent in the first year. Direct-mail donors, by contrast, exhibit higher levels of loyalty, and even though their average gift may be lower than that of DRTV donors, their lifetime value is often higher.

These findings are quite intuitive. It is not at all surprising that donors recruited through the main donor-development medium, the mail, exhibit the highest levels of loyalty when they are again approached through the mail: they are after all mail responsive. The challenge for nonprofits has been finding ways to retain donors recruited through other media. Two strategies have been successful: using media other than the mail, such as the telephone or electronic channels, for follow-up requests and tying donors at the point of acquisition to a regular or committed gift.

Portrayal of Beneficiaries

A particularly sensitive decision in the design of fundraising communications is whether and how to portray the beneficiary group. This decision can have a considerable impact both on giving behavior and on the subsequent attitudes of donors toward the recipient group. The most effective fundraising messages frequently have an undesirable impact on how the recipients of these gifts are perceived within society. This subject has generated much fundraising research as well as a good deal of research in the discipline of psychology on the best communication strategies.

To summarize the strands of this work, we know that donors tend to support those charities that represent the needy in an acceptable way (Eayrs and Ellis, 1990). Pictures of an overtly handicapped child, for example, have been shown to decrease the response to fundraising solicitations. Donors can find such images distressing or manipulative, and rather than donating they ignore the communication.

Other work, by Brehm (1966), suggests that individuals have what they like to regard as behavioral and attitudinal freedoms. In effect they see themselves as being free to donate or not. A hard-hitting campaign can thus fail because it may threaten donors' ability to choose to spend their money elsewhere. A picture of an aided beneficiary can, in fact, be more effective than a picture of a suffering potential beneficiary because donors then feel they have the freedom not to give and are much more likely to give as a result (Bendapudi and Singh, 1996).

Similarly, appeals for charities concerned with disability often emphasize how dependent on the organization's work individuals with the disability are. Considerable evidence indicates that such appeals are successful in engendering feelings of sympathy (Brolley and Anderson, 1986) and feelings of guilt and pity (Feldman and Feldman, 1985). A key issue for fundraisers, however, is the extent to which such dependence should be exhibited. Although one might assume that depicting the maximum degree of dependence on the organization is desirable, the effectiveness of such campaigns is, in fact, a function of whether that dependence is perceived as temporary or permanent. Wagner and Wheeler (1969) found that when the need is perceived as permanent, the level of dependence has no effect on the amount likely to be given. However, if the need is only temporary, increasing the level of dependence depicted in fundraising communications increases the number of donors who give and also the number who give at higher levels.

Miller (1977) found a somewhat different dynamic: helping behavior increases when the need is not portrayed as being widespread and when the duration of the need can be considered short. But some communications from charities are based on the exact opposite position, with appeals stressing the ongoing nature of the need for support and emphasizing the large number of individuals currently being affected by the disease or cause for concern. Such generic appeals do not breed loyalty. Campaigns are most effective when they deal with a distinct portion of the overall need and present donors with a problem they can easily fix. Indeed, many organizations now phrase their campaigns in terms of what a particular donation will buy, giving donors both a discrete problem and an easy, short-term solution.

Adler, Wright, and Ulicny (1991) found that portraying recipients as succumbing to their condition (in contrast to coping with it) has no impact on the pattern of donations. They do however identify a strong impact on the subsequent attitudes of the donor toward the recipient group. In fact, many authors argue that portraying people with disabilities as dependent may well work against the beneficiary group in the long term by reinforcing negative stereotypes and attitudes (Elliot and Byrd, 1982). Positive portrayals, however, seem to engender positive attitudes (Harris, 1975; Shurka, Siller, and Dvonch, 1982). Fundraisers thus need to take adequate steps to preserve the best interests of the community they serve, consulting as widely as possible before running a potentially contentious campaign. Those messages likely to raise the most funds can on occasion be entirely inappropriate given the nature of the cause and the wider needs of the beneficiary group.

Finally, other work on the portrayal of beneficiaries has suggested that attractive people are perceived as more worthy of support than unattractive people (Latane and Nida, 1981) and that female subjects are considered more worthy of support than male subjects (Feinman, 1978; Gruder and Cook, 1971). The portrayal of the responsibility of recipients for their own condition can also have an impact on willingness to give. Piliavin, Piliavin, and Rodin (1975) found that the extent to which an individual could be blamed for his or her needy condition directly affects both the volume and the levels of support offered. Donors sometimes believe that people "get what they deserve."

Strength of the Stimulus

With so many charity appeals each year and with many different organizations competing to break the pattern of loyalty donors exhibit to other organizations, it has become increasingly critical that fundraisers learn how to cut through the "noise" and ensure that their own message is heard clearly. They can do so in a number of ways. First, fundraisers can emphasize the urgency of the need. In general high degrees of urgency engender high degrees of support (see, for example, Chierco, Rosa, and Kayson, 1982). Second, approaches that emphasize personal responsibility on the part of the donor are more effective at getting a response than fundraising appeals that do not have such an emphasis (see, for example, Geer and Jermecky, 1973). This correlation has long been recognized in professional fundraising practice. Exhibit 3.2 is a fundraising advertisement from the time of the First World War that attempts to make such an appeal.

Third, fundraisers can increase the degree of personalization in communications. The most effective fundraising letters are hand-written and signed personally. It is often not practical to write such letters any longer, even to higher-value donors, but personalization can be improved. For example, donors are now routinely written to by name, but, to stand out from the crowd, fundraisers can also refer to the interests of donors, the amount they have given, or the difference their gift has made.

Fourth, fundraising messages succeed when the message is clear and unambiguous. A nonprofit needs to be up front about the fact that it is asking for money. Donors generally understand that the organization needs funds and expect that if they have given before, the organization will ask them again in the future. Successful development communications cut to the chase. Donors want and need

EXHIBIT 3.2. EARLY FUNDRAISING ADVERTISEMENT.

"I'm afraid that's all I can spare"

You're a regular, red-blooded, true-blue American. You love your country. You love that flapping, snapping old flag. You hear hard thumps when the troops tramp by. You're *loyal—100%!*

You intend to—you *want* to—help win the war in a hurry.

"Sacrifice? Sure," you've been thinking. "Just you wait till they really need it." And you've honestly thought you *meant* that too.

But—look yourself in the eye, now, and search up and down inside of your heart—*did* you mean it? *Did* you really mean "sacrifice"?

Listen: You feel poor. This third Liberty Loan, the high prices, the Income Tax—you've *done* your bit. You feel that you've given all that you can spare.

What? Then what *did* you mean? What's that you said about loving your country? What did you think the word "sacrifice" means?

Surely you didn't mean, did you, to give only what you can *spare?*

What about our boys who are giving their lives in the trenches? Are *they* giving only what they can "spare"?

How about those mothers and little "kiddies" in the shell-wrecked towns of that war-swept hell:—hungry—ragged—sobbing—alone? Giving up their homes, their husbands, their fathers.

While *we*—over here with our fun and our comforts—we hold up our heads and feel *patriotic* because we have given—*what?* Some loose bills off the top of our roll. *"We've* given all we can spare!"

Come, come! Let's quit fooling ourselves. Let us learn what "sacrifice" *means.* Let us give *more* than we can spare—let us "give till the heart says stop."

Every cent of every dollar received for the Red Cross War Fund goes for War Relief.

The American Red Cross is the largest and most efficient organization for the relief of suffering that the World has ever seen.

It is made up almost entirely of volunteer workers, the higher executives being without exception men accustomed to large affairs, who are in almost all cases giving their services without pay.

It is supported entirely by its membership fees and by voluntary contributions.

It is today bringing relief to suffering humanity, both military and civil, in every War torn allied country.

It plans tomorrow to help in the work of restoration throughout the world.

It feeds and clothes entire populations in times of great calamity.

It is there to help your soldier boy in his time of need.

With its thousands of workers, its tremendous stores and smooth running transportation facilities, it is serving as America's advance guard—and thus helping to win the war.

Congress authorizes it.

President Wilson heads it.

The War Department audits its accounts.

Your Army, your Navy and your Allies enthusiastically endorse it.

Twenty-two million Americans have joined it.

guidance as to the level of giving that is expected or required. There is thus no need to be embarrassed about closing with a phrase such as "This year, programs of service, information, and training will cost X. Your gift of $30 will provide the gift of sight to. . . ."

Selection Criteria

We have reviewed a variety of donor motives for the support of nonprofits and have noted the impact of a number of campaign variables on the response fundraisers are likely to engender. In this section we consider the criteria that donors use to decide among organizations that compete for their support and the ways that donors evaluate their giving options. As before, we also review the implications for fundraising strategy.

When donors need to decide among organizations, a key facet is the level of performance the organizations have been able to achieve. Donors generally prefer to give to organizations that are both effective (they do what they say they will do) and efficient (they make the best possible use of the resources available to them). Glaser (1994, p. 178) found that the variable "an adequate amount spent per program" was the most important factor in the decision to contribute to specific charities. Donors have their own ideas about what represents an acceptable percentage of income that is applied to the cause as opposed to being "squandered" on administration and fundraising costs. Warwick (1994) found that donors expect that the ratio between administration/fundraising costs and so-called charitable expenditures will be 20:80. Despite this expectation most donors believe that the actual ratio is closer to 50:50. Harvey and McCrohan (1988) found that organizations spending at least 60 percent of their donations on charitable programs achieve significantly higher levels of donations than do organizations that spend less than 60 percent on these programs.

Work by Schervish and Havens (1997) suggests other criteria that donors use to select nonprofits to support:

> Communities of Participation: Donors frequently choose to support causes that are linked in some way to their formal or informal networks. The authors argue that individuals, either by choice or by circumstance, are part of a variety of networks that bring them into contact with specific categories of need. They have links to particular schools, colleges, sports teams, places of worship, and local community groups. When specific causes are linked to donors' networks, the likelihood that they will support those causes increases.

Frameworks of Consciousness: The authors argue that donors have ways of thinking and feeling that are rooted in their individual identity. Their particular ideologies, religious beliefs, and social concerns shape their pattern of thought and assist in developing the conviction to support particular kinds of causes.

Models and Experiences from Youth: Donors may also have familial ties to certain categories of organizations. As we grow up we may learn our parents' and other relatives' attitudes toward the support of specific causes. These attitudes may ultimately shape our own views about which organizations are worthy of support. The authors also note that role models in our current communities of participation can also influence our attitudes toward organizations we are considering supporting.

When donors have made a gift in the past, whether they continue to give depends to a great extent on the quality of the relationship the organization is able to maintain with them. Among both direct-mail and major donors, the quality of the service provided is key. Nonprofits need to respect donors' right to privacy and where appropriate to select the pattern of future communications they receive. The organization also needs to be responsive to requests for information and to deal with any correspondence it receives efficiently and within a reasonable time frame. All these factors have the potential to affect future decisions about whether to support the organization. Donors who value their relationship with the organization and feel valued by the fundraising team are likely to offer gifts in the future. But comparatively few organizations make an effort to measure the quality of the service they provide to donors and to explore in appropriate detail how they can help donors maximize the personal benefit they get from the relationship. The importance of the effective stewardship of the donor cannot be overemphasized.

Another way to ensure that donors continue to give to organizations they have chosen is to match an organization's message to its donors at the point of recruitment with its message in subsequent development. A surprising number of organizations change tack once they have an individual on board. This is a recipe for disaster. Certain types of people prefer certain types of messages, and this preference doesn't change the instant they become donors. Thus differences between recruitment and development messages should be managed with care. If you doubt the wisdom of this advice, conduct a simple experiment of your own: try reactivating lapsed donors with a standard development ask, and then compare the response with that attained by using a message similar to the one that recruited them in the first place. The recruitment message will win every time.

Summary

Three fundamental lessons emerge from this chapter. First, we now know a great deal about donor behavior and the messages and forms of communication that specific categories of people find most attractive. Nonprofits can use this knowledge to their advantage by screening their campaigns for compliance with the knowledge gained from published research.

Second, nonprofits must identify the specific motives, interests, and concerns of their own donors. Some of these may be generic and be similar to those we review in this chapter, but others may be specific and linked to the nature of the cause and the work undertaken. Any retention strategy must take these factors into account and shape communications that provide donors with the benefits they are seeking, either for themselves or the beneficiary group. Failure to provide these benefits simply opens the door for other nonprofits to step in and fulfill this need. Given that we established in the previous chapter that a high proportion of donors are lured away by other nonprofits, this is a highly significant issue.

Third, the fact that donors have started giving to an organization does not automatically mean that they will become loyal donors. As the number of gifts offered increases so too does the feeling of being a part of an organization, and the likelihood of attrition diminishes. Nevertheless these subsequent gifts have first to be achieved, a task that can be accomplished in two ways: making every effort to establish a relationship with the donor and exerting the same care in designing development materials as in designing acquisition materials.

CHAPTER FOUR

ADVANCING THE
RELATIONSHIP REVOLUTION

Transactions Versus Relationships

Until the early 1980s, commercial marketers were focused heavily on the transactions they had with their customers. The aims of marketing were to identify
consumer needs, design products to meet those needs, and develop communication programs that facilitated product purchase. Marketers directed their energy
toward identifying large numbers of potential customers and then persuading as
high a proportion of these individuals as possible to buy. This process was cycli-
cal and ongoing. Having secured one purchase from a customer, marketers would
then begin the process again, identifying individuals who might be interested in
the next round of purchases and developing communication programs accordingly. Each successive campaign was designed to secure as high a volume of sales
as possible, and all potential purchasers were treated alike, often irrespective of
whether they had bought from the organization before.

The mistake these firms made was to focus on transactions rather than relationships. Their approach did not reflect real market behavior because many customers did not view their interactions as a series of transactions. Many were happy
with the products or services the firms provided and were motivated on their own
to continue to purchase from the organization.

By the early 1980s some firms had begun to recognize that this was the case
and to develop marketing strategies that, rather than fostering a series of one-time

transactions, developed a relationship with customers. Marketing activity was designed to recognize and reflect customers' previous purchases and to improve and deepen the bond between them and the organization. This change in emphasis reflects real market behavior: comparatively few purchases are made on a once-and-for-all basis, and most customers (if treated with integrity and respect) will come back and buy again.

The same market behavior occurs in the context of fundraising. Most donors who have been motivated to offer one gift can be motivated to offer second and subsequent donations, yet a surprising number of organizations fail to consider this fact adequately in their fundraising. Each year when they put together their annual campaign, they design thought-provoking and striking communications in order to raise the highest sum of money that they can. They strive to optimize donor response by employing all the latest psychological and design techniques. The response rate and average gift are all that matter, and although they may develop separate communications for the recruitment of new donors and those who are already giving, the messages are in essence the same: "Give now—and give for the following reasons. . . ."

Such messages can lead to an odd and unrewarding experience for donors, particularly those who have been giving for an extended period of time. As Sargeant (2000) notes:

> Imagine yourself at a party where you are introduced to one of your fellow guests. You exchange social pleasantries with the stranger and he tells you something about his life, his job and his interests. After five minutes the conversation ends and you part. A little later in the evening your paths cross again yet he appears not to recognize you. Undeterred he proceeds to exchange social pleasantries and again to tell you something about his life, his job and his interests. After five minutes have elapsed you part again. Towards the end of the evening you meet up for a third time. Again he seems not to recognize you and after a third round of social pleasantries begins to tell you again about his life, his job and his interests.

After the third or fourth such experience, aside from thinking this person might be somewhat strange, even the most tolerant of us would begin to experience some irritation. Why did he not remember the last encounter? Was I really so unmemorable? And why did he give me exactly the same information time after time? Many nonprofits develop communications that reflect this situation all too well. They provide donors with the strongest possible reasons to support the organization, tell them all there is to know about the organization's work, and ask for immediate action. When it comes time for the next campaign, they do it all over again.

Would it not be better to recognize donors by name, acknowledge their prior giving, tailor the communication to reflect their known interests, and let them choose the type of communication they receive and how and when they would like to give? Would most of us not respond better to this approach because it would feel more like an interaction with a friend or acquaintance?

Although the switch from a transaction to a relationship approach to fundraising may sound like little more than semantics, it can have a profound effect both on the outcomes of the fundraising activity and on the attitudes and commitment of donors. Through an ongoing process of exchange, interaction, and genuine choice, donors begin to feel that they are important to the organization and have an important role to play, in return, by supporting the organization's programs.

The differences between these two approaches in their impact on fundraising strategy and budgeting are also profound. In a transaction approach, fundraising strategy is driven by the initial returns expected from each campaign a charity runs (except perhaps where a campaign has been jointly designed to achieve other goals such as awareness, participation, or education). In donor acquisition and in subsequent donor development, fundraisers try to maximize the return on investment (ROI) when the costs and revenues of a particular campaign are calculated. Fundraisers following such a strategy can't afford to offer donors much choice. Little segmentation (grouping) of donors takes place, and so donors typically receive a standard mailing or other communication. The emphasis is usually on the immediacy of each appeal: donors are exhorted to give "now" because of the urgency of the situation. They may then be approached a few months later about another urgent issue the charity feels they should support. Donors thus receive a series of similar communications, each of which is designed to achieve the maximum ROI.

By contrast, a relationship approach recognizes that it is not essential to maximize ROI on the first communication with a donor or even on the second or third. Fundraisers using this approach understand that, if treated with respect, donors will want to give again, and fundraisers are therefore content to live with somewhat lower rates of return in the early stages of a relationship. They recognize that they will achieve a respectable ROI, but anticipate that it will follow naturally in the long term. Although the costs of acquisition and development are still strictly controlled, the initial costs of acquisition are less of an issue than with a transaction approach because the organization recognizes it will make a return on its investment over the full duration of the relationship. Relationship fundraisers are therefore not afraid to spend slightly more on recruitment than their transaction-based counterparts, as even those relationships with donors with a comparatively high acquisition cost may generate perfectly respectable returns over time. This longer-term perspective has prompted many charities to recruit donors into making a comparatively low monthly contribution. Although, on the face of it, the cost of recruiting donors to give only $5 or $6 a month may seem prohibitive, the returns to the charity over the full duration of each relationship are often better than those achieved by more traditional forms of fundraising.

At the heart of the relationship approach to fundraising is the concept of lifetime value, which we explore in more detail in Chapter Eleven. For the moment, however, it is important to understand that when fundraisers have a sense of how much a given donor will be worth to them over the full duration of their relationship, they can develop communication programs that reflect this value and tailor the offering to that donor according to the individual's needs and preferences, and at the same time they are ensuring an adequate lifetime ROI.

The final major difference between the transaction and relationship approaches to fundraising is the degree to which the organization provides service to its donors. The goal of any relationship fundraising program is to retain as high a proportion of donors as possible from one campaign to another and from one year to another. It consequently recognizes that the quality of the communications delivered and the manner in which complaints and general inquiries are dealt with must be second to none. In short the nonprofit must stand out in the minds of its donors for providing first-class service not only to beneficiary groups but also to them. A relationship fundraising approach allows the organization to take account of the different needs of donors and their varying expectations of the organization by developing a relationship with each individual. Modern database technology is now so advanced that it is possible to create this experience for each donor without significantly increasing the costs of communication.

These differences between the transaction and the relationship approaches to fundraising are summarized in Table 4.1.

TABLE 4.1. COMPARISON OF TRANSACTION AND RELATIONSHIP FUNDRAISING APPROACHES.

Differences	Transaction Fundraising	Relationship Fundraising
Focus	Soliciting single donations	Retaining donors
Key measures	Immediate ROI, amount of donation, response rate	Lifetime value
Orientation	Urgency of cause	Donor relationship
Time scale	Short	Long
Customer service	Little emphasis	Major emphasis

Defining Relationship Fundraising

Burnett first coined the phrase *relationship fundraising* in the first edition of his book of that title, published in the early 1990s. He defines it as "an approach to the marketing of a cause that centres on the unique and special relationship between a nonprofit and each supporter. Its overriding consideration is to care for and develop that bond and to do nothing that might damage or jeopardise it. Each activity is therefore geared toward making sure donors know they are important, valued and considered which has the effect of maximizing funds per donor in the long term" (Burnett, 2002, p. 38). From a donor's perspective, this style of approach addresses how an organization

finds you

gets to know you

keeps in touch with you

tries to ensure that you get what you want from it in every aspect of its dealings with you

checks that you are getting what it promised you

seeks your advice and input

shows it values you

Whether an organization develops a relationship with a donor depends on the effort's being worthwhile. Nonprofits on both sides of the Atlantic have found, after calculating lifetime value, that some donors are costing them money. As a result, they sometimes have to make tough choices about establishing donor relationships. A nonprofit organization rarely exists for the benefit of its donors except perhaps in some membership contexts. Trustees, managers, and fundraisers have a duty to ensure that funds are not squandered on those who cost the organization money. This is an increasingly important issue for nonprofits given the high level of public interest in and concern about fundraising ratios. Although no one likes to lose a donor, frequently organizations are better off without some of their donors because they can then free up resources that can be diverted to building relationships with those who do make a difference to their work. For these individuals the benefits that are offered for giving can be greatly enhanced.

Indeed the notion that benefits accrue to both parties in the relationship is central to relationship fundraising. Donors have expectations about how they will be treated by a voluntary organization and about what they will receive either in return for or in recognition of their gift. This is the case even when they are unable to express such needs. In a speech about relationship issues in the service sector, Levitt (1981, p. 100) famously remarked, "The most important thing to know about intangible products is that the customers usually don't know what they're getting until they don't get it. Only then do they become aware of what they bargained for; only on dissatisfaction do they dwell." Although it would be foolish to suggest that a nonprofit should strive to service every potential donor need, it should strive to meet the most basic needs and thereafter to concentrate on developing the specific benefits that appear to be attractive to particular segments of their donors.

Creating a good baseline of acceptable service is an integral part of relationship fundraising. All donors should feel valued and respected, and, as Burnett noted, the organization should do nothing to jeopardize their positive feelings. Nevertheless, many nonprofits get it wrong. Thompson, writing in the May 1998 issue of the Institute of Charity Fundraising Managers journal, bewailed the quality of service provided by many of the charities she supported. "I have been addressed as Mr. Thompson (instead of Mrs.); in two cases I did not receive an acknowledgement of my donation, and one charity still has not banked my cheque that was sent in [the previous] December" (p. 4). Tight control over data-entry processes to ensure that donor details are stored properly and good internal systems that guarantee gifts are processed and acknowledged promptly lie at the core of donor care. Such service is the minimum that all donors, irrespective of value, have the right to expect.

Having achieved a good baseline of service, relationship fundraisers can then focus their efforts on segmenting the donor base, developing tailored service, instituting good quality service for each of the segments they identify, and moving donors up through the segments. The quality of the relationship established should be a function of the value of each segment of donors, and it should be particularly good for higher-value donors because with them retention is key.

Criticisms of Relationship Fundraising

Critics of the relationship fundraising approach argue that many donors do not want relationships or that the cost of tailoring communications to specific segments of donors will be prohibitive. Neither of these arguments holds up to scrutiny. Certainly some donors may offer a one-time gift and expect no further contact with the organization. In our experience, though, this is a rare phenomenon, and in any case organizations can ask individuals at the point of recruitment what further contact they wish to have with the nonprofit and the form it should take. Individuals who are not interested in learning more about the work of the organization and how donated funds are being used can then be excluded from further communication.

The second criticism—that the costs will be prohibitive—assumes that a relationship approach to fundraising results in a proliferation of segments of donors, each of which requires a separate communication mix. As a consequence the organization loses all its economies of scale in producing campaign materials. This is simply not the case. Organizations switching to a relationship approach do so incrementally, offering donors additional choice in communications gradually. The number of segments is therefore not great initially, and the viability of creating further segments can be tested slowly over time. Many organizations find that this approach saves money, as it avoids the need to send every communication to every donor. Donors often want less communication or have an interest in only one or a few of the communications that an organization produces.

The Elements of a Relationship

We turn now to defining a relationship and to describing its components. A relationship is a series of repeated personal exchanges between two parties known to each other; it evolves in response to these interactions and to fluctuations in the contextual environment. The key here is that the exchanges evolve; over time, donors increase their knowledge of the organization, but at the same time their interests change, they reach different points in their life cycles, and they develop different needs and priorities. As Reichheld notes in the for-profit context, "Even though the customer who initially signs onto a firm's product line may have the same name and social security number five years later, he or she will not be the same person from a marketing point of view" (1994, p. 20).

The dynamics of the relationship thus will alter, whether the nonprofit is aware of this change or not. Smart organizations are aware of these changes, and they leverage their understanding of them to build a strong bond with individual donors. Greenpeace, for example, offers a variety of ways for members and supporters to help the organization. They recognize that some individuals are eager to campaign on behalf of Greenpeace but are unable to support it financially, while others are happy to give but are less eager to take personal actions either because they do not have the time or because they are not as passionate about the specific issues. Greenpeace supporters, without donating, can become part of a "cyber activist community," in which they can take a range of actions and be put in touch with other activists, or they can donate and receive news but choose not to subscribe to "activist" communications. All supporters are constantly prompted to visit the central website, where new preferences for engagement and options for support can be registered at any time.

At the core of any relationship is commitment, the extent to which an individual feels he or she has a genuine bond with another and is prepared to continue and to invest in that relationship over time. In the fundraising context every encounter that a donor has with the nonprofit holds the potential to build commitment, and the stronger it becomes, the less likely it is that the donor will lapse or "defect." Committed donors are likely to remain loyal even when the quality of service is not optimal or when there is negative publicity about some aspect of the organization's work. With commitment a donor's support continues through good times and bad.

Commitment can be built through trust, concern, the exercise of choice, involvement, the provision of benefits, and respect. We discuss each of these ways of building commitment here.

To develop commitment donors must have *trust* in the nonprofit's honesty and benevolence. Honesty involves the belief that the nonprofit stands by its work, fulfils its promises, and is sincere. Benevolence reflects the belief that the nonprofit is concerned about the welfare of both the donor and the beneficiary group and will not take unexpected actions to their detriment. Specifically, donors must trust the nonprofit to:

- Provide any benefits that have been promised to them
- Deliver the promised benefits to the beneficiary group
- Use donated funds appropriately
- Deliver an acceptable quality of service
- Behave ethically and in accordance with the organization's mission

Trust is a dynamic factor; it develops as the donor begins to see evidence that these requirements are being met. To engender trust nonprofits need to work hard at keeping their promises, and when donors have no way of assessing results directly, nonprofits should provide feedback in their donor communications.

Commitment also evolves from a feeling that the organization genuinely cares about a particular individual's welfare. Donors are likely to be committed to an organization if they believe they are valued and that the organization has their welfare at heart. This *concern* is easier for some nonprofits to demonstrate than for others. For example, organizations that are involved with medical research or that offer support services to those with disabilities may have donors who give because either they or people they know are afflicted with the condition. Through the provision of timely and personalized information it is relatively easy for these nonprofits to demonstrate that they do indeed have the interests of such individuals at heart.

In major-gift fundraising, where strong personal relationships are built with individual fundraisers, it may also be relatively easy to demonstrate concern. Some fundraisers use their knowledge of a donor's interests to send books or magazine articles that they believe may be of interest to the donor. This can be an excellent way of engaging with individuals at times when gifts are not being sought; it demonstrates genuine interest and concern on the part of the fundraising team.

In other fundraising contexts demonstrating concern may be more difficult to accomplish, but in our experience it can frequently happen naturally if an organization has a consistent focus on donor needs and preferences. The fact that an organization cares enough to identify and satisfy these needs demonstrates that it genuinely cares about its donors. For example, when Iceland decided to hunt whales for the first time in thirteen years, many donors to animal-conservation organizations were greatly concerned. Related charities were able to build commitment by addressing these concerns, informing donors of the issues, and outlining the actions they intended to take. Information such as this should be offered when the matter is of maximum interest to these individuals.

Commitment is also built through the *exercise of choice*. Donors who are afforded the opportunity to choose the frequency and the content of the communications they receive from a nonprofit develop more commitment than those who are not offered such choices. The charity Botton Village has far higher donor loyalty than that achieved by others in its sector because it offers donors a plethora of such choices. When donors begin giving to Botton, they are asked to specify in some detail the form that the relationship will take. They can choose the frequency, timing, and content of communications and even never to hear from the organization again. These choices are subsequently offered in every communication so that donors can change their minds at any point in the relationship. The choices are enumerated in Exhibit 4.1. So successful has this strategy been that the organization regularly achieves a response rate of over 50 percent to its Christmas mailings! Response rates at other times of the year are approximately twice the sector average, and lifetime value and donor longevity also are well above the norm. This record has been achieved because, in offering donors choices, Botton Village has moved away from "intrusion" in fundraising activity to "invitation."

A further key to commitment is *involvement*. Although it could be argued that by exercising choice donors are by definition becoming involved, involvement also includes the interaction of donors with the cause. For some involvement is minimal; they may only send an occasional gift. Others may volunteer for a local group, assist in fundraising, use the services of the nonprofit, lobby or advocate on specific issues, or pledge a bequest gift. We know from research that the greater the number of ways in which an individual engages with a nonprofit the greater the degree of commitment he or she will feel (Sargeant, 2001). Fundraisers thus need to invite donors on a regular basis not only to give money but also to interact with the organization in a variety of different ways. A further key to involvement is novelty. A genuinely new and appropriate idea can often stimulate

EXHIBIT 4.1. BOTTON VILLAGE RESPONSE FORM.

Let The Camphill Family help you

Your support means a great deal to us and we want to help you in return.
Please let us know your preferences by ticking the relevant boxes below.

Choose when you want to hear from us

1. **If you receive four issues of our newsletter each year:**
   ☐ *I would prefer to hear from you just once a year, at Christmas.*

2. **If you only receive a newsletter once a year, you may like us to contact you more often:**
   ☐ *I would like to receive Camphill Family Life four times a year.*

3. **If you would rather not receive appeals:**
   ☐ *I would like you to keep me up to date with news through Camphill Family Life, but I do not wish to receive appeals.*

4. **If you would rather not receive any further information from The Camphill Family:**
   ☐ *I would prefer you not to write to me again.*

To set up or change a regular gift

Giving The Camphill Family your regular financial support helps us to plan for the future. By setting up or amending a Banker's Order you'll continue giving our communities regular help, but your bank will be doing all the paperwork.

5. **If you would like to set up a regular gift:**
   ☐ *I would like to give to The Camphill Family on a regular basis – please send me a Banker's Order form.*

6. **If you would like to amend your existing regular gift:**
   ☐ *I already give regularly by Banker's Order and would like to amend it – please send me a form.*

   Thank you.

Your guide to The Camphill Family

You can be sure of a warm welcome at any of the eleven communities supported by The Camphill Family. This guide gives you all the information you need to plan a visit, including our opening times.
☐ *Please send me a free copy of the guide.*

Do you want a word with someone?

Our office team of Kelly, Fran, Sue, Jackie and Joanne is here to help you. **Just ring our helpline 01287 661294 or our switchboard 01287 660871, 9am to 4pm weekdays,** and one of us will be

pleased to talk to you. Do let us know if you have moved to a new address, if we are sending you more than one copy of our newsletter by mistake, or if there is anything else you would like to tell us.

Find out more about what life is like in The Camphill Family at Botton Village

7. **Our video of life in Botton**
   Botton Village: This is our home is set against the changing seasons in the rural beauty of Danby Dale and will help you to get to know us better. It tells the story of our community through the lives of our villagers and is a charming portrait of special people and the challenges they meet in sharing life together.
   ☐ *Please send me a complimentary copy of the video, Botton Village: This is our home.*

8. **The Botton Village photo book**
   Featuring wonderful images of the people and places that make Botton special. Photographer Keith Allardyce used to live in the village and his close relationship with our community shines through.
   ☐ *Please send me a free copy of the Botton Village photo book.*

9. **Our Sounds of Botton audio tape**
   Our tape follows villager Jane Hill as she tours the village and meets her friends. It gives you a unique insight into life at Botton.
   ☐ *Please send me a free copy of the Sounds of Botton tape.*

10. **Visiting Botton Village**
    Visitors are always welcome at Botton. If you can, please rin us in advance on 01287 660871 and we can give you details of workshop opening times as well as directions.

11. **Sending you past issues of our newsletter**
    Interesting stories from the village's history feature in past issues of our newsletter, *Botton Village Life*. You may ask for any of the past issues you would like, or another copy of ones you may have mislaid.
    ☐ *Please send me issue no._____ (most issues are available).*

The Camphill Family supports eleven communities which help adults in need of special care and understanding, and which are registered as the Camphill Village Trust Limited, a non-profit-making company limited by guarantee 539694 England and registered as a Charity 232402.

Source: Reproduced with the permission of Botton Village.

renewed interest. Exhibit 4.2, a case study of the ETV Endowment, illustrates this point well.

Commitment can also be built through the *provision of benefits.* As we highlighted in the previous chapter, donors give in many cases because they are seeking social, emotional, or tangible rewards. A nonprofit needs to recognize that these needs exist and to create a package of benefits to ensure that they are satisfied. Some donors seek only the warm glow that comes from the knowledge that the beneficiary group will be aided, while others desire access to services, information, or social contacts and networks or recognition within a particular peer or social group. Relationship fundraising requires a fundamental understanding of what donors want, and the mechanics of researching their needs is therefore the topic of Chapter Five. A good illustration of the provision of benefits intrinsically linked to the interests of supporters is provided by the Museum of Modern Art in New York (MoMA). MoMA members can enjoy a guided tour of current exhibitions after hours with a Department of Education lecturer, have free access to current exhibitions, get a 20 percent discount at the MoMA store on specified days, and are invited to preview days, where they can both view the art and socialize.

The final critical determinant of commitment is *respect.* Nonprofits need to demonstrate not only that they care about their donors but that they respect them too. Great care should be taken to ensure that the donor database is kept up-to-date and that data are entered correctly. It is irritating for donors to be addressed incorrectly in a communication from an organization they have supported for years. Simple flaws in the address and salutation can result in the loss of even long-term donors. Respect also entails a regard for privacy and professionalism in the way that personal data are managed and manipulated. A nonprofit needs to adopt the highest standards in regard to such issues, irrespective of local laws concerning data protection and privacy. In addition, donors today are bombarded with multiple communications. However legal they may be, practices such as list sharing and list swaps result in donors being deluged with additional communications. Are these practices appropriate and in the best interests of these individuals? Is this how you would interact with a friend? In general, donors should be treated with the same respect fundraisers themselves wish to receive.

Requirements for Implementing Relationship Marketing

Relationship fundraising cannot be implemented overnight. To succeed in relationship fundraising, a nonprofit needs to ensure that it is adequately prepared to adopt its new perspective, a process that has implications for the whole organization. Fundraisers cannot achieve a relationship approach in isolation. The following prerequisites are essential.

EXHIBIT 4.2. CASE STUDY: THE ETV ENDOWMENT OF SOUTH CAROLINA.

The ETV (Educational Television) Endowment of South Carolina raises funds for that state's public television and radio stations—known for such programs as *Masterpiece Theatre, NOVA,* and *All Things Considered.*

Unlike educational, tax-supported broadcasters in other countries, public broadcasting in the United States is heavily funded by voluntary contributions from viewers and listeners. Nationally, more than 4.2 million contribute about $500 million per year. What's even more unique is that each individual station, more than three hundred in all, each manage their own contribution program.

In South Carolina and elsewhere in the US, members' gifts go to pay for the production of non-commercial radio and TV programs. Appeals are largely made through on-air pledge campaigns and direct mail. Stations are challenged primarily by the amount of time they can reasonably allocate to on-air fund raising, and the continuing need to develop fresh, new direct mail campaigns. For the past thirty years, the recurring fund raising theme has been, "To see and hear these quality programs in the future, please give now." The challenge was to create a new opportunity for members to contribute and strengthen their relationship with the Endowment.

In South Carolina, no campaign had ever been waged between year-end appeals and mid-March on-air pledge drives. So, the agency turned Valentine's Day into a public broadcasting holiday. An affectionate greeting card (complete with separate verses for active and lapsed members) and a follow-up version won over active members and renewed lapsed ones.

The Results

It was love at first sight! The Valentine's Day appeal generated $53,045 in net income on a first-ever project.

Source: This case was kindly supplied by DMW (www.dmwdirect.com). The case and associated materials remain the copyright of DMW and the ETV Endowment of South Carolina. Reproduced with permission.

Supportive Culture

An indispensable requirement is that the organizational culture within the nonprofit be supportive. Everyone must want to seek relationships with donors and must view them as an integral part of the organization. Relationship fundraising is not just another gimmick for making money: it is about strengthening the bond between the nonprofit and its supporters. Board members, managers, and fundraisers must genuinely want to achieve this bond from the outset. Senior staff must be so supportive of the idea that they become advocates for the approach.

Every individual working within the nonprofit should understand the value of a donor in both a personal and in a financial sense. Recognizing the lifetime value of a supporter can, for example, have a sobering effect on the receptionist who is tempted to ignore a complaint or the webmaster who would rather not take the time to find out the kind of information donors want to access online. Each department or division should understand the critical nature of donor care and be prepared to deal with queries in a diligent, friendly, and timely manner. Serving the needs of donors should become as important as serving those of the beneficiary group.

The culture should also encourage individuals from different departments to communicate regularly so that issues that typically get in the way of good donor care, such as data-processing conflicts, budgetary squabbles, and the incompatibility of technical systems, can be reconciled and resolved as speedily as possible. Strong internal relationships among departments and individuals should be fostered, and all internal systems affecting the relationship with donors should be designed to make this relationship as rewarding as possible.

Reichheld and Sasser (1990) argue that if an organization is serious about improving customer retention through the use of relationship strategies, it needs to adopt a "zero defections culture." When we translate their ideas to the fundraising context, we can understand that the entire organization must be focused on eliminating or at least minimizing donor attrition, taking into account the fact that a typical nonprofit loses between 5 and 8 percent of its donors each year because of death or relocation. Even the most creative of relationship strategies will be unlikely to eliminate this loss!

However, there are many reasons for attrition that the organization can do something about. All managers, employees, trustees, and volunteers should know why donors quit and how they might help reduce this attrition. Each department should work with fundraisers to ensure that an integrated plan is developed to deal with and to resolve each reason for attrition. This strategy will frequently require the involvement of senior management and the sharing of information among departments. All fundraisers and senior managers should also be aware of what happens to the profitability of fundraising activity as the attrition rate moves up or down. Some internal research on attrition will thus be necessary, but these data legitimize the focus on retention and help bolster the effort particular individuals are willing to make.

Finally, any internal reward system for fundraisers and related managers should be tied to attrition rates. This change too will assist in focusing the minds of fundraisers on the drivers of loyalty and away from the all-too-common focus on the simple expansion of the database, a focus that breeds transaction-based thinking and that still pervades many organizations.

Willingness to Invest

Developing a strong focus on donor needs and preferences requires research. Offering donors choices in communication increases short-term costs and may even require the creation or updating of a nonprofit's database. Considerable investment in staff training and internal communication is also required. The switch to a relationship approach is therefore not without considerable cost. For it to be achieved, senior management and the trustees must not only be philosophically committed to the process, but must also be willing to make the requisite investment in staff time and monetary resources. Without such a commitment any bid to embrace relationship fundraising will be doomed from the outset.

Adequate Database

To fully implement a relationship approach a nonprofit needs to have a fundraising database. Smaller nonprofits may require only a restricted number of fields that can store information on a relatively low number of donors. For others setting up a donor database may require considerable monetary investment, proprietary software, and the capacity to handle many thousands or even hundreds of thousands of donor records. With large supporter bases it may also be desirable to select a system capable of rudimentary analysis that will support the segmentation of the donor base (as discussed further in Chapter Six) and allow fundraisers to monitor the success of their strategy.

Database selection is beyond the scope of this book, but it is important to recognize the central role that it plays in relationship fundraising. Because of the limited functionality offered by their present databases and the poor quality of the data they have stored, some organizations may be able to adopt relationship fundraising only after they have made a substantial investment in computer hardware and software.

Understanding Why Donors Lapse

We stressed above the need to adopt a "zero defections culture" in order to minimize donor attrition. However, before such a culture can be created, an organization needs to have a clear understanding of why donors stop giving and whether their doing so varies by method of giving or by level of giving. All nonprofits should therefore "watch the door" and determine who is leaving and why. Where practical (and always in the case of major donors), it is worth approaching lapsed donors personally to determine why they left and the weaknesses they perceived in the relationship. When there are many defectors, perhaps from a mailing program, some survey work may be desirable to accomplish this goal. This information should be captured on an ongoing basis and the factors shared with the departments within the nonprofit that need to take action as a consequence.

Using Relationship Fundraising to Maximize Loyalty

We conclude this chapter by examining the practical steps that fundraisers can take in designing a relationship fundraising program to minimize donor defection. Many of the points we make below have been touched on in previous sections, but here we present an action plan.

Match Fundraising Programs to Donor Needs

Having researched the needs of donors, fundraisers should be able to group donor preferences together in such a way as to make it profitable to meet them, while ensuring that all donors feel that their individual needs have been met. We return to this issue in Chapter Six, where we deal with segmentation. Designing fundraising offers to meet donor needs is the opposite approach to simply seeking donors who might have an interest in the offers the organization has previously developed. To paraphrase Levitt, relationship fundraising focuses primarily on the needs of the donor; transaction fundraising focuses primarily on the needs of the organization.

Constantly Reinforce the Value to the Donor

Donors are not loyal because a nonprofit designs great fundraising communications or gimmicks. Donors are loyal because the organization offers them the best value for their money. Typically the value is the impact that their gift will have on the cause, but sometimes the value is the benefits they receive personally or is some balance of these two dimensions. The lesson for loyalty is that the nonprofit needs to identify these sources of value and constantly look for ways to reinforce it.

Develop New-Donor Communications and Ask for Feedback

Many nonprofits realize the value of welcoming first-time donors, but this welcome should include more than a simple thank you note. Some organizations make telephone calls to new donors in which the callers indicate how the donors' money will be used and invite them to ask questions. Others welcome donors by mail and initiate a welcome cycle, a special introductory series of communications that educate new donors about the organization and its work. Whatever the approach, it is important that in this first communication the organization not ask for money. By not doing so, it will stand out from the crowd. Organizations need also to seek the views of new donors to ensure that they were happy with the process of acquisition and (if it has not happened already) to begin to offer them choices about the nature of the relationship they will have with the organization. Levels of donor satisfaction with welcome communications can be high, on occasion so high that new donors become advocates for the organization and actively promote it to others.

Explain to Donors the Full Range of Services

Because the number of engagements a donor has with a nonprofit is one driver of loyalty, the nonprofit should lose no opportunity to promote every way in which the individual can either help the organization or be helped by it. The full range of opportunities to give, volunteer, and, if appropriate, access service provision should be communicated frequently. All these opportunities should be available on the organization's website. In face-to-face solicitation, those avenues that seem most appropriate can be discerned and offered. In direct mail, requests for some categories of support can pervade all communications, while other, more complex forms of giving can be dealt with at specific points during the development cycle.

Develop Donor-Recognition Programs

Programs to encourage and reward gifts at higher levels are now commonplace. They typically involve offering donors various labels, such as *supporter, donor, advocate, partner,* depending on the level of the gift. As we show in Chapter Ten, some nonprofits offer membership in a range of "clubs" with escalating benefits, such as an annual dinner or a seat at the president's table at the annual dinner. These schemes work because donors can see what is expected of them. They can read the names of peers who have given at certain levels and determine the norm for members of their social group. They can also be encouraged to upgrade their membership from year to year, thereby deepening their commitment.

Measure Satisfaction and Retention

Having designed a communication program to meet donor preferences, fundraisers need to ensure that it performs as expected and that individuals receive the right benefits. Ongoing research is necessary to track donors' satisfaction with all the contacts they have with the organization. We return to the topic of perceived quality of service in depth in Chapter Nine, but it is worth noting here that any aspects of service that do not achieve high satisfaction ratings should be redesigned. The impact on loyalty will be profound.

The organization must also establish systems to measure donor attrition or defection in as many different ways as possible. Defection should be measured by value, by method of acquisition, by pattern of development communications received, by region, and by primary demographics. The organization needs to know who is leaving and why so that a plan to optimize retention can be constructed and implemented.

Analyze Complaint Data

Few fundraising departments are fortunate enough not to receive any complaints in the course of a year. Most if not all nonprofits, particularly those dealing with contentious issues, receive a sizable mailbag of complaints every time they run a campaign or publicize their activities in the press. Such communications should not be dismissed as routine. Rather, complaints should be analyzed to determine patterns. Are certain activities more likely to generate dissatisfaction than others? Are there any clues as to why they do? Could some complaints be addressed without compromising either the organization's mission or its ability to fundraise?

A nonprofit also needs to create a policy for dealing with complaints. The approach will depend on the size of the database and the volume of complaints received. Complaints from donors and, in particular, complaints from higher-value donors should be given the highest priority. Complaints from other stakeholders and members of the general public can also be prioritized, and when appropriate and cost-effective, a response can be initiated. Some nonprofits may not be able to respond to every query or complaint, but they must develop a system for categorizing communications that do warrant a personal response. Systems should also be constructed that specify the time an organization will take to respond. Performance against this standard should be measured and remedial action taken where necessary. Timely and appropriate responses to complaints have been shown to improve the chances that individuals will remain loyal (Jones and Sasser, 1995), and hence in many organizations complaints are regarded as opportunities (see Chapter Nine).

Identify Relationship Issues and Failures

Data from the ongoing monitoring of service quality and complaints can be used to develop a list of relationship issues and failures. Many of these may be individual and difficult or impossible to resolve. More frequently, however, a pattern will be detected that can provide guidance as to where the relationship strategy is failing. This information can be converted to an action plan, which (subject to being cost-effective) can then be implemented. Typical relationship failures are as follows:

- Ignoring donors
- Lying to donors
- Failing to return calls or answer letters
- Failing to deliver on promises
- Being uncivil
- Not responding in a reasonable time
- Failing to keep in touch
- Not listening hard enough
- Forgetting a special occasion
- Making unreasonable demands

Nonprofits clearly need to strive to ensure that the incidence of these failures is kept to a minimum if retention is to be maximized.

Measure Profitability

Finally, nonprofits developing an approach based on relationships need to ensure that such relationships are profitable and that in the medium to long term the return on investment exceeds that which would be achieved through a transaction approach. Relationship fundraisers need to measure the returns generated through their strategy and check them against the original forecasts. Smart nonprofits now assess the success of changes in their strategy by the increase in loyalty and donor lifetime value they achieve. Organizations need to move away from short-term measures of performance and toward a longer-term perspective and an assessment of the ultimate impact a change in strategy might have had. Staff rewards and opportunities for advancement should be firmly linked to these measures to ensure that all those on the fundraising team are aware of the importance of retention issues.

Summary

In this chapter we have explored the concept of relationship fundraising and differentiated it from transaction fundraising. Rather than approach donors with a series of well-crafted one-time asks, organizations should build a genuine dialogue with their supporters over time in order to increase retention. The difference between these two approaches is fundamental. Relationship fundraising starts from an understanding of what donors want and an understanding of how these needs can be met cost effectively through a tailored and evolutionary program of communication. A transaction approach, by contrast, involves the organization merely in selling the needs of its beneficiaries and seeking to achieve the best return on investment it can from every set of communication materials produced.

New media are already having an impact on relationship fundraising. With the Internet and e-mail it becomes beautifully simple to tailor communications to the needs of individuals and to do so at extremely low cost. As nonprofits begin to make greater use of web-based fundraising and donors become more comfortable with this medium, relationship fundraising will become standard practice.

CHAPTER FIVE

RESEARCHING WHAT DONORS WANT

A s we saw in the previous chapter, donors are most likely to stay loyal to your
nonprofit and to increase their giving over time if they feel that they have
established a two-way relationship with the organization and that their needs and
preferences have been considered. Achieving this relationship in practice is not
easy. Nonprofits often struggle to design fundraising programs that meet donor
needs and expectations, and they spend considerable sums of money on the development process.

In this chapter we focus on the role fundraising research can play in facilitating the development of a retention strategy. We outline the key information requirements of such a strategy and then consider how this information might be
gathered. However, this is not a text on research. Our interest in the topic here
extends only to the role that research can play in fostering loyalty and the errors
that fundraisers might make when interpreting research. Readers interested in the
topic of research more generally are advised to consult one of a number of excellent texts on the topic, such as Churchill (2000) or Chisnall (1996).

In our view there is no substitute for research. The development of an optimal retention strategy depends on having a thorough knowledge of donors and
the factors that impinge on their decision making. It is not enough to merely take a
guess at what these factors might be. On occasion organizations can get lucky and
select an appropriate strategy by chance, but more frequently poor strategies result
when high-quality fundraising research is lacking. Even where research has been

undertaken, nonprofits can still make mistakes in the development of their retention strategy because they fail to understand the strengths and weaknesses of the work they have completed or because they make errors in interpretation or both.

Even when an agency is used to conduct retention research, fundraisers need to have an informed view about, for example, the advantages and disadvantages of qualitative and quantitative data. Failure to grasp such issues can lead to false conclusions and the development of inappropriate strategies. We address these points and define all the terminology below.

What You Need to Know About Your Donors

We have established that donor loyalty is driven by a (sometimes complex) mixture of factors and that giving is best increased and sustained when a fundraising organization builds a two-way relationship with its donors by offering choice and by responding to donor needs and preferences at an individual level. To develop such a relationship successfully you need constant access to reliable and current donor information. Such data have to be practical to gather and record and easy to interpret. In some cases information is recorded about individual donors, while in other cases data are gathered more generally in order to inform retention strategy and to help segment donors into appropriate groups. What, then, are the characteristics that need to be understood about donors in order to develop the best relationship with them? The following ten key questions about donors need to be addressed:

1. *Why did they start giving to your organization?* Probing the reasons why a first gift was made is essential in determining the relationship that can be developed with donors. Donors may make a first contribution because they have a personal link to the organization; they (or a family member or friend) may be a current service user or may have benefited in the past from the services provided. Their initial gifts have an element of reciprocation or payback. They also already know about the nonprofit's work and the beneficiaries of the work, and it will thus be appropriate to acknowledge that they have this information in the tone and content of the communications they are sent. Other donors may have little knowledge of or experience with the organization; these donors may have spontaneously made a first contribution in response to an emotive or emergency appeal. Their picture of the organization may be accurate, or it may be outdated or incomplete. They may never establish a long-term relationship or may want much more information and require cultivation before they feel comfortable committing themselves further. Such information on the way that a donor was first recruited and data on the

messages or elements of that approach that were important in prompting the decision to give need to be recorded. Donors often complain of a disconnect between the messages used in acquisition communications and those of subsequent (retention) vehicles, and many never give again as a result.

2. *What are their expectations of your organization?* It is important to ask donors what they expect the organization to be doing and achieving with their support. They may perceive it as having a short-term aim to change a piece of legislation or to complete a specific capital project, or they may understand that its mission is long-term and that it is therefore appropriate to offer a longer-term commitment. They may be looking for quick and tangible results or may expect little change to be evident in the short term. You can ensure that you don't disappoint donors only if you first understand what they expect.

3. *What (if any) services do they need from your organization?* Donors may also be service users who require information or assistance, or they may have friends or family members in that position. Donors who are also beneficiaries are often strong advocates for an organization, and their dual status should be discovered and should be recognized in all dealings with them.

4. *What communications do they want to receive?* As we have seen, one of the most important ways that a two-way relationship can be established between a donor and a nonprofit is by offering the donor a choice of how and how often she or he will receive communications. Although it is not practical to implement separate and truly individual communication programs for every donor on the database, nonprofits can offer a range of manageable and deliverable options to their donors. This dialogue not only offers donors a chance to engage and to make their personal preferences known but also demonstrates to them that the organization is efficient, respectful, and careful with its resources. As communication preferences often change over time, it is also important to repeat this dialogue or at least to make it easy for donors to register changes in the future.

5. *How do they want to give?* As part of the dialogue on communication preferences, it is important to offer appropriate giving options. Preferences, for example, for regular giving or for giving through sponsorship or membership should be explored, recorded, and respected in subsequent communications. Many donors stop giving because they feel that they have been asked to donate at a level or with a frequency that is not appropriate for them, or they may feel strongly that they should not be prompted to give certain amounts. Others will be happy to have gift amounts suggested to them. Such preferences should be respected in order to promote loyalty.

6. *How else might they give?* It is also important to ascertain other giving routes that donors might take in the future. Data on the ability of donors to give through planned giving or through major gifts can be gathered and used to inform retention and development work among appropriate donor groups.

7. *Are they interested in supporting your organization in other (nonmonetary) ways?* Donors may want to (or may already) lend support to your organization in other ways than by simply giving money. Information should be gathered on whether they are interested in volunteering, becoming involved in community events, and so forth.

8. *What particular aspects of your organization's work interest them?* As discussed above, the level of knowledge donors have about the work your organization does will vary considerably. As development and retention communications can, at least in theory, cover any aspect of that work, it is important to find out the areas individual donors find most interesting, involving, and inspiring. Once you have a clear idea of the work they consider most attractive and important, you can focus on their preferences in further appeals made to them. Many nonprofits find that donors exhibit clear patterns and contrasts in their interests and that a segmentation strategy built around their preferences is therefore a sensible basis for retention.

9. *Who are they?* Demographic and lifestyle information, such as where donors live, how old they are, what they do at work and outside it, and whether they have a family, is often gathered automatically as part of the acquisition process. All this information is essential in retention work, both in facilitating accurate communication and in establishing the right tone and feel for those communications. A newsletter designed for donors who are between the ages of twenty-one and thirty-five should look different and have a different tone from one designed for a donor group that is over sixty, even if the basic content and triggers are the same for both.

10. *Who and what influences their giving?* Giving may be started or stopped, reduced or increased as the result of an individual or a family decision. A community group, a place of worship, or an employer may influence levels of giving and guide giving preferences. You need to know as much as possible about these influences in order both to understand the behavior of donors and to enable your organization to reach out to those individuals, organizations, or institutions that influence decisions about giving.

The Research Process

These ten key questions can be answered through fundraising research. Figure 5.1 provides a framework for this research process.

Specifying Research Objectives

The first stage of the process is the specification of research objectives. A clear and unambiguous expression of the objectives is essential to ensure that the research is focused, particularly if an external agency is to be employed. Unless the

FIGURE 5.1. THE FUNDRAISING RESEARCH PROCESS.

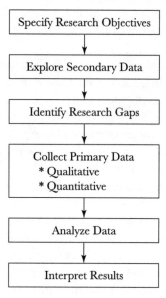

agency has a complete understanding of the issues facing the client, the information produced at the end of the process may be irrelevant if the objectives are not clear. For example, if the problem is that donors recruited through direct-response television (DRTV) tend not to respond to subsequent appeals, the research objectives might be the following:

> To quantify donors acquired through DRTV advertising who have lapsed and to discern trends in retention rates among them
>
> To explore the extent to which these retention trends are unique to the organization or common to the sector as a whole
>
> To discover the motives of the donors recruited through DRTV advertising
>
> To assess the expectations of the donors recruited through DRTV advertising
>
> To obtain a profile of the donors acquired through DRTV advertising
>
> To assess donor perceptions of the DRTV recruitment process
>
> To assess donor perceptions of the communications received after acquisition through DRTV advertising

This list is not exhaustive, and the content will vary in accordance with the particular circumstances facing the nonprofit commissioning the research. The point here is that the problem has to be broken down into a series of objectives that address each of the factors likely to be playing a part in the low levels of response from this donor group. If an agency is to be employed to collect the data, it should be closely involved in shaping these objectives as agency personnel may have insight into the issues and also because they need to understand the rationale underlying each objective.

Exploring Secondary Data

Secondary data come from research that has been conducted in the past for some other purpose either by the nonprofit itself or by third parties, such as research agencies or professional bodies. After research objectives have been set, the next step is always to determine what information already exists. These secondary data are cheap and should therefore always be exploited before costly new research is undertaken. For example, a nonprofit may routinely initiate direct dialogue with donors—for instance, through a survey (as part of a welcome program) that offers choices about future communications and that gives donors an opportunity to express an interest in other ways of being involved with the organization. Information in the existing donor database can also be analyzed to determine the giving patterns and preferences of current donors and the patterns of response and nonresponse among individuals whose donations have stopped. Communications received from donors, such as letters of complaint, and the opinions and experiences of front-line staff are also valuable. Demographic and lifestyle data are often supplied at recruitment by a list broker, or they can be obtained or supplemented through data profiling (as discussed in Chapter Six). In our DRTV donor example, relevant secondary data might include database response records, demographic or profiling data, articles published in the trade press, research reports, and specialist journals. Key sources of secondary data that are relevant to donor retention are listed in Exhibit 5.1.

Collecting Primary Data

In many cases existing information is not sufficiently representative and the data are not recent or relevant enough to be used with confidence in designing and investing in retention programs. In particular, information about donor attitudes and feelings is not likely to be available. If people always made decisions about giving to certain causes and about the value they place on their relationships with certain nonprofits on an entirely rational basis, there would be little need for

EXHIBIT 5.1. KEY SOURCES OF SECONDARY DATA.

Internal Sources
Database records
Profiling data
Management accounts
Internal reports

Sector Journals
FundRaising Management
Nonprofit Times
Chronicle of Philanthropy
Nonprofit Management and Leadership
Nonprofit and Voluntary Sector Quarterly
International Journal of Nonprofit and Voluntary Sector Marketing

Academic/Research Institutions

Indiana Center on Philanthropy
http://www.philanthropy.iupui.edu/

The Urban Institute
http://www.urbaninstitute.org/

Mandel Center for Nonprofit Organizations, Case Western Reserve University
http://www.cwru.edu/mandelcenter/

Hauser Center for Nonprofit Organizations, Harvard University
http://www.ksghauser.harvard.edu/

Social Welfare Research Institute, Boston College
http://www.bc.edu/research/swri/

The Aspen Institute
http://www.aspeninstitute.org/

Independent Sector
http://www.independentsector.org/

Fundraising-Information Websites

www.Charityfundraising.org

www.givingcampaign.org.uk

www.charitynet.org

www.fundraising.co.uk

www.guidestar.org

www.caritas.co.uk

EXHIBIT 5.1. KEY SOURCES OF SECONDARY DATA, Cont'd.

Think Tanks

The Future Foundation
http://www.futurefoundation.net/

Social Market Foundation
www.smf.co.uk

Professional Associations

Association of Fundraising Professionals (AFP)
www.afpnet.org

Institute of Fundraising
http://www.institute-of-fundraising.org.uk/

Association for Research on Nonprofit Organizations (ARNOVA)
www.arnova.org

International Society for Third Sector Research (ISTR)
www.istr.org

Council for Advancement and Support of Education (CASE)
www.case.org

Other

American Association of Fundraising Counsel (AAFRC), Trust for Philanthropy
http://www.aafrc.org/philanthropy/

Directory of Social Change
www.dsc.org.uk

Better Business Bureau
www.bbb.org

research, as fundraisers could just make an educated guess about donors' motivations and be proven correct on most occasions. However, human beings often behave irrationally and base their decisions on emotional and subjective responses. In these cases, developing a research program is the only way to uncover their motives for giving or for not giving.

When information gaps remain after a search for secondary data, fundraisers need to commission primary research in order to obtain new data to answer the research objectives. This typically expensive exercise should not be entered into unless the information is likely to be of considerable value. Two broad categories of primary research can be commissioned—qualitative and quantitative. These research types and the methods that can be used are outlined below.

Qualitative Research. Qualitative research provides insights into feelings, opinions, and motives. It is therefore appropriate to use qualitative methods if you are looking for information such as how donors view your organization, how they feel about the communications they receive, or what motivated them to respond to a particular fundraising approach. The most common qualitative methods are depth interviews and focus groups (group discussions).

Depth interviews are conducted with individuals from the group whose opinions are being sought. They are arranged on a one-to-one basis so the interviewee is not put under any pressure to respond in a socially responsible way and does not need to worry about what other research participants think of his or her views. Researchers using this technique are trained to put their subjects at ease and to ensure that the process is open and unthreatening. Depth interviews can be unstructured, semi-structured, or very structured depending on how much knowledge the researcher has at the outset about the factors likely to be discussed. When the researcher does not have detailed knowledge, an unstructured approach can facilitate a general discussion around the research question. The interview topics can then be narrowed down as pertinent factors emerge. The disadvantages of this technique are cost, which may be up to $30 per interview, and the potential for bias if interviewers put their own interpretations on the answers being given.

Focus groups, or group discussions, require the researcher to assemble six to ten individuals who have agreed to take part in (typically) a one- to two- hour discussion that addresses the research objectives. This discussion can be held at the organization's offices or at a separate venue located conveniently for participants. Focus-group researchers carefully facilitate the discussion, ensuring that every participant takes part. They may have to deal with individuals who attempt to dominate or lead the discussion and with those who fail to express a point of view. Facilitators need to be highly skilled so that the views of every participant are considered equally. Focus-group sessions are usually either audiotaped or videotaped for subsequent analysis. The main drawback of this technique is the cost. A typical focus group costs between $1,000 and $1,200 and six to eight groups are usually necessary to address a given research question. Basing decisions on a smaller number of groups is inadvisable, as individual focus groups can be unrepresentative of the donor group as a whole.

Because qualitative research does not quantify the impressions and feelings it uncovers, qualitative research alone may not constitute valid market research. The sample sizes are too small, the method of questioning can be inconsistent, and the interpretation of results is unavoidably subjective. Two or three individuals (or agencies) doing the same qualitative research often come up with different results because the views of a small number of individuals are rarely representative of the population as a whole (the entire group whose views are being researched). For example, a group of DRTV donors brought together in a focus group to probe the issue of nonresponse to subsequent appeals might come up with a valuable list of factors, but it could not provide any indication of the proportion of the total DRTV market that would feel a particular way. Focus groups are an excellent way of finding out how donors feel, but they cannot indicate how many individuals hold these views. The value of qualitative research lies in the generation of hypotheses about how the relevant donor population as a whole might feel or might behave. Typically these hypotheses are then tested using quantitative techniques.

Quantitative Research. Quantitative research involves the gathering of numerical information. The goal is to provide data on the number of members of a group who hold certain views, donate in certain ways, or are motivated by certain issues or factors. Quantitative-research techniques include face-to-face interviews, telephone interviews, and postal and e-mail questionnaires.

Face-to-face interviews may be conducted in the home, on the street, or in an office. Both qualitative and quantitative data can be collected in this way, although time constraints often mean that it is practical to concentrate on quantitative data. The interviewer, working with a set script, poses a series of questions and writes down the replies, which are then analyzed numerically.

Increasingly marketing research is carried out through *telephone interviews*. As with face-to-face interviews, telephone researchers follow a set script. This process is now usually automated through a system known as computer-assisted telephone interviewing, which presents the interview questions on computer screens in front of the interviewers so they can input responses quickly. Depending on the response recorded, the system prompts the next question to ask.

Postal questionnaires provide a less personal route to the selected audience. A questionnaire is mailed out with a postpaid reply envelope included, and responses are often encouraged in some way. Mailed questionnaires have the advantage of being low-cost, but response rates are often poor. It is not uncommon for these rates to hover around 5–10 percent, and they can be even lower if younger people are being surveyed.

Many researchers believe that *electronic surveys* will replace telephone and postal surveys by the 2010s. Questionnaires can be e-mailed to donors, or longer questionnaires can be included on an organization's website (or a password-protected part of the site), with donors being sent an e-mail asking them to complete it and providing the requisite link. If the organization already has the necessary technology, these surveys have the merit of being low-cost, but nonresponse can also be an issue here, with completion rates being typically only 5–10 percent, even with the present benefit of novelty.

In commissioning postal or e-mail surveys a fundraiser should always ask how the researcher intends to handle nonresponse bias: that is, how the researcher will account for the fact that the people who respond may be different from those who do not. This is a particular problem in retention research. One way of handling this problem is to do a telephone follow-up of a small sample of nonresponders. The results from this sample can then be compared with the results for the larger mail sample to see whether any differences emerge. If there are no differences, then the fundraiser can safely rely on the results of the postal survey. If differences do emerge, the research may need to be repeated employing a different method.

Some researchers deal with nonresponse by comparing the answers of the last 25 percent of responders with those of the first 25 percent. The theory here is that those who respond last to the survey are likely to be the most like nonresponders. If differences emerge between these two groups, a problem probably exists with the results. If no differences emerge, the results are most likely representative of the views of the total population being surveyed.

In quantitative research it may be possible to ask the relevant questions of everyone in the target population—for example, all DRTV responders. The researcher is then essentially conducting a *census*, as everyone is given the opportunity to express his or her views. However, in most donor research a census approach is not possible because the total population is often large; the cost of reaching all of the members of the group under study is therefore prohibitively high, and the logistics are unmanageable. In this case researchers take a *sample* of the population. They then calculate statistics from that sample that allow them to make statements and provide estimates about the views or behavior of the population as a whole without the need to contact everyone.

A variety of methods can be used for taking a sample, the technicalities of which are beyond the scope of this book. Fundraisers who are commissioning or interpreting donor research need to know, however, the advantages and disadvantages of each method; a good research agency will work with its clients in choosing the most appropriate method.

Once the nature of the sample is determined, the researcher needs to decide how large the sample will be. The size of the sample depends on a number of factors, such as the type of statistics that will be calculated, the degree of accuracy required, the population being studied, and the resources available. A number of tools (including tables, calculator functions, software programs, and on-line tools) can be used to generate appropriate sample sizes. Sample-size calculations, surprisingly, do not have much to do with the size of the population; they are based instead on the variability within that population. If ten thousand people all respond in an identical way to solicitations, you need to take a sample of only one to predict the behavior of the others. However, if the ten thousand people respond at one hundred different levels and in several different ways, the sample required will be larger. The more variants involved, the greater the sample size needs to be.

Choosing the Research Method

Having a clear understanding of research methods allows a nonprofit (or its research agency) to match its research objectives to the appropriate methods for reaching them. Returning to the DRTV example, we can now specify how each of the objectives might be met through the range of research techniques we have discussed. The objective "to quantify donors acquired through DRTV advertising who have lapsed and to discern trends in retention rates among them" can be met by using database records to count the numbers recruited and the numbers lapsing over time. The objective "to explore the extent to which these retention trends are unique to the organization or common to the sector as a whole" can be met through desk research of secondary data presented in the sector press, journals, and published reports. The objective "to obtain a profile of the donors acquired through DRTV advertising" can be addressed using existing database information or through data profiling (see Chapter Six). The other objectives are best addressed through a two-stage research program, with focus groups designed to generate a set of hypotheses and a quantitative project designed to test these hypotheses among a larger audience representative of the entire base of DRTV recruits.

Interpreting the Data

When a research agency presents the data it has gathered, clients should approach the report with a healthy degree of skepticism. Even when a high degree of trust exists between the agency and the client, the organization should expect a thorough justification of the findings presented. If qualitative data have been collected, the conclusions that the agency draws should be grounded in the data. The organization should look for illustrative quotes drawn from the transcripts of the focus groups or interviews that justify the specific conclusions and should be able to understand why each of the conclusions has been drawn. If evidence is lacking in the agency's report, organizations should ask for transcripts of one or more of the discussions to ensure that they can follow the rationale adopted by the researchers. If, as is typical, the organization is using the agency for an "objective" view, it should not second-guess the agency. The organization does not have to agree with a particular interpretation, but it should be able to follow the agency's logic.

The same points can be made with respect to interpreting quantitative data. Organizations need to check that the conclusions drawn are thoroughly grounded in the numbers and statistics presented. It may be difficult for a nonexpert to grasp the nuances of particular statistics, but it should be possible to check whether the conclusions reached seem logical given the data. In one report we were involved with, the research agency had conducted a survey of individuals who had pledged to leave a legacy (or bequest) to a nonprofit. The purpose of the research was to determine what communications the organization should use when it asked its existing donors to consider such a gift. The agency found that direct mail was the preferred medium of the existing pledgers they surveyed and thus concluded that direct mail should be used in all future solicitations to the rest of the fundraising database. They had forgotten an earlier part of their survey, however, which showed that all the individuals who had responded had been recruited as donors originally through the medium of direct mail. It is therefore not surprising that they considered direct mail the most appropriate route: they had all previously demonstrated responsiveness to this medium! Donors brought into contact with the organization through other media might well hold different views about how the issue of a legacy or bequest should be raised with them.

Selecting and Managing a Research Agency

Rarely does a fundraising organization have research expertise and technical support available in-house, so, as we have noted, it is frequently necessary to employ external specialists in the collection and analysis of research data on donors. In these cases the organization should involve the agency from the start in defining the research problem and developing the objectives. These goals should be agreed to formally as part of a brief. If the nonprofit has an existing relationship with a research agency, the brief can be given to that agency. Alternatively the organization may wish to ask a range of agencies to respond to the brief in a competitive tendering process. Research is expensive, and a tendering, or pitch, process is often the best way to ensure that your organization gets value for its money. When asking agencies to pitch, you should request that they respond with a proposal document, which interprets the research objectives, specifies the data requirements, and lays out the methods to be used in gathering the data. Costs and schedules should be part of this document, along with (in the case of quantitative research) an estimate of the level of accuracy of the findings that will result.

The decision about which agency to use for a project should be based on a number of considerations, including cost, the quality of the proposal (see the discussion of ways to assess this quality below), the reputation of the agency (especially regarding the specific research methods to be used), and the experience of the agency in the nonprofit sector and in researching donors in particular. The seniority and experience of the staff offered by the agency should also be considered, as should the extent to which the agency has worked with competing organizations. Although familiarity with a nonprofit's competitors is an advantage, issues of confidentiality and conflict of interest need to be addressed.

When reviewing a proposal document, a nonprofit needs to consider all aspects of the research program:

- Are the *methods* proposed appropriate? As we have seen, qualitative and quantitative techniques have their own strengths and weaknesses. Qualitative methods can produce useful ideas and hypotheses, but they should not be used on their own to shape strategic change. In research on retention it would be dangerous to make decisions about communication frequency and content on the basis of depth interviews or focus groups alone because the responses may not be representative of the views of your donor base.
- In quantitative research, is the *sample* proposed representative of the donor population you are concerned with? Researchers should identify at the start the key variables (for example, age and gender) that will be used to select individuals for a sample. The nonprofit and its research agency need to ensure that the sample includes an appropriate mix of individuals and that this mix mirrors the donor population under study.
- The *size of the sample* should also be checked. As we have discussed, a large sample size is not necessarily indicative of robust research. The correct sample size is a function of the variability of the population, the techniques that are being used, and the degree of accuracy you require. If the population of donors to be studied is large, be suspicious of proposals to research fewer than two hundred individuals. When samples are too small, the results are unrepresentative. Basing decisions on these data would expose your organization to significant risk.
- You should probe the agency to discover what *response rate* it is seeking to achieve and how it will handle nonresponse bias. A report may, for example, describe "a survey of one thousand donors," but the response rate may have been only 10 percent, and the results therefore are based on the views of just one hundred people. This research would be invalid, however, only if the one hundred people who responded are not representative of the audience being researched. If, for example, the donor base is made up of 20 percent males and 80 percent females, 30 percent of donors are over seventy, and 75 percent have a household income over $100,000 a year, and the same proportions are true of the one hundred responders, the results are probably representative.
- Agencies and researchers should be able to provide an estimate of the likely *accuracy* of the research results. There is always some possibility that the findings

of any study could have occurred by chance. Before making any changes to a donor-development program based on research findings, it is important to be confident that the results have a high probability of being accurate.

• Simple *variables* like age, gender, and income can each be measured by a single question. Complex phenomena, such as the degree of trust an individual has in an organization, cannot be measured through one question. Such *constructs* should be probed through a number of different questions to ensure that the researcher ends up with a meaningful response. Asking donors whether they trust an organization through a simple yes/no question is meaningless. What does it mean to trust a nonprofit organization, and isn't it, in any case, a matter of degree? Exhibit 5.2 includes a group of questions that might be used to address this issue more effectively. If one measure of trust is required, taking the mean (average score) of the answers to these questions would be an appropriate way to get to it. Nonprofits should thus question agencies about how they intend to measure complex social phenomena. If the research concerns retention, the measurement of constructs such as trust, commitment, loyalty, or the motives we referred to in Chapter Three, such as sympathy, empathy, and the desire to conform to social norms, is a far from straightforward task, but a good agency should be able to explain and justify its approach.

Having selected an agency on the basis of its response to the brief, the nonprofit next has to set up the necessary communication links for managing the project as it progresses. Usually an individual at the agency is designated the client liaison. The person managing the project from the nonprofit end should monitor progress against the schedule and should provide all the information and access the agency requires to facilitate its work. When research projects have two stages, with a qualitative phase preceding a quantitative phase, the nonprofit should re-

EXHIBIT 5.2. SAMPLE QUESTIONS FOR MEASURING TRUST.

To what extent would you trust organization X to undertake each of the activities listed?

	Low Degree of Trust						High Degree of Trust
To always act in the best interest of the cause	1	2	3	4	5	6	7
To conduct its operations ethically	1	2	3	4	5	6	7
To use donated funds appropriately	1	2	3	4	5	6	7
Not to exploit its donors	1	2	3	4	5	6	7
To use fundraising techniques that are appropriate and sensitive	1	2	3	4	5	6	7

quest an interim report at the end of the first stage so that the results can be subjected to a "reality check" prior to the start of the second stage.

Summary

You need to be able to access a wealth of accurate and up-to-date information about your donors in order to build programs and structures that establish a relationship with them, deliver on that relationship, and encourage and build donor loyalty. This information can be gathered in a number of ways: through database analysis of donor behavior, through the initiation of a direct dialogue with donors, and through research. Research can involve a desk-based investigation of existing sources, or it may require the gathering and analysis of new information in order to answer a particular question or set of questions.

In this chapter we have looked at the techniques and methods available for donor research, at the strengths and weaknesses of each, and at the process that should be followed in undertaking a research project. Research is a specialist area of knowledge requiring specific tools and experience. In many cases nonprofits wishing to undertake research have to buy this expertise from an external agency. We have provided some recommendations for selecting an agency and some pertinent questions to ask when considering research proposals and reports.

In the next chapter we describe how the findings of retention research can be used to inform fundraising strategy.

CHAPTER SIX

USING DONOR SEGMENTATION TO ENHANCE LOYALTY

I n the previous chapter we examined how market research can be used to gather information about donor motives and preferences. Here we consider how this information can be used to inform retention strategy. In particular we examine techniques that can be used to cluster donors into specific segments, which can then be used to tailor communication programs. True one-to-one communication with the majority of donors remains impractical (although it is essential with the highest-level givers), but your donor base can be segmented and development programs can be initiated to enable your organization to meet donor preferences in such a way that it appears to every donor that you are indeed responding on an individual basis. This perception can help build loyalty for a number of reasons. First, if the needs of donors are met by the organization, they have no reason to switch their support elsewhere. Second, as donors perceive that the organization is responsive to their needs, they feel obliged to reciprocate by continuing or extending their giving. Third, because donors have chosen the degree of interaction that takes place, they are likely to remember and value their encounters with the nonprofit and to continue to give accordingly.

In this chapter we look at how the perception of one-to-one communication may be achieved across a donor database. We review some of the most common donor groupings used by fundraisers and outline the kinds of programs currently used to best effect in retaining and developing each group. Although we use the term *perception* of one-to-one communication throughout this chapter, we do not intend for you to somehow mislead donors into believing that they are important enough to warrant one-to-one communications. Donor needs may be intensely personal, but if an organization has hundreds, thousands, or even hundreds of thousands of donors, groups of these donors will have similar if not identical needs. These bundles of need can be separately and successfully addressed so that from their perspective donors have a relationship with the nonprofit that is an exact reflection of the relationship they prefer.

Defining Segmentation

Segmentation has been defined as "the task of breaking down the total market (which is typically too large to serve) into segments that share common properties" (Kotler, 1991, p. 66) and as "the process of dividing a varied and differing group of [donors] or potential [donors] into smaller groups within which broadly similar patterns of needs exist" (Wilson, Gilligan, and Pearson, 1992, p. 91). The rationale for segmentation is simply that by focusing on a distinctive set of needs or interests, a nonprofit can develop a fundraising program that uniquely addresses those issues. This adaptation makes it attractive for donors to give to the organization and enhances response rates; increased gift amounts and loyalty levels are likely to result.

Segmentation Criteria

A wide variety of criteria can be used to segment a nonprofit donor base.

Demographic Criteria

Donors can be clustered together on the basis of variables such as age, gender, socioeconomic group, family size, family lifecycle, income, religion, race, occupation, and education. Collectively, these are called demographic variables. In most cases a combination of some or all of these variables is used in building a donor profile. Because demographic data have been collected over many years, a great deal is known about the giving behavior of each group and their likely needs, wants, sympathies, and preferences. Thus, if some demographic information can be gathered, a lot of other information about the group can be inferred with a fairly strong level of confidence. Age, gender, income, and occupation are the most commonly employed demographic variables.

A huge proportion of the support for nonprofits comes from the older sections of the population. *Age* tends to be a reliable indicator of the sources of information people use, the communication routes they are most comfortable with, and the social influences they are susceptible to, as demonstrated by the sample donor profiles in Exhibit 6.1. The profiles are ones that were developed by a non-profit dealing with the welfare of deaf and hearing-impaired people for key segments of its supporter base. As can be seen, nonprofit donors in different age groups start their association with the organization through a variety of routes and often want different benefits and activities to keep them interested and loyal. This sort of breakdown by age group, using sketches of "typical" individuals, can be a useful guide in planning media and in writing and designing communications. Imagine, for example, the damage that would be done by sending an identical communication to all the groups mentioned in these donor profiles!

Many studies have demonstrated *gender* differences in giving. Women tend to spread their giving among a greater number of charities and so tend to give smaller amounts to each one (Sargeant, 1999). Most nonprofit donor databases are weighted markedly toward females. Studies of for-profit marketing have shown that the way women respond to information is radically different from the way men respond (see, for example, Marx, 2000, or Braus, 1994). Making use of these studies, some nonprofits segment their mailings by gender and develop "male" and "female" copy. With direct marketing the benefits of segmenting on this basis can easily be tested and at a relatively low cost.

Income has also proved to be a useful base for segmentation; despite difficulties in identifying a true picture of income for any particular group, it is a powerful indicator of propensity to give and of likely donation levels. The higher and the lower socioeconomic groups tend to give a higher proportion of their income to good causes than do those in the middle. A common fundraising approach based on income is segmenting the level of the fundraising ask. We know from professional experience that higher earners may be less likely than low earners to respond to low-level gift requests. Many want to give at a level that will make a difference. Thus, the level should be appropriate for the selected audience.

Geodemographic Criteria

Geodemographic information combines data on geographical location and type of housing with lifestyle data; this type of information can be used to ascertain the purchasing (and giving) behavior of particular neighborhoods. Suppliers of geodemographic segmentation systems categorize households by a number of different types (typically forty to seventy). These systems work because people who live near each other typically are at a similar stage in their lifecycle and have similar interests and behaviors. In the United States the approach is typified by the PRIZM system, which was developed by the Claritas Corporation. Claritas collects a vast amount of information on the populations of the forty-two thousand zip code areas, including standard demographic data, product and service purchases, and

EXHIBIT 6.1. SAMPLE DONOR PROFILES.

Elders 70+
Most with low incomes, but free of debt. They like to support many charities, but because of their limited discretionary funds, often at low gift levels. They like children's groups, animal-welfare, and health causes related to their personal experiences. They hold traditional values and appreciate special efforts made for them, such as personalized acknowledgements of support.

Dorothy is aware of the work of this organization because her physician gave her a leaflet when she was fitted for a hearing aid. When she recently received a leaflet from the nonprofit asking for her opinions on deafness, she was happy to respond, and to give a small gift. The little address labels printed with her name especially touched her; she uses them when she writes to her friends.

Seniors 60–70
Respond well to appropriate direct mail from charities, particularly those concerned with children, animals, and local causes. Have a strong waste-not, want-not philosophy, hold traditional views, and hope for a better future for their children and grandchildren.

Joan had been badgering her husband, Ken, to have his hearing tested for years. Eventually her persistence paid off, and Ken was fitted with a digital hearing aid. When the appeal came she was happy to give, particularly when she saw that the organization had been involved in the development of the new technology that was benefiting her husband.

Thrivers 50–60
More affluent than any previous 50+ group, healthier, and more active. They're not old. They own their own homes and are recent beneficiaries of legacies from their parents. They are comparison shoppers and put a high premium on service. They give to overseas charities and health charities and to groups that preserve heritage and the environment.

Sarah wouldn't normally have thought to give to the organization, but she's noticed it's becoming harder to hear conversations at the social events she attends with her husband. She regularly throws appeal letters away, but she thought this nonprofit's plea for research funding was a little different.

Settlers 35–50
They are building their careers and families; they have good incomes but spend most of their money on house payments and their children. Charity support is likely to be based on personal interest or special interest rather than generalized philanthropy. They are most likely to support human rights or children's charities.

Lucy has a six-year-old son who has been deaf from birth. Her relationship with the organization is as a service user: she gives donations and receives information. She wants to be spoken to in an open and honest way. She understands the language of marketing.

Starters 20–35
Experiencing and enjoying their independence, starters have expenditures that often exceed their incomes and that tend to be self-focused rather than philanthropic. They are concerned about inequality in the world and about the environmental legacy of past generations. They are looking forward to career opportunities, a high income, good health, and a good retirement.

Kerri works hard and plays hard. She's sorry her grandmother is deaf but thinks that's what happens when you get old. Kerri loves going to nightclubs but was a bit worried when she saw a news item about prolonged exposure to loud music leading to deafness.

media use. Clustering procedures were then used to group zip code areas into sixty-two categories and fifteen social groups, which are given names such as "Shotguns and Pickups," "Money and Brains," and "Second City Elite." Fundraisers can use the PRIZM system to prospect for new donors, and the coding system can be purchased as an addition to a nonprofit database so that geodemographic data is appended automatically to every donor record. Other systems such as ACORN (A Classification of Residential Neighborhoods), ClusterPlus, and MicroVision are available in the United States, with similar systems available in the United Kingdom.

From a retention perspective, appending geodemographic codes to the database can help build a picture of who supports an organization. It is normal to find that support tends to come from particular categories of households. The additional data the suppliers are able to provide about the kinds of individuals who live in these clusters of households can provide a rich picture of the typical donor and therefore of the kinds of development and retention messages likely to have the most appeal.

Lifestyle Criteria

Lifestyle has been defined as a pattern of living in the world as expressed in one's activities (work, hobbies, social life, entertainment, shopping, sports), interests (family, home, job, community, recreation, media, achievements), and opinions (of oneself, social issues, politics, business, education, products, culture). Lifestyle data portray the whole individual and how she or he interacts with the environment.

The basis of lifestyle profiling and segmentation is that substantial numbers of people have been persuaded to provide research agencies with comprehensive information about themselves: their households, possessions, behavior, and interests. A huge amount of lifestyle information on millions of people is therefore available commercially. Databanks are compiled from sources like product registration cards and large-scale consumer surveys.

These data are most often used by charities in donor recruitment; they rent or purchase lists of prospects with profiles that closely resemble those of existing donors. However, lifestyle data can also be appended to donor records and used in retention segmentation. The key to using this information for retention lies again in understanding the kinds of individuals your nonprofit has as supporters. By building up a picture of them you can decide on the messages most likely to act as a stimulus to action. Too many fundraisers write copy and design communications that they enjoy themselves, not copy and communications that a particular lifestyle group will enjoy.

Preference for Communication Route and Frequency

As we discussed in Chapter Four, one of the most effective ways to establish a two-way relationship with donors is to give them the opportunity to choose how they are communicated with and how often they want to hear from you. Donors who have identical demographic and lifestyle profiles may have completely different preferences for methods of communication. Many younger donors, for example, may opt for e-mail as the best route for charities to use in contacting them, but among this same age group some may still prefer the mail. Some donors react extremely badly to telephone fundraising calls, considering them an invasion of privacy, while for others, who may have the same lifestyle and giving history, the telephone is a convenient and appropriate way to be approached.

Your organization should be able to offer donors a range of options, workable for you, that can then be used as a basis for segmentation. These alternatives are often best explained in a welcome packet sent to donors shortly after their first gift has been received. Most donors are receptive during this "honeymoon" period and are delighted to have the chance to express their preferences. Asking for this information also makes donors feel that your organization does not waste resources and is courteous and is therefore a worthy recipient of their charity giving. This sort of welcome is often the key to beginning a long-term relationship with a donor. As some donors will not express any preferences, a "standard" program should be developed that reflects the wishes of the majority or of those in the middle segment; this program should be reviewed in the light of subsequent donor behavior and responsiveness (or nonresponsiveness).

Once information on donor preferences has been collected, it should be recorded and used in the creation of segments. Here is an example of segmentation based on preferences for frequency and type of communication:

Segment 1 Once a year by e-mail
Segment 2 Once a year by mail
Segment 3 Once a year by phone
Segment 4 Twice a year by e-mail
Segment 5 Twice a year by mail
Segment 6 Twice a year by phone
Segment 7 Quarterly by e-mail
Segment 8 Quarterly by mail
Segment 9 Quarterly by phone
Segment 10 No communications required

Donors should be made aware that they are free to change their preferences at any time and should be given the means to make such changes. They should also be presented with the opportunity to review their instructions on a regular basis as their circumstances change.

A number of warnings and caveats should be added. Your nonprofit must be able to deliver the choices offered efficiently and economically. A common mistake is to promise donors options that the organization cannot deliver or can deliver only at a high cost. Database systems have to be in place to record the preferences expressed and to generate the appropriate communications at the right time, and suitable communications must be available for use or must be easily produced by modifying existing materials. Not following through on promises produces far worse donor relations than not offering all options to begin with.

Nonprofits designing segmentation strategies around donor communication preferences should also be mindful that the resulting segments have to be big enough to make the exercise worthwhile. Planning should include thinking through every possible combination to ensure that small segments are not likely to be created. If they are, the options offered should be modified. Most donors would rather get quarterly e-mails, for example, than have their preferred monthly e-mail service cost the nonprofit a disproportionately high sum to deliver.

Area of Interest

Many nonprofits have broad missions and are involved in dozens of specific projects to further their mission. Their donors, however, may be especially interested in only one part of that work, in only one project (which might be a local one or might have some personal relevance), or in only certain types of projects. The areas of particular importance to a donor either can be discovered by directly asking the donor or can be inferred from the donor's response to the solicitations that have been sent over time. Inferring a preference can be as simple as identifying that some supporters of an animal-welfare charity tend to support projects featuring dogs rather than horses or as complex as ascertaining that a donor to a social welfare organization is developing a preference for projects benefiting specific communities or areas of need.

Segmentation on the basis of areas of interest can be beneficial to an organization in that it can send appropriate appeals and information to those individuals who feel the strongest involvement with and connection to a specific element of the mission. However, some pitfalls also exist with this strategy. Although some donors have special areas of interest, others are more broadly engaged in the nonprofit's work, and it would not therefore be appropriate to channel specific communications to them. Many donors who are initially attracted through one area of work or one project that repeatedly engages them may also enjoy receiving information about other areas, and their loyalty can be encouraged through a process of education about the full range of the nonprofit's activities. If you choose to group your donors into interest groups, you must also be confident that sufficient and appropriate activity is being undertaken in these areas to sustain a specific communication program about each area over time.

Benefits Expected

Donors can also be grouped according to the benefits they seek. Some donors are service users and want regular information; others require high levels of feedback and recognition in return for their contributions. This form of segmentation is most clearly demonstrated by nonprofits that allocate different levels of benefits and care in accordance with the category of donation made. Such fundraising products and recognition vehicles are discussed at greater length in Chapters Eight and Ten, respectively.

Level of Interest or Knowledge

Donors can also be grouped according to the nature of their interest in the work of the nonprofit. For example, the Royal Society for the Protection of Birds (RSPB) segments donors according to their level of interest in and knowledge of the subject. The organization sends communications to committed bird watchers that are different from those it sends to individuals who like to attract birds to their gardens but understand little about them. Some donors to charities involved in medical research are motivated to respond to information about the science behind the work, while others prefer to hear about the results through case studies and human-interest stories about individuals who have benefited. Some of this information on level of interest and knowledge can be gathered directly through donor research, but some has to be inferred over time through the study of donor responses. Tailoring messages in line with the approach to a subject that individual contributors prefer is an effective way to keep donors' interest and support over time.

Type of Activity

Some nonprofits provide services and also lobby to promote change. Because different donors are motivated by each category of activity, many of these nonprofits find it beneficial to segment their supporters along these lines to ensure that lobbying and campaign messages and calls to action are received by the donors most likely to act on them and that other fundraising or information communications are not drowned out by campaign material. Many nonprofits ask donors to self-select by opting-in in advance of the receipt of campaign and lobbying communications. In addition, some donors who fall cleanly into the campaign category demonstrate mixed responses to different campaign messages, perhaps according to the specific project or area the campaign is addressing. Other "campaigners" may be among the most generous donors, responding to any and every kind of message the nonprofit sends them.

Donors can also respond differently to certain types of fundraising activity such as competitions, prize drawings, and raffles; fundraisers need to select those who are solicited for this sort of activity carefully, bearing past response and donor preferences in mind. Although some donors view raffles as an enjoyable and entirely appropriate vehicle for charity support, others find them objectionable.

Exhibit 6.2 is a survey that a membership-based environmental nonprofit might use to gather information on members' activity preferences. Responses to these sorts of questions can be used to group members into segments according to their primary interests. Answering these questions is also likely to make donors feel involved and to believe that the nonprofit is interested in their opinions. Such surveys strengthen the bonds between the organization and its supporters by giving donors the chance to reaffirm their belief in the mission of the organization.

Giving Criteria

Supporters' giving history and giving potential also provide a way of segmenting your donor base.

Recency, Frequency, Value (RFV). One of the most common forms of segmentation is the grouping of donors by how much and how often they have given. Data on recency (the time since the last gift was given), frequency (the number of gifts that have been given), and value (the value of the gifts given) are calculated and are used to provide for each donor a score that can then be used to determine whether that donor should receive a particular solicitation. RFV analysis assumes that (1) higher-value donors are more valuable than lower-value donors, (2) donors who give frequently are more likely to respond to a communication than those who don't, and (3) donors who have given in the last six months are more likely to give than those who have not given for the past two years. RFV scoring can reflect differences in individual donor behavior and give the fundraiser considerable insight into whom to include in particular donor-development programs, whom to address with specific solicitations, and how much to ask for.

Many charities use RFV scoring in conjunction with other criteria, such as donor communication preferences and ratings based on the sort of appeal themes the donor has responded to (or rejected) in the past, to drive segmentation. RFV can also be used effectively to identify those donors most likely to lapse, to look

EXHIBIT 6.2. SAMPLE SURVEY FOR DETERMINING DONORS' PROGRAM AND ACTIVITY PREFERENCES.

In order to achieve the goal of protecting, preserving, and enhancing our environment, which of the following activities should we emphasize?

☐ Public education programs

☐ Land purchase

☐ Advocacy and lobbying

☐ Research

Check items that describe the relationship you would like to have with us.

I would like to:

☐ Support your work financially and read about environmental issues in your magazine

☐ Be notified quickly about urgent environmental issues so I can write to public officials

☐ Take an active role in building support by nominating others for membership

☐ Help establish a local activists' network

☐ Be involved in habitat-preservation efforts near me

☐ Other _____

Of the following, which is your single most important reason for contributing to us?

☐ To learn more about environmental issues through your magazine

☐ To help protect the environment with a financial contribution

☐ To help protect the environment through personal actions

for patterns of lapsing, and to prompt reactivation. Pre-lapse campaigns can be generated for those donors who have not given recently or whose frequency and value patterns have been interrupted. The charity Help the Aged (described in Exhibit 6.3) provides an example of the use of RFV segments in structuring a mailing program.

Predicted Lifetime Value (LTV). One of the weaknesses of using RFV is that it focuses attention on a donor's past behavior. The better approach, when the quality of in-house data permits it (although it frequently doesn't), is to segment donors according to how much the organization believes they will be worth to it in the future. This measure is donor lifetime value (LTV). The calculation of LTV is complex; we discuss this calculation and the uses of LTV in detail in Chapter Eleven.

EXHIBIT 6.3. HELP THE AGED:
AN EXAMPLE OF THE POWER OF RFV SEGMENTATION.

Help the Aged works to address issues that matter to older people. Their four main priorities are (1) combating poverty, (2) reducing isolation, (3) defeating ageism, and (4) challenging poor standards of care.

Help the Aged ran a system in which donors were selected for mailings by recency: their mailings went out to anyone who had donated in the last four years. But this was too broad a measure. Marketing analysts at Help the Aged realized that if they had two donors who last gave four years ago, they should be separating the one who had given a single gift of $5 from the one who had previously given an annual gift of $50.

By including frequency and value variables in the analysis, Help the Aged now has a much better indication of supporters' worth to the charity, and the analysts are able to match this worth against the cost of mailing to determine whether particular donors should be included in a given communications program.

Help the Aged segments its donor base (using SPSS) by ranking the file from highest to lowest using Recency, Frequency, and Value. Each file is then split into equal bands, and a score from 1 to 5 is appended to each band. Frequency is defined as the number of gifts a supporter has made over their lifetime, and Value is defined as the average (mean) gift over their lifetime. This latter measure proved to be a more discriminating factor than the total value of their gifts. Each supporter was allocated an RFV score accordingly.

Method of Giving. Most North American donors give by check or by credit card to mail or telephone solicitations received at several points throughout the year. A smaller number now give over the Internet, and major donors give through sometimes complex planned-gift vehicles solicited in one-to-one meetings. In each case donors are usually responding to a new request each time. Some organizations ask donors to pledge regular gifts, but even in these cases the donor must frequently take action in order to make the gift on each occasion.

Monthly giving through automated bank payment has revolutionized donor fundraising in the United Kingdom since the mid-1990s. This new approach is also beginning to pervade fundraising in the United States (where the banks are less amenable to automated payments) as monthly-sustainer or pledge programs (McKinnon, 1999), and it is prevalent in Canada. Such programs are likely to be a key feature in the expansion of fundraising in the coming years.

Monthly givers, once recruited, should be treated differently from single-gift donors, as they are likely to respond differently to the communications they receive and to require a different development program if they are to be kept loyal and upgraded successfully. Retention programs for regular givers should feature feedback and recognition, courtesy communications, an upgrade appeal (perhaps once a year or every two years), and an occasional cash appeal only if the theme is appropriate. Like other pledgers, regular givers have a wide range of communication preferences, which should be respected wherever possible.

Implications for Development Strategy. So far we have focused on the characteristics of individual donors. In this section we explore opportunities for segmentation by giving group and explain how retention can be fostered among each of the giving categories: major givers, bequest/planned-giving prospects, high-value donors, and low-value donors.

Most U.S. charities (and an increasing number in the United Kingdom) deal with potential and actual *major donors* through a discrete program of personal contact, stewardship, and events. This program is often carried out by specially selected staff, board members, or volunteers or by a separate department or division within the development function. Ongoing RFV or LTV analysis will identify donors who have already made a major gift or a number of high-value gifts. These donors can be flagged and provided with a personal level of stewardship and recognition. They can also be profiled to provide guidance for prospecting. The main donor base should be "trawled" for major prospects on a regular basis. The cultivation, retention, and development of major givers is a different process than that used in the development of the bulk of the donor base. Much of the contact is face-to-face and often involves individuals from within the nonprofit who are friendly with the donors in question. The uniquely personal nature of this form of solicitation makes it unlikely that there will be a great deal of overlap in the communications that are used for major givers and for the rest of the supporter base. Occasionally the same event invitations, feedback vehicles, and special appeals may be sent to major givers and to lower-level donors, but major givers generally receive an enhanced or more highly personalized version of the package. The keys to retention in this context are donor involvement, ongoing cultivation through personal relationships, and the professional stewardship of these donors.

Those donors who pledge to leave *a bequest or other planned gift* to a nonprofit organization form a special supporter segment and should receive a tailored program of development communications designed to retain their loyalty and interest and to recognize that they have made a major commitment, even though it may not be realized for many years. Such donors do not necessarily possess high levels of disposable income, as their estate may be in the form of property or other nonliquid assets.

Designing a strategy for this segment of supporters can be challenging, as they often have a wide variety of opinions as to how they should be treated and can be demanding. Many prefer not to receive public recognition during the lifetime of their commitment (which they see as confidential), while others expect regular and prominent acknowledgment of their status. The content of any program therefore depends on the accurate recording and use of individual preferences.

Many nonprofits invite donors pledging gifts of this kind to join a "legacy club." The Nature Conservancy legacy club, for example, provides its members with personalized membership certificates, copies of special publications, and invitations to exclusive conservation journeys and events. This practice is beginning to grow in the United States, where legacy gifts have historically been the preserve of the planned-giving department and have been solicited primarily from major donors. The lesson from other countries is that all donors have the potential to offer a bequest, and while these gifts may be smaller than those from higher-value donors, they can still be substantial. Soliciting lower-value legacies from the mass of the fundraising database can be a successful strategy.

Programs of care for this category of giver typically involve a limited number of appeals, regular feedback and updates, plus courtesy communications, such as invitations to special events and Christmas cards. The key to retention is to develop a differentiated standard of care and to avoid excessive requests for additional donations. These individuals have provided to your organization in their wills probably the largest single gift they have ever made to a voluntary organization, and they expect their generosity to be rewarded.

Many charities identify a segment of *high-value donors*, those who have given at above average levels but have not given a major gift. Each nonprofit has its own definition of the amount that qualifies as a major or high-value gift; as an example, a major gift might be defined as $10,000, and a high-value gift as $250–$9,999. High-value donors may be researched to see whether they are likely to become major donors in the future. They are valuable to the organization and should receive an appropriate program of communications that educates them about the cause and guides them toward a planned or major gift. Such communications should address areas in which these donors have demonstrated an interest and should include invitations to events, and courtesy and feedback mailings. Appeal packets should have a higher production value than the standard and may include additional items. All communications should be personalized, should refer to the previous giving history of the donor, and should recognize the value of these previous contributions.

One of the main advantages of RFV or LTV analysis is that *low-value donors* can be identified, and programs can be developed to ensure that more is not being invested in this group than is warranted by the gifts expected from them over time. Individuals who give small amounts can easily be generators of a negative ROI (return on investment). In a commercial setting such customers might be ignored or divested, but in the nonprofit arena this option is never advisable; a great deal of anecdotal evidence suggests that sizable bequests can come from donors who have given little during their lifetimes.

Efforts should therefore be made to maintain a relationship and to retain the loyalty of low-value donors if this is possible while also obtaining a positive ROI.

Low-value donors might therefore receive a restricted number of appeals and updates each year and might also be approached to convert their giving to a regular commitment in order to reduce administration and retention costs.

Low-value donors, as the least-valuable segment, can also be used in reciprocal mailings (list swaps). Using these donors (where data-protection law permits) in exchanges with other nonprofits may minimize recruitment costs. Our experience, however, suggests that the decision to swap lists should not be taken lightly. Each donor whose name is swapped typically loses between 10 and 20 percent of lifetime value, and a nonprofit may unwittingly be giving away a bequest prospect, as noted above.

Where to Start? Determining Segments and Assessing Their Suitability

As we have seen, donors can be segmented in a variety of ways. We have examined segmentation by category of giving and by demographic, lifestyle, and behavioral variables. Faced with all these options a nonprofit may have difficulty knowing where to start in developing a successful segmentation strategy. It is impossible to prescribe the exact criteria that should be used by a particular nonprofit; most select a mix of these variables.

The best approach to selecting donor segments is to look at donors within each giving category to determine their needs and preferences. Your organization can thus develop, for example, subsegments of regular givers interested in specific aspects of your work. You can also profile these groups by demographic or lifestyle variables or both to determine not only the profile of each category of giver but also other ways in which the organization can interact with them.

It is important not to be so carried away by this process that you continue segmentation to the point where all economies of scale are lost and where as a consequence your fundraising becomes uneconomic. Donor needs and preferences should be met only where it is profitable to do so. This tactic is nothing less than what the donors themselves would expect.

Thus, although an organization can consider many ways of segmenting its donor base, only a few of them will be worth developing. The difficulty facing fundraisers is how to evaluate the possibilities. Four criteria can be used to analyze the potential of each proposed segment. Only if the analysis is favorable in each case should the segment be pursued. The segment must be:

1. Measurable: The segment should be easily measurable and information about its characteristics should therefore exist or be obtainable cost effectively.
2. Substantial: It should be cost effective to fundraise from the segment. In other words, the segment should have a large volume of donations (or be small with sufficiently high contributions) to warrant separate development.

3. Stable: The segment's behavior should be relatively stable over time to ensure that its future development may be predicted with some degree of accuracy for planning purposes.
4. Unique: The segment should have a unique response to fundraising activity so that it can be distinguished from other segments.

Criterion 4 warrants explanation. A segment may meet all the other criteria but may behave identically to other segments in its response to different types and timing of appeals. If this is the case, you need to recognize that although it may be conceptually useful to develop separate segments in this way, it is not managerially useful (Kotler and Andreasen, 1996). As an example, many charities now have two distinct demographic groups in their direct-marketing databases: older individuals (sixty and over) and younger donors (twenty-five to forty). The fundraiser responsible for donor development can look at the differences, decide that the segments are distinct, and develop a separate communication program for each. However, if donors in the two segments react in an identical way to receiving direct mail, find the same topics/issues relevant, and are stimulated to give by the same motives, it does not make sense to treat these two groups differently. Segmentation is not necessary.

Summary

In this chapter we have discussed the role of market segmentation in donor development and retention. We have summarized a range of criteria that can be used to segment a fundraising database and have illustrated how each major segment can be developed. One of the keys to successful donor retention lies in developing a thorough understanding of who gives to the nonprofit and why. Segmentation simply applies this knowledge to the database and allows the fundraiser to develop a detailed focus on each group of individuals. Fundraisers find it a lot easier to communicate with each of these groups if they understand who the donors in each segment are, their likes, dislikes, preferences, and so on. One experienced fundraiser we have worked with keeps a photograph of an individual representative of each major segment of donors on his computer. Whenever the organization develops a new communication he reflects on how the relevant individual will feel receiving that communication. This practice can yield considerable insight into the design and likely impact of campaigns, and, in fact, commercial marketers have been using this tactic for years.

CHAPTER SEVEN

GROWING MONTHLY GIVING

One of the largest growth areas in individual giving is regular, or monthly, giving. Many nonprofits have already recognized the value of a monthly-giving program, and we predict that by the mid-2010s the majority of individual-giving solicitations will be for this kind of gift because regular giving can enhance donor loyalty and lifetime value. With regular giving donors do not have to be approached for gift after gift as the months and years go by. They sign up instead at the outset to give a specified amount at specified times. Because the payment is taken automatically from their bank or credit-card account, they cannot forget to make their gift and are therefore not likely to lapse—a factor that improves the economics of fundraising for the nonprofit. Regular giving also frees up time and resources so that the organization can focus on designing communications to build a relationship as opposed to being driven by the need to secure yet another gift. The combination of these factors makes the development of a regular-giving program a powerful part of any strategy designed to foster donor loyalty. This chapter looks at why and how monthly giving works and presents best practices in this area. We provide a step-by-step process for the introduction of monthly giving and list the major pitfalls to avoid when establishing this sort of scheme.

Why Monthly Giving Works

From the point of view of many donors, a monthly gift is an attractive option. It effectively spreads the load, enabling donors to plan their finances and to spread their philanthropic commitment evenly throughout the year. Making a monthly gift by automatic payment means that donors do not have to think about their giving once the initial decision to contribute has been made—the administration of the gift is taken care of for them.

Monthly payments are also convenient and "painless" in their impact on a donor's finances; the debiting of a small regular gift is barely noticed. The donor will, therefore, often not consider it worth the time and effort to cancel the arrangement if his or her financial situation gets tighter. Inertia in this case works for the nonprofit, especially when the amount of the gift is low.

When promoting monthly-giving programs, many nonprofits highlight the fact that this form of support is cost effective for the charity to administer and that monthly givers need not receive additional appeal communications. The prospect of fewer appeals is definitely an attraction for many donors, and an increasing number of supporters are aware of the costs of communication and administration and are therefore supportive of automated giving as an effective way to maximize the funds directed toward programs. Thus, an effective case for monthly support can be constructed by linking the giving of a regular gift to the long-term, sustainable funding needs and core work of an organization.

From the perspective of the nonprofit, monthly giving provides a reliable income stream that can help with budgeting and cash-flow projections. Monthly gifts grow over time to substantial contributions. Monthly gifts are also economical to administer once the systems are in place, and communication programs for monthly givers are cost effective as there is no need to create and send a new appeal each time the donation comes up for renewal.

Monthly givers can be upgraded on a regular basis by asking that they increase their gift from time to time. Monthly givers can also be sent occasional appeals for one-time cash gifts, but these solicitations tend to elicit a good response only when the need is urgent, such as after an environmental or other disaster, or extraordinary, such as for a capital project. Generally speaking, if donors have accepted the logic of giving through a monthly payment, they prefer to increase their giving through the same route.

How Monthly Giving Works

Automated monthly payments can be made in two basic ways in the United Kingdom: through bankers orders or direct debits. With a bankers order, after the donor signs a paper agreement, the bank sets up and controls the payment from the donor's account, and any alterations to the arrangement have to be made by the donor. Direct debits are electronic transactions. The agreement can be set up without a donor signature, and the payment is debited from the donor account by the charity. Alterations can be implemented by the charity. In the United States, automated checking-account transfers (electronic funds transfers) work in much the same way, with the major difference being that to start the arrangement the donor is required to provide a voided check for bank coding purposes. Generally speaking, the banks on both sides of the Atlantic are eager to promote paperless and electronic systems to reduce their own administration costs and workloads, and they are actively encouraging and investing in these options. Paperless payment systems are therefore likely to increase in number and simplicity. From the perspective of fundraising, paperless systems are greatly preferable to bankers orders, as they are more cost effective, give more control to the nonprofit (less to the bank), and present the donor with fewer steps to take in establishing a gift arrangement. Monthly payments can also be set up with a "continuous-authority" arrangement, through which the payment is deducted from a credit-card account. Habitat for Humanity's HopeBuilder on-line application (Exhibit 7.1) provides reasons for monthly giving and an explanation of its monthly-giving options.

Impact on Donor Loyalty

A monthly-giving program has a major impact on donor loyalty for two reasons. First, monthly givers tend to keep giving for a long time, staying on the donor base for an average of four to seven years. As we mentioned above, inertia plays a part, as donors tend not to cancel an established giving arrangement even though they might have failed to respond to new requests for one-time gifts sent to them during the same period. Therefore, their lifetime value to the organization is much higher than that of most donors who give occasional gifts.

Second, monthly giving alters the dynamics of the donor-charity relationship. With the continual need to appeal for funds removed, the communication balance can be changed; the charity has more opportunities to give the donor feedback, information, and updates without the need to attach a donation request. Such communications also offer the ability to cross-sell other opportunities for the donor to engage with the organization, such as through trading (that is, offering products by mail order), volunteering, or event attendance.

A proportion of monthly givers will stop giving over time. Experience suggests that the reasons are generally changes in financial circumstances, changes in banking arrangements, or errors by banks or credit-card companies. The lapse rate needs to be carefully monitored to find patterns. Lapsed monthly givers can

EXHIBIT 7.1. HABITAT FOR HUMANITY MONTHLY-GIVING APPLICATION FORM.

Habitat For Humanity International - Online Donation Area - Microsoft Internet Explorer provided by Wiley P...

File   Edit   View   Favorites   Tools   Help

← Back ▼ → ▼ ⊗ ☐ ⚹ | ⚲Search ⚹Favorites ⚹Media ⚹ | ⚹▼ ⚹ ⚹

Address ☐ https://www.habitat.org/donation/hopebuilder/donation_1_form.aspx ▼ | Links »

Habitat for Humanity® International

Home | Donate Online | Gifts From The Heart | HopeBuilders | Click & Build

One Family, One Home at a Time!
Your gift helps lift people out of poverty housing.

Rest Assured

Security
All personal information you submit is encrypted using industry standard technologies.

Privacy
Please click here to review our complete privacy policy.

Good Stewardship
We take seriously our responsibility to contributors, to those counting on our help, and to God to be wise stewards of funds entrusted to us.

Quick Gift Guide

See what your gift could buy.

$10 = Box of Nails
$35 = Shingles
$50 = Low Flow Toilet
$75 = Window
$100 = Kitchen Sink
$150 = Front Door
$500 = Siding
$1000 = Wallboard
$2000 = Flooring

Our online donation process is secure and easy!

Our simple online donation process makes it easy to help deserving families — your tax-deductible donations represent a contribution to Habitat for Humanity's entire mission to eliminate poverty housing worldwide.

* = required field

First Name* ☐
Last Name* ☐
Address* ☐
Address ☐
City* ☐
State/Province* ☐
Zip/Postal Code* ☐
Country* ☐ USA
Phone ☐
E-Mail Address* ☐
(Required so we may send you your receipt.)

Monthly Donation Amount* $ ☐ 0

Gift Card Option ☐ Select if you would like to make this donation in honor or memory of a special person. If so, you will be able to select your gift card and sending method (e-mail or post card) on the next screen.

Stay Informed ☑ Keep me updated on the latest Habitat news - Send me bi-monthly Habitat Extra! e-mail newsletters and updates on how I can continue to support Habitat programs around the world.

HopeBuilder Terms of Agreement
This authorization to charge my credit card is just like writing a check to Habitat for Humanity International or making a charge on my credit card, except that it will be done directly.
I understand that each transaction will appear on my monthly credit card statement.
I further understand that this agreement will remain in effect until I notify Habitat for Humanity's HopeBuilder Coordinator that I wish to change or suspend it, and Habitat has a reasonable amount of time to fulfill my request.

[Click Here to Proceed]

Site Index | Donate Online | Local Affiliates | Search | E-Mail Updates | Habitat World
Get Involved | Where We Build | How It Works | Support Habitat | True Stories

To contact Habitat for Humanity International, please see our contact information page.

© 2003 Habitat for Humanity International

Done   Internet

Source: Reproduced with the permission of Habitat for Humanity International.

be successfully reactivated and persuaded to either give a regular gift again at a lower level or to give a cash gift.

Changes to the Donor Database

The introduction of monthly giving (especially when new fundraising routes are employed to recruit monthly-giving donors directly, as discussed later in this chapter) is likely to alter the balance of your fundraising database because automated monthly giving is especially attractive to younger donors, who are more familiar and comfortable with electronic banking arrangements than older donors and who also appreciate the speed of this form of giving. For example, the Royal Society for the Prevention of Cruelty to Animals (RSPCA) had a large donor base built through direct-mail single-gift asks; the average donor in this database was fifty-five to seventy years old. RSPCA fundraisers found, however, that moving to a monthly-giving appeal in their direct-mail recruitment packets attracted donors aged thirty-five to fifty-five.

Although this drop in the average age of donors is viewed by many nonprofits as a welcome development, it can pose problems. Younger donors are often not responsive to direct mail, preferring the telephone and e-mail. Donors at an earlier life stage are also much harder to maintain contact with over time, as they tend to move and to change banks more frequently. They also exhibit more fluctuation in their financial situation as they change jobs or take time out to travel or start a family, so their gifts may lapse at a higher rate than is the case with older donors. In the worst cases new, young audiences are attracted, but then the relationship with them either is not sustained through the right communication routes or is sustained only at a prohibitively high cost as they require a program of development communications different from that required by the rest of the supporters. Fundraisers who are prepared for the arrival of these new, younger donors can avoid these problems by developing relevant routes such as e-mail in good time and can build realistic expectations of lapse rates into the planning and budgeting process.

A further possible problem is that when regular giving is promoted across a selection of existing supporters, it tends to "cream off" the best donors; those most committed to the organization or with the highest levels of disposable income are the most likely to take up the offer of a regular payment arrangement. Consequently, the response rates and average gift sizes generated from appeals to the single-gift donors who remain will decline. In addition, it is also more difficult to gather data on the giving behavior of monthly donors than of single-gift supporters, who can be selected for specific appeals according to whether and how much they have given to previous appeals on related subjects. Regular givers obviously have no such clues about their personal interests built into their giving history, and thus they have to be asked to provide information on their preferences directly if these are to be used in selecting communications for them. However, these problems are generally side issues, as the introduction of regular giving has an overwhelmingly positive impact on retention and lifetime value. As long as fundraisers are prepared and forewarned, these situations can be allowed for, and their costs can be factored into plans accordingly.

Using Established Media to Promote Monthly Giving

Monthly giving can be introduced and enhanced by using the same media that you have been using for single-gift solicitations.

Direct Mail

When the aim is to convert current one-time donors to the new form of giving, most fundraising organizations have found it worthwhile to create a special direct-mail packet that thanks donors for their previous support and that runs through the benefits both to the donor and to the nonprofit of the new method of giving. The packet can include a section on frequently asked questions to address doubts about the administration and mechanics of the process and to explain clearly how the method works. Requests for monthly giving get the best results when the gift is solicited for the main mission and ongoing work of an organization—a long-term gift to meet long-term aims and needs—rather than being associated with a particular appeal. It is hard to craft a request for a monthly gift on the theme of emergency relief or a one-time capital project, as these situations call more logically for a single contribution. The aim is to use monthly giving to increase retention rates and lifetime value, so great care should be taken to ensure that the monthly amount suggested is appropriate; it would be disastrous to downgrade higher-value givers by converting them to a low monthly amount! The monthly ask should be related to the annual value of past gifts. Once a mailing to upgrade single-gift donors to monthly giving has been created, it can be tested on a variety of segments of the donor base.

In recruiting new supporters through the mail to give a monthly gift, many organizations simply amend an existing recruitment packet. We have found that it is better to feature a single ask in a recruitment packet, either for a one-time gift or for a monthly commitment, rather than offering both options.

As in appeals for single gifts, monthly-giving direct-mail recruitment solicitations are especially powerful when the gift amount requested is tied to a particular outcome. Donors may be suspicious of a request for a low monthly amount, fearing that it will not make much of a difference. By tying a gift to a particular outcome, charities are not promising donors that their individual gifts will be put to a specific use but are enabling them to visualize exactly how their monthly contribution might be used:

> For just $2 a month you can help provide food, medicines, and clothing to older people who are desperately in need.
>
> Your $4 a month can help us train two health workers in Bangladesh and will as a result safeguard the health of hundreds of people.
>
> In Sudan $4 a month will help provide enough tools for villagers to dig a well that will give their whole community a permanent supply of clean, safe water.
>
> Can you spare $10 a month to help us cure cancer faster?
>
> Giving a small regular gift is one of the best ways you can help because every advance we make takes many months.
>
> If you can spare $6 a month, it will pay for seven operations a year.
>
> $10 a month can help save her life.

Many successful charities recruit new donors by mail to give this sort of low-value monthly gift. The donors subsequently receive communications designed to increase their loyalty, are sent requests for additional one-time contributions only in extraordinary circumstances, and are upgraded by asking them every year or every eighteen months, usually by phone, to increase the monthly amount.

Upgrade requests can also be made through the mail. Most donors are aware that costs tend to rise over time and that it therefore makes sense for them to review their gift level on a regular basis. The following example comes from a mailing packet to monthly givers from an animal-welfare charity:

> I know how passionately you care about the plight of all the unwanted and abused animals we help each year. I know, because every month you show us with a valuable gift of £10 that is much appreciated.
>
> Although you already help us so generously, I felt I had to write to you today. You see, I need to ask for more help urgently.
>
> In front of me I have the latest figures, and I'm sorry to have to tell you that last year was one of our busiest on record. We saw an alarming increase in cruelty to animals, and we now receive a call for help every 20 seconds.

I am talking about a significant and disturbing increase in our costs, which we have to deal with swiftly if we are to prevent more animals suffering. That's why I need you to consider increasing your monthly gift by an extra £4.

Telephone

Telephoning existing donors can be an effective way to convert them to monthly giving and can also be effective in campaigns designed to increase the regular gift amount of existing monthly payers. As in a direct-mail approach, the benefits and mechanics of monthly giving can be explained in a telephone script, with callers primed to answer any objections or concerns the donor might have. A key advantage in telephone promotion of regular giving is the ease of the fulfillment process when a paperless payment system is in place. Donors can make their commitment over the phone, and all the charity needs to do is to write to donors immediately after the calls to confirm the arrangement. If donors do not respond to the letter by opting out of the arrangement within a prescribed time period, the payment can be set up with their bank. If the donor is required to sign and return a confirmation of the arrangements or to provide a sample check, a further step is introduced into the fulfillment process, and the telephone campaign is likely to be less profitable. Fulfillment is also key in telephone solicitations in which the aim is to increase the monthly amount given. If an amendment to a gift arrangement can be made by the charity without the donor's signature, the process is much more cost effective than when a signature is required because a step is cut out of the procedure. As with mail solicitations, upgrade requests are relatively easy to script.

Other Recruitment Media

New monthly donors have also been acquired successfully by means of direct-response television (DRTV), press advertisements, websites, and inserts in newspapers and magazines. In DRTV, as in direct mail, the monthly-giving request often merely replaces a previous single-gift prompt, with the rest of the creative concept left unchanged. Again, the number of stages that have to be gone through in the telephone fulfillment operation is key to the success of DRTV.

Press advertisements are used less commonly in recruiting regular givers, except where a sponsorship or membership product is being offered (as discussed in Chapter Eight). The size and complexity of the reply card required usually dictate that the advertising space be comparatively large and therefore expensive, and consequently the advertisement is not likely to generate an acceptable level of profitability. As with other media, press advertisements tend to be most effective when the request is based on an immediate and urgent need rather than being a less dramatic plea for a low-value, ongoing commitment.

The opportunity to give a monthly gift can be presented on a charity website, although few sites currently offer this as an on-line giving option; instead, the donor must print out a form for completion and return it to the charity.

Newspaper and magazine inserts can work well in recruiting regular givers, and, as in direct mailings, the regular-gift request can initially be added to an existing successful insert as a low-cost and low-risk test.

Exhibit 7.2 demonstrates that a monthly solicitation can also be used where higher-value gifts are being sought. The Australian Bush Heritage Fund uses this insert to recruit new givers at a suggested minimum of $25 (Australian) a month, payable by direct debit or by credit card.

EXHIBIT 7.2. AUSTRALIAN BUSH HERITAGE FUND MONTHLY-GIVING INSERT.

Source: Reproduced with the permission of Australian Bush Heritage Fund.

New Fundraising Routes

As we have seen, monthly giving can be used to recruit donors in all media where single-gift recruitment has been successful. In the United Kingdom and Europe two other forms of monthly-gift fundraising have developed since the mid-1990s and have made a difference in the philanthropic picture: face-to-face fundraising (also know as direct-dialogue fundraising) and door-to-door (or doorstep) fundraising. These routes are now growing in popularity in the United States as well.

Face-to-Face

Face-to-face fundraising is a simple idea that was developed originally in parts of Europe where strict data-protection regulations made the use of direct mail impossible. It is estimated that one in ten people in Europe now give to charities by this method, and it is also used in Australia, Canada, and the United States (Jay, 2002). Small teams of trained fundraisers, employed by a fundraising agency and representing a nonprofit, are positioned on busy streets and at shopping areas, commuter areas, and festivals in order to make direct contact with members of the public. They ask passersby to talk with them about the work of the charity they are representing and to consider supporting the work of the charity with a monthly gift from their bank account. The fundraisers wear brightly colored vests or T-shirts bearing the charity logo; they carry badges that identify them as professional fundraisers and give information as to how their legitimacy can be verified. The solicitation is for a regular gift only, so no cash changes hands.

The fundraisers are trained to make the solicitation approach nonaggressive and as nonintrusive as possible. Only passersby who appear interested are approached, and refusals are met positively. The idea is that the solicitation should be a genuine dialogue and a positive representation of the work and attitude of the charity. Fundraisers are typically young, enthusiastic, and upbeat; they communicate a passion for the cause and exhibit a resilient cheerfulness, whatever the weather!

From the point of view of the nonprofit, face-to-face is attractive because it delivers regular donors, signed up to give a sustainable donation. The charity is represented positively and prominently in busy public places by young and enthusiastic professional fundraisers. Payment to the fundraisers is per donor, so nonprofits pay for the activity only when it is successful—there is no waste and costs can be tightly controlled. The method also delivers a new, younger audience. Donors recruited by face-to-face fundraising tend to be "charity virgins": many do not support any other charity and the majority are new to regular giving. In the United Kingdom over 85 percent of face-to-face recruits are under forty (Jay, 2002).

Face-to-face was first tested by Greenpeace in Belgium and then rolled out throughout Europe. With a fundraising-agency partner, Greenpeace tested the concept in the United Kingdom in the spring of 1997. Initial tests were carried out at events such as the Glastonbury music festival, where large numbers of likely Greenpeace sympathizers were gathered in one place. It was a huge success. Both recruiters and those recruited fit the classic Greenpeace profile of young, passionate, and intelligent members. The new medium was then tested in busy streets and shopping centers, wherever pedestrian traffic was high. This successful tactic delivered young, committed donors at a return on investment that was as good as or better than any other form of donor recruitment in operation at the time. The parallel development of web-based communication and fundraising techniques helped to retain and develop the supporters recruited on the streets. Greenpeace is now using face-to-face recruiting on university campuses and at events in the United States.

Door-to-Door

Door-to-door is essentially face-to-face fundraising carried out on the doorstep. Trained professional fundraisers knock on doors and ask householders to consider giving to charity. If a gift is agreed to, a form is completed. The donor is given a copy of the form and a package of information to keep. The recruiters carry clear identification and are trained in nonaggressive solicitation. While face-to-face recruiters always represent a single charity, some door-to-door fundraising agencies run solicitation programs in which the fundraiser represents a range of different causes. The prospective donor can therefore choose to give, for example, to a children's charity, an animal charity, a health care cause, or a Third World–development cause. In another variation on the approach, the fundraiser makes two visits. On the first occasion the concept of monthly giving is introduced and the charity or charities are described. If the householder expresses an interest, the recruiter leaves some information and arranges to come back the next day. This approach allows the prospective donor time to consider the decision and to discuss it with family members.

A Step-by-Step Guide to Establishing a Monthly-Giving Program

Although the details of planning and implementing monthly-giving programs vary greatly based on the size and complexity of the fundraising organization, its current fundraising mix, its mission, and its donor profile, several basic steps should be followed. Much of the success of monthly giving lies in the smooth running of banking, database, and donor-care routines. The creativity of fundraising communications and the selection of media are also central, but in the implementation of monthly giving internal processes tend to prove the hardest barriers for fundraisers to overcome.

Step 1: Research and Plan

In any new venture the more time and effort that can be given to research and planning, the more likely that the project will succeed and run smoothly. Any nonprofit considering implementing monthly giving should research the activities of competitors and of charities of the same size in different fields to determine what if anything they are doing to promote regular giving. Relevant data on the preferences, giving patterns, and profiles of existing donors should also be assembled, and results from any past pledge or sustainer promotions studied.

Implementing monthly giving will affect many parts of the organization, including the finance department, database administrators, and those engaged in supporter care as well as the fundraisers. It will also change the working patterns and priorities of external suppliers, from fulfillment houses and creative agencies to media buyers and list brokers. Thought should be given to all these implications and a plan drawn up to brief the relevant stakeholders on the reasons why monthly giving could be important for the organization and the cause and on the part they will be required to play. If you can achieve "buy-in" from all parties at the beginning, you increase your chances of success.

Step 2: Make Cost Projections

To compare financial projections of the value of monthly gifts over time with the current value of your single gifts requires that you have accurate data on the current performance of your donors. You may know, for example, that you receive a 1 percent response rate to your direct-mail recruitment packet on average and that 55 percent of those you recruit never give a second gift. Against this background you might estimate that a monthly-gift solicitation will generate half the response rate. However, if you know, as we mentioned in Chapter One, that the lapse rate for monthly givers is 20 percent in the first year, then you can estimate that 80 percent of the responders will still be giving at the end of the first year. In year two, fewer will lapse—say 10 percent will be lost during the second year, and a further 5 percent will lapse in the third year, and so on. Such figures build a positive financial picture and a sound argument for regular giving as an aid in the promotion of retention and lifetime value. It is important not to be overoptimistic in projecting future income however. Monthly givers may give for years and may increase their monthly gift amount over time, but they are unlikely to respond to other appeals. And although their lifetime value will be high, the organization will incur costs in creating new communications for them.

Step 3: Set Up Payment Arrangements

Your organization's bank should be one of the first suppliers you contact. Its payment processes will be at the core of a regular-giving program, and these operations will need to run smoothly. Costs for payment processing should be established. In some cases the charity will need to apply for authority to operate certain electronic systems from the relevant financial-services organizations. This can be a time-consuming process and should be investigated at the start. Similarly, new software may need to be purchased and loaded before payments can be taken.

Step 4: Establish Database and Reporting Routines

There is little point devising promotions for monthly giving if the information needed to run the program cannot be stored efficiently on the donor database. For each monthly donor, your system needs to be able to hold a record of the gift arrangement and the payments made; these records can then be used for donor care, financial management, and the calculation of lapse data. Ideally management information should be available to facilitate the tracking of lapse rates by source media, by month, by donor segment, and by gift size. In devising communication programs for monthly givers it may be necessary to add new donor preferences, and the recording of gifts made during upgrade campaigns needs also to be considered at an early stage.

Step 5: Emphasize Donor Care

All monthly givers should receive a high standard of care, with high-value givers selected for special treatment. In particular, staff should receive training on the steps to take to investigate problems with regular-payment mechanisms. When monthly gifts lapse, you might assume that the correct system is to follow up as quickly as possible with the donor to try to reinstate the gift. But the lapse may be the result of a bank error that will be corrected in a month or two. Contacting the donor as soon as a monthly gift has been missed can therefore be counterproductive, as many donors will feel they have wasted their time trying to ascertain how to get the error corrected.

Step 6: Test of Existing Donors, Existing Media

Once the back-end systems are in place, the first monthly-gift offers to donors can be made. To minimize risk it is best to start by trying to convert existing donors to the new method of giving and to use media that the organization is already familiar with. In order to test the results of these offers, it is essential to limit the number of elements that are changed at one time. In most cases telephone and mail (or a combination of the two) are used for an initial offering to existing donors. A variety of donor segments should be tried, with care being taken that the amount requested does not downgrade donors but instead increases their giving.

Step 7: Test of Donor Recruitment

When a successful program is working among a section of the existing donor base, monthly-gift options can be offered in campaigns to recruit new donors. In most cases existing recruitment materials will feature the core work of an organization, and these can be amended to make the case for supporting that work through a regular rather than a single contribution. At this initial stage of offering the monthly-giving option to prospective donors, we recommend that you use media that can be tightly controlled, such as direct mail; you can then address any fulfillment issues before moving on to widen the net through DRTV, press advertisements, or inserts.

Step 8: Test of New Media

Once monthly giving is established, new media can be used, such as door-to-door fundraising. Before embarking on this project, however, further research should be undertaken, especially regarding the profile of the donors likely to be acquired. If much younger donors are to be recruited, your organization must be able to communicate with them in the ways they prefer in order to retain them over time.

Step 9: Monitor and Evaluate

As with any new fundraising enterprise, monthly giving programs should be monitored with care from the beginning and evaluated carefully. New measures, such as the calculation of lapse rates over time and the success of upgrade campaigns, need to be instituted. Evaluating the impact on lifetime value involves the costing out of ongoing communications, which in turn depends on the preferences of donors. Savings in and costs of fulfillment and donor-care operations should also be calculated.

As discussed earlier, it is also important to keep careful track of the overall impact of regular giving on the nature of your donor base. Donor-recruitment officers may be delighted at the success of new routes in attracting young donors, while donor-development staff struggle with operating different retention programs for a wide range of age groups, and planned-giving staff find far fewer bequest prospects to approach.

Step 10: Expand the Program

Despite all the provisos above, monthly giving should in time be rolled out through all viable recruitment routes using all possible fundraising methods.

Caveats

Although monthly giving is a powerful way to increase donor loyalty and lifetime value, there are some pitfalls; charities planning on introducing regular-giving programs would be well advised to be aware of the issues we discuss below.

Beware of Bank Charges

Monthly gifts of low amounts of money have proved popular with donors, but these gifts are profitable for charities to administer only if their banks do not charge a disproportionately high amount to set up the payment arrangements. If this is the case, and the bank charges are not negotiable, a minimum limit can be set for a monthly gift.

Automate the Process

The success of monthly-gift fundraising depends on the speed and accuracy of the organization's administrative and donor-care systems. Monthly gifts have to be set up quickly and acknowledged appropriately, and each monthly payment has to be received, logged onto the donor's record, and banked. Administrative, database, and software systems should be capable of automating this process. Manual reconciliation of hundreds or thousands of small monthly gifts can be a nightmare, and donors will expect charities that request monthly gifts to be able to debit them efficiently.

Expect Banks to Make Mistakes

Although some donors stop their regular gifts for various reasons, many payments cease through bank error. Payments can also be duplicated or be made at the wrong time. Again, the answer is to move as soon as possible to an electronic system that allows the charity, rather than the bank, to set up or change the arrangement and to draw down the funds each month. In the meantime, any communication to a donor about a lapsed payment should allude to the possibility that the donation has ceased through bank error rather than through the deliberate decision of the donor.

Allow Sufficient Time to Process the First Gift

The first time they sign up for a monthly gift, donors are likely to be unsure of the process, especially if the gift has also been secured through an unfamiliar fundraising approach. If the first payment is not made, they will immediately be suspicious. Even in the most well-organized nonprofits it can take weeks to set up a new payment. Therefore, you need to be sure that the date the donor sets for the first gift to be debited is sufficiently far in the future for the payment to be arranged. Many nonprofits also set one day in each month to take all their regular payments, a process that makes administration easier.

Explore the Practical Problems of Upgrades

As with payment set-up, increasing the amount of a monthly gift can be challenging for some database systems. In the early planning stages of an upgrade campaign, fundraisers should work closely with database administrators and supporter-care staff to run through the systems required to increase a gift and to ensure that the donor and bank records can be altered to reflect a higher gift amount within an acceptable time period.

Identify Lapsers and Calculate Attrition Rates

The success of monthly-gift programs should be measured in part through the calculation of the lapse rate, especially if these donors were recruited by door-to-door and face-to-face agencies, which receive a payment for every new donor. Paying per donor helps to make these methods affordable and accountable, but many donors obtained through this method do stop giving, perhaps because the payment has not been set up successfully, because donors change their minds, or because their financial situation changes. Some agencies guarantee that they will refund the payment (or part of the payment) made for obtaining any donor who lapses within a specific period, usually three months. The operation of this sort of mechanism depends on the nonprofit's having systems in place to track and identify lapsed payers quickly.

Summary

In this chapter we have reviewed the nature of regular, or monthly, giving. We cannot stress too highly how in countries such as the United Kingdom and Canada such forms of giving have revolutionized the economics of fundraising activity and have affected in a positive way donor lifetime value and loyalty levels. Although initially more expensive to recruit than single-gift donors, regular givers are much less likely to lapse and can generate lifetime values that are twice as high. We have mapped out the best of professional experience with this type of giving, illustrating how it can be developed and pointing out the major pitfalls to be avoided.

CHAPTER EIGHT

BUILDING EFFECTIVE FUNDRAISING PRODUCTS

The current focus of the nonprofit sector on fundraising products is another factor that has had a dramatic impact on donor retention. A fundraising product is a package of benefits that the donor receives from the organization. These benefits may accrue to the donor personally, but more usually a product is a package of beneficiary needs that donors can feel they have satisfactorily addressed. Examples of products include "sponsor a child," "adopt a dog," "adopt a granny." In each case the nonprofit maps out a specific set of needs that each beneficiary has and invites the donor to invest in resolving these needs.

The introduction of products to the fundraising mix can encourage donors to give over longer periods and to give in higher amounts than they would if products were not offered. Fundraising products breed donor loyalty for two key reasons. The first is the link that is forged between the donor and the beneficiary. This bond can be powerful, particularly in child sponsorship when the donor receives communications from the youngster being sponsored. The second reason is the immediacy of the feedback that these products create for donors. Donors know exactly what they are giving for and can reassure themselves at the time that the gift is made that a specific impact will follow. This feedback too can be powerful.

Because products present key tasks of the organization and associated outcomes as packages, with relevant costs attached, using them can make the work of a complex nonprofit easy for the donor to understand. Products can be focused on donors' special areas of interest, such as advocacy, and thus can maximize the support and involvement of a segment of donors by providing them with feedback and opportunities to make a difference in a specific area that matters to them personally.

However, although some fundraising products have proved successful in fostering and increasing donor loyalty, this route is not suitable or possible for every nonprofit; the development, launch, and management of a fundraising product can be difficult, costly, and time-consuming. Some wonderful success stories can be told in this area of fundraising, but there have also been many expensive failures.

In this chapter we outline the key characteristics of successful fundraising products and provide some examples of best practice. We then look in more depth at the processes that underpin this kind of initiative, and we close by pointing out the pitfalls to avoid in initiating this form of fundraising.

Characteristics

A wide range of successful product programs have been created by fundraisers worldwide; the best of them share a number of features. In general, they do the following.

Involve a Commitment to Regular Giving

Products are based on the donor's commitment to giving a regular gift monthly, quarterly, or annually. In the previous chapter we discussed the advantages of this form of giving and the positive impact that regular giving through automated bank payments can have on income generation and donor loyalty. This guaranteed payment is essential because the donor usually receives relatively expensive products, such as child sponsorship, and a high degree of care from the nonprofit, and the costs of set-up can be high. The contribution is therefore set at a relatively high level, with this cost spread by means of a monthly payment to make the commitment manageable for the donor.

Represent an Organization's Core Work

The best fundraising products represent the core mission of the organization. Examples are the Whale and Dolphin Conservation Society's "Sponsor a Whale" product, ActionAid's "Sponsor a Child," and Help the Aged's "Adopt a Granny." In each case the products are a fair representation of what the organization is all about. Products programs that are tangential to the core work or unrepresentative of the major efforts of the organization are likely to fail and may make it hard to fundraise successfully for other aspects of the organization's work. For this reason nonprofits that have a wide or long-term mission (such as some conservation charities) or that work on a reactive basis (such as emergency-disaster-relief organizations) find it difficult to package an aspect of their work into a product that can be easily grasped by their donors.

Provide a Direct Link to Beneficiaries

Fundraising products work best when they provide a link from the individual donor to an individual beneficiary. This is the basis of most sponsorship and adoption schemes. Such a link provides donors with a personal connection and gives them the chance to see and understand the good that their gift is doing. One of the initial attractions of these products is the involvement provided to donors at the outset, when they are asked to choose a child or person or animal to support.

Although the emotional link to an individual beneficiary is a key part of the success of these programs, product fundraisers have to be careful to make the use of funds under such schemes completely transparent to donors. In child sponsorship, for example, most programs direct the funding to the child's village or to projects in the vicinity that will benefit the child and the wider community rather than directly to the child or his or her family. In most cases many individual donors are in fact sponsoring the same child or animal, and the funds raised are destined for wider projects. In this way the case of the individual beneficiary serves mainly as an illustration of the problems facing a group. When a wild animal is sponsored, it is often not possible to track the progress or to directly affect the welfare of the individual creature, and sponsorship income thus may be used to purchase safe havens, to lobby for legislative protection, or to research behavior. This use of donations is entirely valid but only as long as it is made clear to the donor and the product is not mis-sold in any way.

Some sponsorship programs explicitly make the link between the donor and a group of beneficiaries. Oxfam's Project Partners was an example. Donors were asked to sponsor over time certain projects, such as irrigation or farming schemes; in return Oxfam provided them with reports of the progress of their project and of the impact it had on a specific community and on individual members of that community. Sponsorship of teams of workers, such as cancer nurses or scientific research teams seeking a cure for Alzheimer's disease, can also be offered. Although some of these programs have worked well, they tend not to be as effective as those that tie the donor to a named individual. Linking givers to groups or projects can make the cause tangible and immediate, but it does not bring the donors as close to the beneficiaries as when they have a perceived relationship with another person.

Set Appropriate Donation Levels

Many of the most successful fundraising products involve beneficiaries in the developing world because the impact that a relatively small gift can have is huge. For instance, a $15 per month gift to Oxfam's work in the poorest countries of the developing world (where more than 1.2 billion people live on less than $1 a day) can make a vast difference. Other effective product programs set a fairly high monthly amount, reflecting the enhanced feedback and level of service donors can expect and the seriousness of their commitment. In either case, the cost of the product has to be credible. If the cost appears to be too low or too high, the credibility and ethics of the scheme may be questioned.

Offer Identity Groups

Part of the appeal of products lies in the fact that donors can self-select to become members of a special "club" or "community" and hence can gain an identity from their philanthropy. Sponsors/adopters/members of clubs can be given recognition and be made aware that they are part of a group of individuals with shared interests and a common commitment.

Provide Tangible Results and Feedback

Fundraising products that link the donor to the beneficiary set up a dialogue between the donor and the recipient. In child-sponsorship programs the donor is often free to write to the child and receives in return personalized letters and reports of progress at school and at home, as well as regular updates from the charity on the impact of specific projects on the community in which the child lives. Supporters of the Wildfowl and Wetland Trust sponsor birds and receive updates on the birds' progress as they undertake their seasonal journeys of migration. Some animal-sponsorship programs even invite the sponsor to visit the animal.

Feedback and direct news of the beneficiary keep donors informed of what their support means and help them visualize the impact they are having. This sort of feedback essentially removes the organization from the picture; donors can see what their money is doing rather than suspecting that some or all of their gift may be diverted to organizational and overhead costs.

When a product is offered, a promise is made to the donor, and changing the nature of that promise later by altering the product is likely to have a negative impact on donor loyalty. Because fundraisers are aware of this possibility, they sometimes decide to offer unspecific, open-ended products: "Give $30 a month to sponsor a child, and we will send you regular reports on that child's progress."

Unfortunately, such offers are not as attractive as those that can make specific promises: "Give $30 a month to sponsor Jane, and we will send you a certificate and a monthly magazine and will put you directly in touch with her. She will write to you with her news at least twice a year."

Provide Enhanced Service

Donors who have made a regular financial commitment through a highly personalized program, especially when their gift is of a relatively high value, expect good service from the fundraising team and recognition from the organization. They want their record to be kept updated, their preferences to be noted and adhered to, and their queries to be answered promptly. Donors who feel they have a personal link to a project or a beneficiary can be demanding, and those programs that have succeeded most fully over the years incorporate a high standard of donor care plus recognition devices, including privileged access to information and the opportunity to attend events and functions.

Expect a Long-Term Commitment

Successful fundraising products tend to involve the donor in a regular commitment over a relatively long period. Child sponsorship may end when the child starts school or when a particular community project is over. Animal sponsorship may end on the death of the animal or when a home for it has been found. We estimate that such programs last on average for at least three years. Part of the appeal to donors of this sort of product is the serious nature of the undertaking. The expectation that the donor will be giving over a significant time period is both indicative of the importance of the gift and a major driver of donor loyalty.

Examples of Successful Products

The examples that follow help illustrate the features we mention above through descriptions of some of the most successful product programs.

ActionAid's Child-Sponsorship Program

ActionAid began work in 1972. Since that time, it has constantly refined and developed its approach to child sponsorship. It now has over one hundred thousand child sponsors and generates over £30 million a year. With the ActionAid plan the donor is linked to a named child and receives information about that child. (Exhibit 8.1 shows the cover of an ActionAid booklet.) Sponsorship costs £15 per month. ActionAid makes it clear to donors at the beginning that this money does not go directly to the children or to their families but is used to fund the projects

EXHIBIT 8.1. ACTIONAID'S CHILD-SPONSORSHIP PROGRAM.

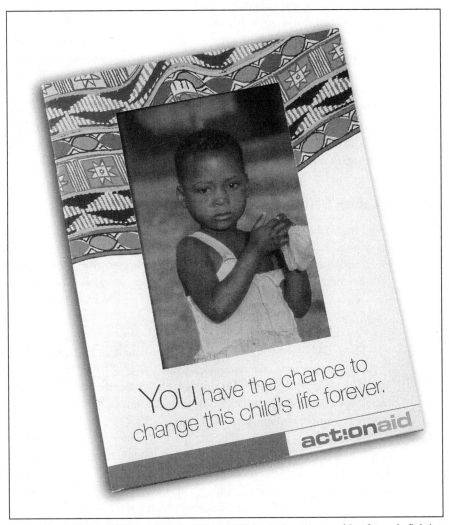

Source: Reproduced with the permission of ActionAid, a unique partnership of people fighting for a better world—a world without poverty.

that are most needed in the area where the children live. It also tells donors that 90 percent of the sponsorship payment goes overseas, with just 10 percent retained and spent by the organization on fundraising, advocacy, and education work.

A sponsor receives letters twice a year from the community where the child lives, including personal messages from the child or from ActionAid staff working with the child. Sponsors are encouraged to send messages to the children they support. Child sponsors are given a high standard of care, including access to dedicated staff and web resources.

The materials sent to prospective sponsors stress the importance and seriousness of the commitment. Sponsors are told that their commitment is expected to last for about three years and that, if their circumstances change and they have to cancel their gifts, they should let the charity know as soon as possible so it can arrange another sponsor.

An analysis of the lifetime value of ActionAid's child sponsors found that they tend to stay with the organization for an average of seven years. At the end of the sponsorship, donors are encouraged to give their regular support to other projects in the same community or alternatively to sponsor another child.

National Canine Defence League's Sponsor a Dog Program

The National Canine Defence League (NCDL) is one of the oldest charities in the United Kingdom. Although in the past the organization generated high levels of income through bequest gifts, its donor base was made up predominantly of older people and the organization was increasingly viewed as old-fashioned. The NCDL was also competing in a crowded and confused animal-welfare sector and was finding it increasingly hard to maintain a voice in the market and a share of donor support.

The NCDL devised a new logo and launched its Sponsor a Dog program. Potential sponsors are asked to give a small gift of £1 a week to sponsor a dog at one of the NCDL's centers. Inquirers are sent a brochure with pictures and details of a range of dogs they can choose from. In return for their sponsorship they receive regular communications (including Valentine's and Christmas cards) from their adopted dog, which is, in effect, their virtual pet. A particular feature of this program is the humor that is used, both in the advertising and promotional materials, that introduce the product and in the subsequent communications between the sponsors and their dogs. Humor can be used in this context because there is less of a concern for the beneficiaries to be represented fairly and with absolute dignity than is the case in human sponsorship or adoption schemes. The sponsorship brochure (Exhibit 8.2) promises donors a certificate, a badge, a sticker, a sponsor's card, and a regular magazine ("*Wag!*—Packed with Doggy News!") as well as "a friend for life who will love you unconditionally."

In the Sponsor a Dog advertisement on DRTV a dog is the main character. The dog addresses the viewer directly and explains the plight of his friends at NCDL centers. Some examples are provided of dogs needing care, and viewers are told that they can change the life of a dog with a low-value, regular gift. The ads are unashamedly funny, light, and sentimental.

EXHIBIT 8.2. BROCHURE FOR SPONSOR A DOG.

Source: Reproduced by kind permission of Dogs Trust (formerly the NCDL).

The program has been successful, especially in attracting younger people who would love to have a pet dog but cannot because of where they live and the hours they work. Sponsor a Dog has brought in thousands of new donors and has raised the profile of the charity. It has also differentiated the charity from its main competitors in the animal-welfare sector. These other organizations are unable to mimic the product because they operate in a different way: they tend to re-home or destroy the unwanted dogs that arrive in their centers rather than hold them for long periods, and they also tend not to use humor in their fundraising materials, which are serious rather than playful. (Since introducing this program, the NCDL has changed its name to Dogs Trust.)

Freedom Village's Adopt-a-Teen Program

Supporters of Freedom Village in the United States and Canada can donate to the Adopt-a-Teen program. This faith-based organization offers help to troubled teenagers and their parents and provides a residential home for teenagers, many of whom have struggled with drugs and alcohol or have suffered sexual abuse. The Freedom Village residential home is a 150-acre campus described as "an intensive care ward for troubled lives." Up to 150 teens can live there. The main residential program runs for a year. Freedom Village is funded through contributions by parents as well as supporters.

The Adopt-a-Teen program provides the backbone of support for the organization. For $22 a month, which can be an automated payment, a donor can "help feed, clothe, educate and care for a young person who otherwise would have no help at all." Donors receive an "adoption packet" with a picture of the young person, a data sheet "giving information about your teen," and a certificate of adoption. Every month donors receive a letter with testimonies from several young people so that they can see "exactly what your monthly gift is accomplishing."

San Francisco Zoo's Adopt-an-Animal Program

The San Francisco Zoo offers its Adopt-an-Animal program as a "unique and wild gift for a business associate, friend, family member or loved one." Supporters can choose from a range of animals and receive in return a package that includes a certificate of adoption, a photo of their animal, and a set of "Nature Notes" about the species. They are also recognized on the zoo website and receive a regular publication. All sponsors are also invited to an annual event, Zooparent Day, which includes behind-the-scenes tours of the zoo, animal feedings, keeper talks, and free rides on the zoo's carousel and steam train.

In this case sponsorship involves only an annual gift, priced from $40 to $1,000 with different benefits attached to each level of gift. The zoo makes it clear to sponsors that their donations will be used to support "vital animal enrichment and wildlife conservation projects including the breeding of rare and endangered species."

Steps to a Successful Product Launch

Nonprofits considering the introduction of a product to their fundraising and communications mix should follow a rigorous planning system. Products can work, but fundraising is also littered with examples of poorly planned product launches that have proved expensive failures and with products that are maintained at a low return on investment (ROI) for the benefit of only a small number of donors. The planning process should include research, costing out, testing, and monitoring.

Research

Researching the feasibility of a fundraising product should involve as much looking at the internal processes and work of the fundraising organization as it does
assessing the potential external audiences for the product. As we mentioned above,
the best products use the core work (or some of the core work) that the organization is already doing and present this work in an attractive way to donors. The
first step thus is to revisit the organization's mission, work practices, and outputs
to see whether they lend themselves easily to this sort of presentation and treatment. This appraisal has to be honest: for most fundraising nonprofits a product
is not an advisable route to take, and it is better to come to this conclusion at an
early stage than to invest further in attempts to manipulate the organization's work
into a contrived package.

Presenting individuals as products may be highly effective for fundraising, but
the moral implications of doing so may contravene aspects of an organization's
mission. UNICEF, for example, has many opportunities to develop a form of child
sponsorship, but the head of fundraising for UNICEF in the United Kingdom
believes that it is inappropriate to view children as products and has thus resisted
introducing any such scheme. Such strong feelings are far from rare, and organizations should thus explore the sensitivities of all its different stakeholder groups
before developing any fundraising product.

For any new program, fundraisers have to create promotional materials, set
up new systems, and "package" the core work of an organization, but having internal systems of feedback and information provision already in place to help with
these tasks is indispensable. If program staff are required to alter their work practices or to undertake a great deal of extra work to provide the information the
fundraising team needs to sustain the product, it may not be worthwhile investi-
gating the idea any further. The product also has to be sustainable over a long period, so using as a product projects or work areas that may be withdrawn or
changed substantially over time are not suitable. Often "lobbying clubs" or "action groups" on single issues, for example, do not succeed because the organization
finds that it cannot provide, over the long term, enough specific information and
opportunities for activists to satisfy the keen cohort of donors who have subscribed
to the program.

If a product idea appears to be workable from the point of view of the organization internally, external research should then examine the activities of
competitors and compare products offered by nonprofits in the same or similar
fields. The donor database should be analyzed to identify potential segments
where, were the product introduced, a substantial increase in contributions would

result. Consideration should also be given to the impact the product might have on the organization's brand and image should it eventually be used in donor acquisition.

Costing Out

The introduction of a fundraising product has to be costed out with great care. Although most organizations cost out the promotional materials that will be required and set these against the gift levels needed, in many instances the costs of staff time and of process and system changes are not included. Organizations need to recognize that complex products such as sponsorships can, for example, involve program staff and donor-care staff as well as the fundraising team. In addition, if the product attracts many subscribers, the temptation may be to roll it out as an acquisition tool to a wide audience without recalculating the associated costs in both materials and staff time. Although in most cases the unit cost of published materials will fall as greater numbers are produced, the costs of additional staff time and of changes in internal systems may be high.

In costing out a new product, several projections should be made of the number of subscribers the product might generate. A minimum quantity can then be calculated, below which the ROI will not be acceptable. Fundraisers should also factor in a number of lapse rates, which can be based on the lapse rates with similar products (if this information is available) and on the lapse rates the organization currently experiences with other donor activities.

As we have already discussed, the level of the donation request has to be credible; it has to reflect the nature of the product and the quality of the commitment by the donor to the beneficiary (and by the organization to the donor). It also has to be realistic for a significant number of the organization's existing and prospective supporters.

Pilot Testing

As in all direct marketing, a new product should be pilot-tested with a small group before a major investment is made. Before testing donors, it may be wise to do some qualitative research. For example, the relevant staff should check through every aspect of processing and fulfillment to be sure that these tasks can be performed efficiently.

Next, tests should be carried out with sections of the existing donor database. Segments should be selected with care to ensure (1) that the donors are not already giving more than or as much as the product would require them to—that is, that committing to the product would upgrade their support—and (2) that they are likely prospects—that is, that existing data show that the donation level required would be possible for them to meet. Testing on existing donors before potential new ones provides the warmest possible audience (as should be remembered when projecting response rates if the product is subsequently offered to a "cold" audience in acquisition). Testing on existing donors is also far cheaper to undertake, and it removes some of the variables from the test so that it is clear that the response rate generated is a function of the product offer rather than of the media selection.

If the product gets a positive response from the existing donors chosen for the initial test, and if fulfillment and processing are carried out with them successfully, the product can be rolled out with care to other donors and can be tested as a donor-acquisition tool. Again, it is best to pilot-test in a controlled way, perhaps split-testing the product against the current acquisition device among a small sample of prospects. Testing of both the presentation of the product and the media used should continue throughout the promotion of the product. Any testing of the product offer itself should be carefully controlled, with fulfillment and processing implications rehearsed on each occasion.

Monitoring

The key measurements to monitor, as with any committed-giving offer, are the rate at which donors lapse and the lifetime value of each donor. As products tend to be expensive to operate, especially in the early stages of the relationship with a new donor, it is essential that lapse rates and reasons for lapse be monitored. Lapse rates for a good product should be fairly low, as donors tend to invest emotionally in this product, the payments should ideally be automated, and the level of care and feedback donors receive should be high. However, a certain number of donors will always stop giving over time because of changes in financial or personal circumstances. Lessons should be learned from lapses. For instance, if donors lapse because the product does not deliver what they expected or because competitor offerings appear more attractive, the organization may need to reevaluate its product offer.

Over time the loyalty and value of the donors giving via products can be calculated and the results analyzed. When lapse rates are low, and profitability and loyalty are high, the organization may be able to invest more in the promotion of the product, to accept a lower ROI from acquisition campaigns where the product is utilized, and to increase the level of donor care.

Pitfalls and Restrictions

Although products can prove successful in fundraising and can increase donor loyalty and lifetime value dramatically, drawbacks and pitfalls need to be considered. The major downsides of using fundraising products are summarized briefly here.

Restricted Funding

Fundraising products succeed best when they are specific. Donors are therefore entitled to expect that their gifts be used precisely as described in the information they have received, and the nonprofit is required to use the income generated through the product only for that work and the associated costs. Donors also expect a nonprofit operating a product to be honest about the proportion of the donation that is used to cover administrative and other nonprogram costs. If the product is clearly related to the central mission of the organization and the nonprofit can efficiently deliver its core programs through the operation of the product, using funds as promised will not be an issue. However, if the product represents a tangential or minor part of the work, the organization may have difficulty raising funds for other work areas, as it will have diverted the gifts of supporters of its product to tangential projects.

High Costs

Fundraising products are relatively expensive to operate. They may require amendments to be made to databases and recording systems and a suite of special materials to be used in promotion and in ongoing communications with donors. A successful product will probably need dedicated staff, and as we have mentioned earlier, donors who give through products tend to need high-quality service and fast turnaround on queries. Cost-efficient product programs, therefore, make use of systems that are already in existence. One example is the sponsorship of an animal at a zoo. The regular reports on an animal that are sent to a donor can be captured from the veterinary and scientific reports that are constantly generated as part of the core operation of the organization. Project reports used internally can also be adapted for this purpose, with the added advantage that they will automatically carry the sort of "inside track" information and authentic tone donors appreciate.

Questions that product fundraisers should constantly ask are whether the ROI the product is generating is acceptable and whether the product is being promoted correctly. Many higher-value products will be attractive only to a restricted donor segment, but products have to attract a significant cohort of donors to be viable. As we stressed above, careful testing, costing out, and monitoring are essential.

Although products may be useful in upgrading donors, sometimes a product (with its associated high costs to the organization) is promoted to donors who would have been content to contribute a regular gift without the trappings. One animal charity invested heavily in an adoption scheme, setting up new systems for donor feedback and creating a raft of attractive materials. The scheme was launched and attracted a great deal of support. The organization subsequently promoted a regular gift with no product attached; the gift went toward the core mission, and the donor received nothing special in return. The two programs had the same monthly donation level. Over time the general gift was as popular as the adoption product. Donors giving through the adoption scheme did stay with the organization for an average of a year longer, but the ROI was far healthier for the straightforward gift than for the complex product.

Changes in Branding and Identity

Some products, especially when they are promoted extensively to acquire new supporters, are so successful that they become the main face of the organization, its identity. Such branding may be welcome, but often these products outgrow their parent nonprofit, and the situation may then be far from positive. Some fundraising products can be seen as oversimplifying the work of an organization, as belittling the importance of the areas of work that they do not represent, or as an inaccurate representation of the values and mission of the nonprofit. In some cases products are specially designed to appeal to certain sections of the donor base, such as younger people, women, men, or activists. The organization needs to make sure that this sort of product remains secondary to the main organizational brand and does not make it harder for the nonprofit to promote and fundraise for less packageable work.

Difficulties with Upgrading and Development

Donors who give through products are effectively supporting a package of benefits for a fixed gift amount. Having explained that it costs a certain amount to adopt a child/sponsor a dog/pay for a bed in a hostel, the organization may find it difficult to alter that cost at a later date and ask the donor to give additional money for the same project. Upgrading may not be necessary if the gift level is set relatively high to begin with, but doing so requires that the product be costed out with great care at the outset.

Another issue is how to deal with the donor when the product is ending—when the child goes to school or the animal dies or is re-homed. Some nonprofits take the opportunity to try to broaden the product—for example, from supporting a child to supporting a community—and thereby to lift some of the restrictions on the funds and to increase its flexibility in using the contribution. However, donors may have developed loyalty to the beneficiaries they have been helping rather than to the organization that acts as an intermediary in getting funds to the beneficiaries, and so donors may move their support to another nonprofit offering the same type of product.

Given that many products involve regular and specific communication between the donor and the beneficiary, it can also be difficult to find opportunities within the program to introduce new ideas and provide information on alternative ways for the donor to give support and become more involved.

Summary

In this chapter we have discussed the contribution that fundraising products can make to retention. The rapid growth in such approaches, with a number of both large and small nonprofits now designing products for the first time, is attributable to the improvement in donor lifetime value and the associated higher rates of retention that can be achieved through product offerings. When properly designed, fundraising products can have a dramatic impact on the profitability of an organization's fundraising, with a concomitant rise in donor satisfaction as individuals find themselves linked to the beneficiary group.

CHAPTER NINE

MANAGING SERVICE QUALITY

I n this chapter we look at the role that service quality can play in donor retention, examining in further detail the findings of our research project. We also
explore the lessons to be learned from the for-profit environment and offer frameworks and models that can be used to inform the development of higher-quality
service.

Nonprofits and charities have shown surprisingly little interest in the notion
of service quality. Since the mid-1980s corporations have been striving to develop
and enhance the quality of service they provide to their customers, but nonprofits have given the matter little thought. The interest they have expressed has
tended to be in the context of service provision to beneficiary groups and to a
lesser extent in relation to government contracts. Although many nonprofits plan
in great detail how a service will be provided to beneficiaries, ensure that this service matches their needs, conduct surveys and focus groups to measure performance, and plan for annual enhancements to upgrade service quality, they rarely
pay as much attention to the quality of service in the context of fundraising.

Why are fundraisers not taking the same interest in service quality as their
for-profit counterparts or even those in their own organizations involved in provision to beneficiary groups? Perhaps they do not recognize the relationship between the quality of service provided and donor loyalty, or perhaps they find it
difficult to apply many of the standard models and frameworks for service quality
to the realm of fundraising. In this chapter we explore each of these issues.

What Is Service Quality?

Several definitions of service quality are offered here.

> The delivery of excellent or superior service relative to customer expectations [Zeithaml and Bitner, 1996, p. 23].

> A behaviour—an attitude—that says you . . . will never settle for anything less than the best in service for your stakeholders, whether they are customers, the community, your stockholders or the colleagues with whom you work every day [Harvey, 1995, p. 24].

> Providing a better service than the customer expects [Lewis, 1989, p. 4].

At the heart of these and other definitions lies the fact that the perception of service quality depends on the experience of the customer or, in our case, the donor. It does not matter how well the organization believes it delivers a particular service, it is the customer's perspective that matters. Quality is a perception not an absolute, and so donors' perceptions, no matter how accurate or inaccurate, drive subsequent attitudes toward the organization. Perception also drives behavior—how long donors remain loyal and how much they give.

These definitions also make clear that assessments of service quality depend on two specific factors: expectations of performance and perceptions of performance. Consider an example. Suppose you have received an invitation to attend a charity fundraising dinner. A good friend who is one of this particular organization's fundraisers has told you that you "must absolutely attend" this event. She tells you that it is for a worthy cause, that the people you will meet are friendly, that a number of celebrities will be there, that the entertainment and conversation will be excellent and the food delicious, and that overall your experience of the night will be outstanding. Imagine how you would then feel if you attended the event and discovered that in reality it was mediocre. Although the people were friendly, conversation was difficult, few interesting people were there, the food was acceptable but not to your particular taste, and the entertainment passed the time but could hardly be described as outstanding. On balance you would probably leave the event dissatisfied with the quality of your experience. Imagine, in contrast, that your friend had told you that the event was worthwhile, but that you would have to be wary of a few "difficult" people who would be there, that the food would be bland, the entertainment relatively poor, and good conversation lacking. If your experience of the event matched this description, you might be quite satisfied with the experience as it matched the quality you had been led to expect.

This simplified example illustrates that perceptions of quality are not carved in stone. Individuals form a view by comparing their expectations of a service with the service that is delivered. This need not be a conscious process and frequently it isn't, but it has been observed in enough settings and contexts for us now to accept that perceptions are indeed formed in this way.

Academics refer to this perspective on service quality as the "disconfirmation paradigm," and it has a number of implications. Peters (1987), for example, argues that, given this paradigm, organizations should "under-promise" and "over-deliver." Customer expectations will thus be low and perceptions of delivered service quality high; as a consequence customer satisfaction will also be high. The problem with this argument is that expectations are based on experience, so this process will work only once. As soon as donors perceive a high standard of service, they expect it on later occasions and can be dissatisfied if their new expectations are not fulfilled. As a result we contend that by far the safer (and more ethical) way of ensuring customer satisfaction is simply to consistently deliver on one's promises.

Another consequence of the disconfirmation paradigm is that it forces organizations to identify the criteria against which consumers build expectations, which is not an easy task. And even when the factors important to overall satisfaction can be identified, organizations still have to set objective measures of quality and ensure that the services they deliver meet the targets set. This is also a difficult task. Although the quality of physical goods can be measured quite satisfactorily by monitoring variables such as durability or the number of physical defects, in the case of services objective methods of assessment are almost totally absent.

However, some consolation can be drawn because it is not only providers who have difficulty assessing the quality of their services. Consumers can have equal difficulties in formulating their own individual assessments. Although the disconfirmation model looks neat in theory, in practice consumers can make quality assessments on the most superficial bases. To explain why they do, it is worth looking at the work of Nelson (1974), who drew a useful distinction between two categories of consumer goods: (1) those high in search qualities—which consumers are able to evaluate prior to making a purchase (for example, size, color, feel, and smell) and (2) those high in experience qualities—which consumers can discern only during use and hence in most cases after purchase (for example, taste and wearability). For our purposes Darby and Karni (1973) helpfully add a third category: (3) those high in credence qualities—which are difficult to evaluate even after consumption. Many nonprofits offer services that are high on credence qualities—for example, a heart operation or a charity donation.

These qualities can best be conceptualized on a continuum. Figure 9.1 is a continuum for different products and services that have varying degrees of experience and credence qualities. With products and services high in credence qualities, consumers may find it all but impossible to evaluate their experiences. Nevertheless, marketers should not lose heart because in such cases consumers use a variety of surrogate variables to make their evaluations. In the case, for example, of a bypass operation, consumers are unlikely to have the technical knowledge to appraise the skills of the surgeon; they might therefore judge service quality on the basis of the perceived professionalism of the staff, the level of technology employed, the decor of their ward, and so on. This is a simple but important concept to grasp, as these criteria can be radically different from those that the hospital might use to evaluate the quality of the same operation (for example, survival rates, number of medical complications, technical proficiency, use of resources, and so on). Nonprofits, therefore, must monitor service quality not only against their own internal criteria but also against those that are likely to be used by the customer. For services that are high on credence qualities, these dimensions can usually be identified only through research.

Many forms of charity giving can be high in experience qualities. Major donors, for example, may be shown around a facility and invited to see service provision in person. Attendees at a charity gala or dinner are also in a position to appraise the quality of various aspects of the event and to formulate an overall view. However, the experience of donors responding to direct mail and other less personal forms of fundraising is different. Most have no choice but to trust the nonprofit to use their gifts in the way they or the organization have specified. They have no direct way of assessing how the money has been spent. Thus the service provided is high in credence qualities, and donors' perceptions of how the service they purchased has been delivered are based on surrogate variables, such as how they were thanked for their gift, the time it took the organization to answer queries, the friendliness and professionalism of any staff they might have encountered, or the quality and clarity of any global or individual feedback that was offered. Although fundraisers may rightly suspect that donors are more concerned with beneficiaries than they are with the quality of service provided to them personally, it is important to recognize that donors' perceptions of how good the organization is at program delivery and administration are driven to a great extent by completely unrelated variables. Fundraisers should care about the quality of service they provide to donors both for its own sake (after all, donors do matter!) but also because how they treat donors determines global perceptions of their organization, whether they like it or not.

FIGURE 9.1. EXPERIENCE AND CREDENCE QUALITIES IN SERVICES.

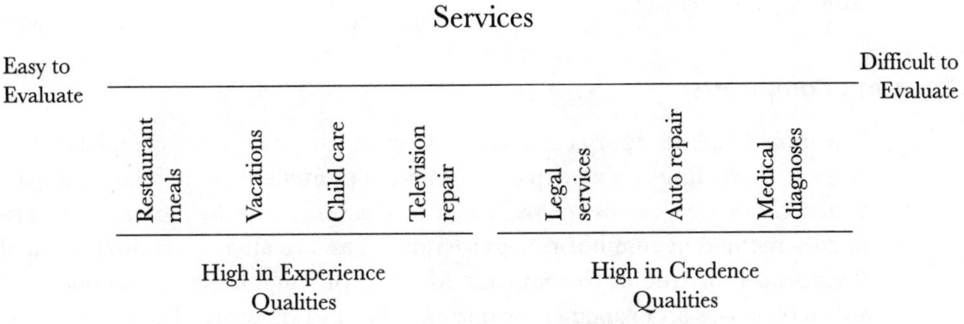

The Measurement of Service Quality

Given the difficulties we have mentioned, you could be forgiven for believing that the measurement of service quality is an almost impossible task. This is not the case, as we now understand a great deal about how to measure the quality of a service. A variety of methods of measurement have been advocated, each with its own strengths and weaknesses and each involving a greater or lesser degree of complexity.

In measuring service quality, asking donors general questions such as "How do you rate our service?" is, at least in isolation, worse than useless. Ovretveit (1992, p. 23) argues that "the question is not the general 'What do customers think about our service?' but the more specific 'Which features of our service are the most important to potential, current and past customers in relation to the actions which the service wishes to influence, and how does the service compare to the alternatives on these features?'" Thus, organizations need to understand how customers feel about each aspect of the service, the elements of it that they find particularly important, and how they compare the service provided with that of other providers in the market. For those services high in credence qualities, the picture is even more complicated because the organization has to understand the surrogate variables that customers use to appraise the service being delivered.

Three broad approaches to the measurement of service quality are possible: counting complaints, rating service attributes, and using what is known as the SERVQUAL method.

Counting Complaints

The most simplistic approach is simply to count the number of complaints that come in to the fundraising department and to examine these in relation to particular campaigns, the use of particular media, and so forth. This is an unsatisfactory method of monitoring service quality, as a relatively low proportion of donors take the trouble to complain. Most simply rate the service as poor and switch their support to another organization. We also know that dissatisfied donors tell about seven of their friends or relatives about the experience they have had, and thus they can seriously damage the nonprofit's image and standing in the local or national community. Simply counting complaints is therefore a futile exercise.

Rating Service Attributes

A rather more sophisticated method of measuring service quality consists of deriving a list of service attributes (or surrogates) and asking customers to rate their perceptions of each attribute, typically on a five- or seven-point scale. Using this method, a fundraising team can separate out each of the components of the service that it provides to donors and ask donors to rate its performance on each component. This method yields useful data, but refinements are necessary because donors can be very satisfied with components of the service that they find of little consequence. They can also be very dissatisfied with components of the service that they consider to be absolutely critical. To make decisions about improvements to the quality of service provided, the fundraising team must thus gather data about both the performance and the importance of each component. The statements in Tables 2.3 and 2.4 (Chapter Two, pp. 22 and 23) could constitute a survey question that would elicit responses about both variables.

If this question were administered as part of a donor survey, the results could be analyzed and plotted graphically as illustrated in Figure 9.2, which displays the mean (or average) scores for each component obtained from the survey in a two-by-two matrix. Items falling in the top left-hand corner are rated highly by donors on both dimensions. They regard these components as important elements of the service and also believe that the organization is very good at satisfying their needs in these areas. The prescription from the matrix for these items is to "keep up the good work." Items falling in the bottom right-hand corner are rated poorly by donors, but they also consider these components relatively unimportant. In these

FIGURE 9.2. IMPORTANCE/PERFORMANCE MATRIX.

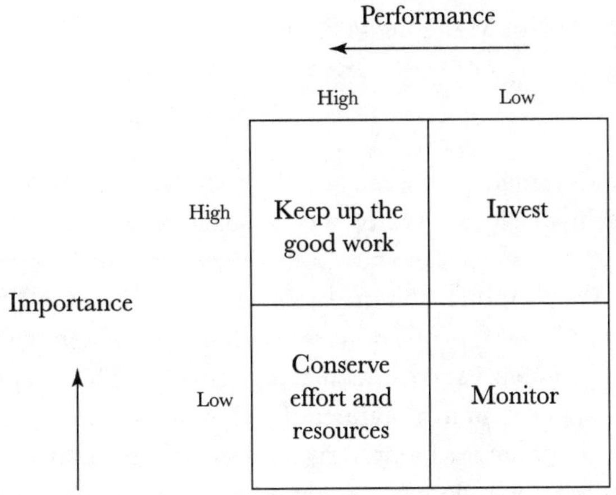

Performance

High   Low

	High	Low
High	Keep up the good work	Invest
Low	Conserve effort and resources	Monitor

Importance

areas, it is not worth investing in future improvements. The prescription here is simply to monitor donor needs and preferences because these components may become important in the future. Donors rate items falling in the bottom left of the matrix high on performance but low on importance. This is a case of overkill. The prescription is to conserve effort and resources in these areas and apply them instead to those components that are of importance. Finally, items falling in the upper right-hand quadrant are of high importance to donors, but they rate performance in these areas as comparatively poor. Not surprisingly the prescription here is to invest in these services in order to retain donors.

Using the SERVQUAL Method

Perhaps the most well-known technique for service-quality measurement is that proposed by Parasuraman, Zeithaml, and Berry (1988). It is based solidly on the disconfirmation paradigm. The authors posit the existence of four service gaps that are together responsible for any differences between expected performance and perceived performance. The authors define these gaps as follows:

Gap 1: Not Knowing What Customers Expect—The difference between customer needs and management's perceptions of those needs.

Gap 2: Not Selecting the Right Service Design—The difference between management perceptions of customer needs and the service standards set.

Gap 3: Not Delivering to Service Standards—The difference between service specifications and service delivery.

Gap 4: Not Matching Performance to Promises—The difference between the service promises made in external communications and the service delivered.

Parasuraman, Zeithaml, and Berry evolved this concept of gaps into a quantitative technique for measuring service quality known as SERVQUAL. They designed a generic twenty-two-item questionnaire that covers the broad dimensions of service quality. We reproduce this questionnaire as Exhibit 9.1. The items whose numbers are preceded by E probe donors' expectations of service quality; the P questions probe donors' assessment of actual performance. This is a generic questionnaire suitable for application in a number of different sectors. Therefore, many of the items are inappropriate for fundraising, and some items may be relevant for face-to-face contacts but not to donors communicated with through direct mail. Virtually all the items need some adaptation to the specific needs of a nonprofit organization.

If you take the time to tailor this questionnaire to your organization, you will be able to see at a glance where the organization fails to meet customer expectations. After all, the idea behind the questionnaire is essentially that

$$Q = P - E$$
where
Q = the perceived quality of each item
P = the performance achieved for each item
E = the customer's expectations of performance for each item

To measure the quality of each service dimension one thus subtracts the expectations score from the performance score for each item. A high positive result indicates a high perceived standard of service, while a high negative score indicates a low perceived standard of service.

In testing the responses to this instrument, the authors determined that service quality could best be viewed as having five underlying variables:

1. Tangibles—physical facilities, equipment, and appearance of personnel
2. Reliability—ability to perform the promised service dependably and accurately
3. Responsiveness—willingness to help customers and provide prompt service
4. Assurance—knowledge and courtesy of employees and their ability to inspire trust and confidence
5. Empathy—caring, individualized attention the firm provides its customers

EXHIBIT 9.1. THE SERVQUAL QUESTIONNAIRE.

Directions: This survey deals with your opinions of _____ services. Please show the extent to which you think firms offering _____ services should possess the features described by each statement. Do this by picking one of the seven numbers next to each statement. If you strongly agree that these firms should possess a feature, circle the number 7. If you strongly disagree that these firms should possess a feature, circle 1. If your feelings are not strong, circle one of the numbers in the middle. There are no right or wrong answers; all we are interested in is a number that best shows your expectations about firms offering _____ services.

		Strongly Disagree						Strongly Agree
E1	They should have up-to-date equipment.	1	2	3	4	5	6	7
E2	Their physical facilities should be visually appealing.	1	2	3	4	5	6	7
E3	Their employees should be well dressed and appear neat.	1	2	3	4	5	6	7
E4	The appearance of the physical facilities of these firms should be in keeping with the type of services provided.	1	2	3	4	5	6	7
E5	When these firms promise to do something by a certain time, they should do so.	1	2	3	4	5	6	7
E6	When customers have problems, these firms should be sympathetic and reassuring.	1	2	3	4	5	6	7
E7	These firms should be dependable.	1	2	3	4	5	6	7
E8	They should provide their services at the time they promise to do so.	1	2	3	4	5	6	7
E9	They should keep their records accurately.	1	2	3	4	5	6	7
E10	They shouldn't be expected to tell customers exactly when services will be performed. (−)	1	2	3	4	5	6	7
E11	It is not realistic for customers to expect prompt service from employees of these firms. (−)	1	2	3	4	5	6	7
E12	Their employees don't always have to be willing to help customers. (−)	1	2	3	4	5	6	7
E13	It is okay if they are too busy to respond to customer requests promptly. (−)	1	2	3	4	5	6	7
E14	Customers should be able to trust employees of these firms.	1	2	3	4	5	6	7

EXHIBIT 9.1. THE SERVQUAL QUESTIONNAIRE, Cont'd.

		Strongly Disagree						Strongly Agree
E15	Customers should be able to feel safe in their transactions with these firms' employees.	1	2	3	4	5	6	7
E16	Their employees should be polite.	1	2	3	4	5	6	7
E17	Their employees should get adequate support from these firms to do their jobs well.	1	2	3	4	5	6	7
E18	These firms should not be expected to give customers personal attention. (−)	1	2	3	4	5	6	7
E19	Employees of these firms cannot be expected to give customers personal attention. (−)	1	2	3	4	5	6	7
E20	It is unrealistic to expect employees to know what the needs of their customers are. (−)	1	2	3	4	5	6	7
E21	It is unrealistic to expect these firms to have their customers' best interests at heart. (−)	1	2	3	4	5	6	7
E22	They shouldn't be expected to have operating hours convenient to all their customers. (−)	1	2	3	4	5	6	7

Directions: The following set of statements relate to your feelings about XYZ. For each statement please show the extent to which you believe XYZ has the feature described by the statement. Once again, circling a 7 means that you strongly agree that XYZ has that feature, and circling a 1 means that you strongly disagree. You may circle any of the numbers in the middle that show how strong your feelings are. There are no right or wrong answers— all we are interested in is a number that best shows your perceptions about XYZ.

		Strongly Disagree						Strongly Agree
P1	XYZ has up-to-date equipment.	1	2	3	4	5	6	7
P2	XYZ's physical facilities are visually appealing.	1	2	3	4	5	6	7
P3	XYZ's employees are well-dressed and appear neat.	1	2	3	4	5	6	7
P4	The appearance of the physical facilities of XYZ is in keeping with the type of services provided.	1	2	3	4	5	6	7

EXHIBIT 9.1. THE SERVQUAL QUESTIONNAIRE, Cont'd.

		Strongly Disagree						Strongly Agree
P5	When XYZ promises to do something by a certain time, it does so.	1	2	3	4	5	6	7
P6	When you have problems, XYZ is sympathetic and reassuring.	1	2	3	4	5	6	7
P7	XYZ is dependable.	1	2	3	4	5	6	7
P8	XYZ provides its services at the time it promises to do so.	1	2	3	4	5	6	7
P9	XYZ keeps its records accurately.	1	2	3	4	5	6	7
P10	XYZ does not tell customers exactly when services will be performed. (−)	1	2	3	4	5	6	7
P11	You do not receive prompt service from XYZ's employees. (−)	1	2	3	4	5	6	7
P12	Employees of XYZ are not always willing to help customers. (−)	1	2	3	4	5	6	7
P13	Employees of XYZ are too busy to respond to customer requests promptly. (−)	1	2	3	4	5	6	7
P14	You can trust employees of XYZ.	1	2	3	4	5	6	7
P15	You feel safe in your transactions with XYZ's employees.	1	2	3	4	5	6	7
P16	Employees of XYZ are polite.	1	2	3	4	5	6	7
P17	Employees get adequate support from XYZ to do their jobs well.	1	2	3	4	5	6	7
P18	XYZ does not give you individual attention. (−)	1	2	3	4	5	6	7
P19	Employees of XYZ do not give you personal attention. (−)	1	2	3	4	5	6	7
P20	Employees of XYZ do not know what your needs are. (−)	1	2	3	4	5	6	7
P21	XYZ does not have your best interests at heart. (−)	1	2	3	4	5	6	7
P22	XYZ does not have operating hours convenient to all their customers. (−)	1	2	3	4	5	6	7

Note: The statements should appear in a random order in a questionnaire and those phrased in the negative (−) should be reverse-scored prior to data analysis.

Source: Parasuraman, Zeithaml, and Berry, 1988. Used by permission. Copyright New York University, Stern School of Business.

A number of the statements in the questionnaire can be viewed as addressing the issue of reliability, while others together address the issue of responsiveness, and so on. As a result the scale has a number of applications within a service or, in our case, a fundraising environment:

- Tracking service trends. SERVQUAL can be used over time to plot changes in donor perceptions of key service components (that is, trends in the responses to individual questions).
- Analyzing each service variable. Average difference scores (the difference between expectations and performance) can be calculated for each of the five variables. These scores can also be averaged to arrive at an overall measure of service quality, which can then be tracked over time.
- Identifying the relative importance of each service variable. A statistical technique known as regression can be used to isolate the variable customers feel to be of the greatest importance. Resource allocation can then be planned accordingly.
- Determining whether specific groups of customers prioritize the variables differently. If this should be the case each group can be profiled to determine its demographic characteristics or lifestyle characteristics or both. (See Chapter Six.)
- Benchmarking against competitors. A separate series of questions about performance can be included in the instrument for each key competitor, and the resulting information can be used for benchmarking purposes.

SERVQUAL has been found to be effective in a variety of different contexts; as we noted above, in the fundraising context the questions need to be carefully tailored. When we did our own research on the quality of direct marketing in fundraising, for example, we designed the series of performance statements in Exhibit 9.2. The tangibles variable and to a lesser extent the assurance variable are of little relevance in this context and can safely be dropped.

The Satisfaction–Loyalty Link

We have so far in this chapter discussed customer perceptions of service quality and identified three ways in which these perceptions might be measured. We have as yet said little about why you should be interested in the issue of service quality and have provided no hard evidence that it is an important factor in donor loyalty.

The key work on service quality has been conducted almost exclusively in the for-profit sector and has been inspired in particular by the relationships that large multinational companies have with their customers. Although it is impossible to apply this work directly to the charity context, many nonprofits are involved in

EXHIBIT 9.2. DONOR SERVICE-QUALITY QUESTIONNAIRE.

Thinking about your recent ongoing relationship with X, please indicate the extent to which you agree or disagree with the following statements. Please circle the appropriate point on the scale.

Dimension	Strongly Disagree				Strongly Agree
I feel confident that X is using my money appropriately	1	2	3	4	5
X keeps me informed about how my money is being used	1	2	3	4	5
X always responds promptly to requests I have for information	1	2	3	4	5
X cares about the needs of its donors	1	2	3	4	5
X makes me feel that it is always willing to help me if I have a query	1	2	3	4	5
X doesn't ask me for funds too often	1	2	3	4	5
X asks for appropriate sums	1	2	3	4	5
X's communications are always courteous	1	2	3	4	5
X's communications are always timely	1	2	3	4	5
I feel safe in my transactions with X	1	2	3	4	5
The behavior of X's employees instills me with confidence	1	2	3	4	5
Employees at X are always courteous	1	2	3	4	5
Employees at X have the knowledge to answer my questions	1	2	3	4	5
X gives me individual attention	1	2	3	4	5
Employees of X seem to understand my specific needs	1	2	3	4	5
When I have a problem, X shows an interest in solving it	1	2	3	4	5

some form of trading activity (that is, through mail-order sales or charity shops) to raise funds so it is instructive to take a brief look at some of the key findings of the leading authors in this field, Jones and Sasser (1995).

As we discussed earlier, many organizations measure customer perceptions of various aspects of their service. Frequently they also ask a final question such as "Overall how satisfied are you with the quality of service supplied?" and then ask customers to answer on a scale of 1 to 5, with 1 being "very dissatisfied" and 5 being "very satisfied." Measuring overall satisfaction in this aggregate way as well as in the specific way already described allows the organization to explore the relationship between specific aspects of the service and overall satisfaction. The statistical analysis required, however, may well be beyond the expertise of many fundraisers, but an agency or an analyst can easily be found to perform this analysis on an organization's behalf.

More immediately, asking a question of this type allows an organization to plot graphically the overall perception of the quality of service provided. Consider Figure 9.3. Here we have plotted the percentage of customers who gave a hypothetical organization each of the five scores we listed; 2 percent of customers are very dissatisfied, 4 percent are dissatisfied, 12 percent feel neutral, 37 percent are satisfied, and 45 percent describe themselves as very satisfied.

Putting yourself in the position of the manager of this organization, would you be happy with these figures? The conventional wisdom is that you should be. After all, 82 percent of your customers are either satisfied or very satisfied. Consider an additional question: Which category of customers should you be most concerned with? Again, the conventional wisdom is that you should work to improve the scores of those in categories 1 to 3, who are clearly not satisfied with the quality of service.

However, this would be far from the best approach. In their study (which embraced a variety of different sectors) Jones and Sasser concluded that individuals who indicate that they are very satisfied are six times more likely to repurchase

FIGURE 9.3. SAMPLE LEVELS OF CUSTOMER SATISFACTION.

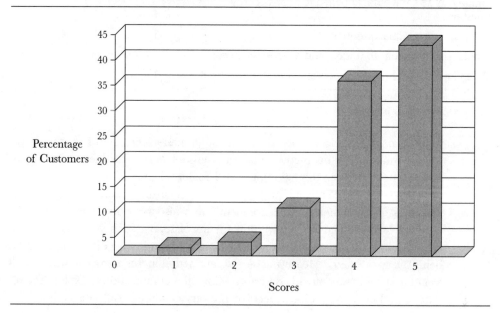

than those who indicate they are merely satisfied. In this example, then, if all the customers who rated their satisfaction 5 (very satisfied) repurchase, only about 17 percent (one-sixth of 100 percent) of those who rated it 4 (satisfied) will do so. This revelation focuses your mind on the group of customers who should clearly be regarded as most important. If an organization can increase the percentage of customers who rate their satisfaction at the highest level, it can substantially improve the amount of loyalty that will be exhibited as a result.

The factor of six mentioned above in connection with the difference between the repurchases of those who gives scores of 4 and 5 is not static across all industries and sectors; that factor depends on the availability of substitute services and the nature of the competition. For many organizations providing comparatively unique services the factor is likely to be considerably lower, but even if it should prove to be as low as two or three, a significant difference still exists between the loyalty patterns of customers who consider themselves satisfied and those who consider themselves very satisfied.

The reason for elaborating on this research is simple. The key to moving customers from a 4 to a 5 is customer value. If you think about some of your own experiences with service organizations and in particular those that you might have been asked to evaluate, you can probably quickly recall why you gave a particular organization a 4 rather than a 5. The organization almost certainly met your basic requirements but probably did not excel in one area that was of particular importance to you. As a result organizations need to be particularly alert to those aspects of their service offering that customers perceive to be most important and ensure that they engineer in value in these key areas. If loyalty is to be preserved or enhanced, customers must be made to feel that they have received exceptional service. Nonprofits engaged in some form of trading will find it worthwhile to invest in ongoing research to check on levels of satisfaction with the service provided. If many customers are rating the service as merely a 4, the subsequent management of loyalty will be problematic.

And what of customers who offer a 1, 2, or 3 rating? Individuals who give scores at the lower end of the scale possibly have encountered service issues; they do not have the relationship that they thought they would have with the organization. We deal with customers who fall into this category in the next section, but for now it is worth noting that the route to retention here is satisfactory complaint resolution.

Another group of individuals who give scores at the lower end probably shouldn't be donating to the organization. They may never have understood the service that was offered when they signed up and will never find their needs satisfactorily met by the organization. If a high percentage of an organization's customers fall into this category, the organization probably has a problem with what marketers refer to as positioning. In effect it is sending out the wrong messages to potential donors about what it can legitimately provide. Such messages confuse potential purchasers or donors and don't allow them to select other organizations that would be better suited to their needs. A new positioning strategy may therefore be required.

So far in our discussion we have been talking largely about a trading environment, although many of the points we make apply equally to the fundraising context. In our retention research we specifically explored the application of Jones and Sasser's work to fundraising. Figure 2.2 was our plotting of the overall level of satisfaction of donors to a range of different nonprofits. As you will recall from Chapter Two, a high percentage of donors felt neutral about the quality of service provided. A smaller percentage indicated that they were satisfied, and a much smaller percentage that they were very satisfied. Exploring the giving histories of respondents, we found that individuals who were very satisfied were twice as likely to offer subsequent donations as those who described themselves as merely satisfied. The multiple is thus not as high as the one Jones and Sasser identified in the commercial context, but overall satisfaction does have a marked impact on subsequent giving.

The lesson here is that fundraisers need to measure donor satisfaction on an ongoing basis and to ensure that as high a proportion as possible of an organization's donors describe themselves as very satisfied. Even more important is gaining this score from high-value or major givers, whose retention is essential for an organization's survival.

Complaints as Opportunities

We have already suggested that one approach, albeit a simplistic one, to the measurement of service quality is either counting or tracking trends in the volume of complaints. Because complaints signal dissatisfaction, many nonprofits tend to shy away from them. Fundraisers often feel uncomfortable dealing with individuals who are unhappy with the way they have been treated. None of us likes conflict. Fundraisers thus often downplay complaints and ignore all but the most serious ones. Certainly fundraisers should never actively encourage complaints about their work—or should they?

Consider Figure 9.4, in which we have plotted the percentage of donors with complaints who will continue to offer donations to a hypothetical organization under specific sets of circumstances. From our work in this field we know that donors behave in similar ways. Although the exact percentages of individuals in each category who will donate again vary substantially from one organization to

FIGURE 9.4. PERCENTAGE OF DONORS WITH COMPLAINTS WHO WILL GIVE AGAIN.

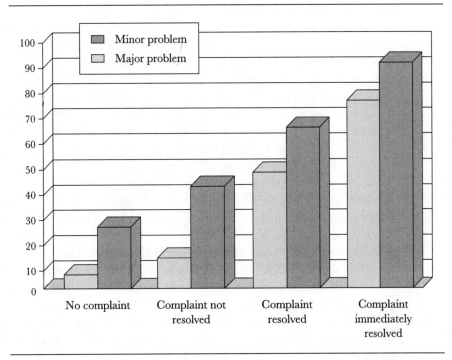

another, the relationship between the various categories that we describe holds true. So too does the relationship between donors exposed to immediate complaint resolution and the average retention rate, as explained below.

In the first column is a group of donors who experienced a major problem with the organization and failed to complain. Only about 8 percent of these individuals will offer a further gift. However, if they encountered only a minor problem, the percentage of individuals who will offer a further gift climbs to 31 percent. Next is a group of donors who have had a major problem, and although they have complained to the organization, the complaint has not been resolved. About 18 percent of these donors will offer a subsequent gift. If the problem is minor, the figure will be 47 percent. Moving along the graph we find a group of donors who have had a problem and have complained to the organization, which resolved the issue to the donors' satisfaction. Of these donors, 53 percent will give again if the problem is a major one, and 69 percent, if it is a minor problem. Finally we have a group of donors who had a problem and complained to the organization, which instantly dealt with the matter to the donors' satisfaction. The percentage of these donors who will offer a subsequent gift is 82 percent for a major problem and 94 percent for a minor problem.

Now if we consider that the average percentage of donors who will continue to give to this organization irrespective of whether they have had a problem is 78 percent, we can draw a number of conclusions. First, the better an organization is at resolving donor complaints or queries the higher its rates of retention will be. Second, donors who complain are generally more loyal than those who do not, even though they are not able to obtain any satisfaction! Psychologists tell us that individuals who complain have been able to express their feelings and thus tend to feel better after making the complaint. The enhanced levels of loyalty simply reflect this psychological "release." Third, notice the relationship between average loyalty (78 percent) and the loyalty of those individuals who have had their complaint speedily and satisfactorily dealt with (82 to 94 percent). These results suggest that if a nonprofit wishes to secure loyalty, it should simply create thousands of problems for its donors and then develop true excellence in resolving them! We are not advocating any such drastic measures, but this result does illustrate why, in the commercial sector, many firms now refer to complaints as opportunities—opportunities to keep customers loyal. The same opportunities exist in the context of fundraising.

The lessons for donor retention are clear. Rather than regard complaint handling as a necessary evil, regard it as an opportunity to build donor loyalty and to personalize the relationship between your organization and the donor. It will not be possible to resolve every issue a donor might have, particularly those that relate to actions taken in pursuit of the organization's mission. The research does show, however, that prompt and careful handling of these individuals can greatly enhance donor loyalty even in these difficult circumstances.

More typically, though, complaints from donors to the fundraising department are about a particular communication, the number of communications that are being sent, or a problem with either their data or the way information about them is being used by the organization. In such cases an organization should be able to respond promptly to donors' concerns. Given the significance of the issue for retention, the fundraising team has a duty to set up appropriate protocols for the handling of complaints and inquiries.

The Role of Staff

A final lesson that can be learned from the commercial world relates to staffing. Fundraisers are not usually the most highly paid members of an organization's staff, yet the skills and expertise they can offer are unique. Moreover, as they gain knowledge and experience in dealing with an organization's donors, fundraisers often improve their ability to predict behavior and begin to sense intuitively how donors will react to certain appeals. They also gain a firm grasp of the most attractive aspects of the organization's cause and which of these aspects will appeal to different segments of donors. As fundraisers deal with inquiries each day, they become better and more efficient at offering responses and take less time to research the detail needed to reply. They can minimize complaints, as they understand the nuances and weaknesses of internal policies and procedures. In short they can get better at providing service and building relationships with donors the longer they remain in their jobs. The operative word here is *can*. If properly rewarded and motivated, fundraisers not only remain loyal to the organization but are just as enthusiastic about their work as they were the day they first joined. Indeed, the more they develop experience with the work undertaken, the more they may develop an even stronger motivational bond with the organization.

Because research has consistently shown that customer retention is positively correlated with staff retention, fundraising teams with high turnover are significantly less likely to attract and retain donors (Reichheld, 2000). Senior management and board members thus need to give adequate consideration to their human resource policies and to assess how individuals feel about their work, their rewards, and their opportunities for advancement. UNICEF, for example, is particularly good at retaining key staff, and all fundraisers are afforded the opportunity at some point to visit the work the organization undertakes. This is an excellent way of adding value for staff and of reinforcing the effect their day-to-day fundraising efforts are having on the cause. The impact on motivation and on their desire to communicate their commitment to donors is profound.

Latest Thinking

As we have seen from the preceding sections, in order to develop a higher-quality service, it is essential for an organization to have a firm grasp of issues such as donor expectations, perceptions of the current provision, and the importance that they place on each dimension. This information can be used to make investment decisions and to help develop a plan for the quality of service that will be provided in the future to each key category of donor.

However, the latest thinking on retention is that, while important, issues such as service quality and complaint handling are only part of the picture. However good the quality of service provided, some donors will always defect and often for no apparent reason. The same is true of customers in the for-profit context. Why should this be?

The short answer is that these individuals have no real commitment to the organization. They may have given once, twice, or even more frequently, but the cause is not one they feel particularly passionate about. Commitment is a complex phenomenon and is certainly in part a function of issues such as service quality, but it is also driven by factors such as the following:

- A personal connection to the cause (perhaps through being a sufferer of a particular disease or having graduated from a particular university).
- The degree of personal empowerment the organization offers. Individuals develop commitment when they believe that they can and are making a real difference to the beneficiary group.
- Engagement with the organization in a variety of different ways, perhaps through campaigning, lobbying, volunteering, and so forth.
- The sense of the existence of a genuine relationship between the nonprofit and the donor (see Chapter 4).

Organizations seeking to retain donors thus need to give adequate consideration both to enhancing service quality and to building commitment. Delivering a high quality of service is only one way in which donor commitment and hence loyalty can be built.

Summary

To summarize our preceding discussion, service quality is clearly a critical issue for fundraisers to address. Donors who are very satisfied are twice as likely to remain loyal as those who are merely satisfied. In this chapter we outlined a variety of ways in which the quality of service can be measured, including the rating of specific attributes and the SERVQUAL approach. Quality of service is particularly critical when the solicitation process is impersonal and when as a consequence the service being "purchased" by the donor is high in credence qualities.

An organization seeking to manage service quality should follow these steps:

1. Identify customer groups or segments
2. Identify components or surrogate components of the service
3. Assess the relative importance of each component for each donor segment
4. Set performance targets for each component
5. Measure service performance against each target

6. Prioritize necessary improvements
7. Allocate investment accordingly

Following such a procedure should ensure that when performance deviates from the desired targets, scarce resources can be allocated to only those aspects of the service that are perceived as of greatest importance. Because these factors are not static over time, this process should be iterative.

CHAPTER TEN

RECOGNIZING AND
REWARDING DONORS

No book about donor loyalty would be complete without an examination of the role of donor recognition and feedback. In this chapter we therefore examine how and under what circumstances various forms of donor reward and recognition methods are likely to be appropriate, and we provide some examples of best practices in this area. We also discuss different categories of donors and the varying levels of care they expect if they are to remain loyal over time. And we explore how donor motivation can be linked to rewards and recognition.

Basic Vehicles for Recognition and Feedback

Any conversation with charity donors is likely to include some reference to the importance of feedback. Donors need and want to know what is being done with their money, how much of it is getting through to the beneficiaries or the cause, and what it is achieving. Most donors want some form of positive communication in return for their giving, if only to confirm that their gifts have been received and that the organization is legitimate. In donor research, supporters constantly stress the need for courtesy in the relationship between the donor and the organization, and it is, after all, only polite to recognize a gift appropriately, express gratitude for it, and provide information about what it is used for. This basic feedback begins with the acknowledgement of a first gift.

A brief glance through the thank-you notes that we have received in return for our giving indicates a great diversity in the approaches that nonprofits adopt. Some fundraisers simply say "thank you for the kind donation." Others use it as an opportunity to introduce the donor to other aspects of the organization's work, while some particularly hungry colleagues use the communication as an opportunity for a further ask. Our experience with donor retention suggests that it is unwise to ask for a further gift without first properly acknowledging and thanking the donor for a previous gift. Even the most charitable of donors is likely to feel somewhat exploited by this kind of approach, and we know from our focus-group research that some individuals find it offensive.

Our experience also suggests that the thank-you (both for the first and for subsequent gifts) is a critical form of communication. As we stress elsewhere in this book, donors frequently have no direct contact with the beneficiary group, and they therefore assess how good the organization is at keeping its service promises by how well they themselves are treated. It is thus essential that the organization respond to donors in a timely, friendly, and appropriate manner.

Exhibit 10.1 describes how a thank-you was used effectively to increase response and build loyalty for an organization concerned with both animal and child welfare.

EXHIBIT 10.1. CASE STUDY: AMERICAN HUMANE ASSOCIATION.

The American Humane Association (AHA) is an organization based in Colorado with approximately 80,000 donors across the United States. The 127-year-old organization has had a dual focus since its creation. The first is to protect and support shelter animals and prevent further abuse through both direct support as well as indirect support through advocacy. Its second focus is to protect children and prevent child abuse through advocacy efforts. In addition, American Humane has identified a clear link between animal and child abuse and is actively generating awareness in communities to recognize the signs of child and animal abuse and giving people information on how to alert the authorities.

AHA mails to its donors often and faced a continuing struggle of sending timely acknowledgements. In the past, the American Humane Association mailed appeal-like thank-you packages six weeks after a gift was received and was suffering continuously declining donor retention rates.

The thank-you packs consisted of an outer envelope, a double reply slip, and a reply envelope. Typically, the donors were not broken out by level of gift. Response rates were an average of 4 percent and average gifts were approximately $15.

The organization and their direct marketing agency (DMW) both agreed that cutting response time between the gift and a thank-you and improving the pack were the keys to improved loyalty and increased revenue.

First, the agency created a more visually striking acknowledgement package designed to build loyalty, improve response, and more quickly bring a second gift. A series of four 4-color cards was created for the donor acknowledgement package and stock was printed for a whole year, to be most cost-efficient. The four cards were prepared to accommodate those donors who give more than once a year.

EXHIBIT 10.1. CASE STUDY: AMERICAN HUMANE ASSOCIATION, Cont'd.

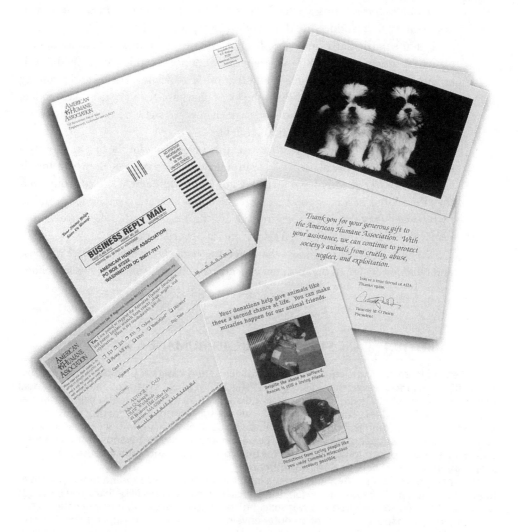

The time between receiving a gift and mailing an acknowledgement was cut from six to two weeks. Gifts of $250 or higher are acknowledged immediately. This is accomplished through a daily communication between the data-entry house and AHA, which sends a personal letter the next day.

Every two weeks, selections are made of the respondents, and donors are broken out by new versus repeat and by level of gift. Ask amounts on the reply slip are then laser-printed, based upon their last gift (and prompted for a slightly higher amount).

Before the card series was introduced, a donor would give an average number of 1.5 donations a year with an average annual gift value of $26.63.

EXHIBIT 10.1. CASE STUDY: AMERICAN HUMANE ASSOCIATION, Cont'd.

Response rates were increased by more than 50 percent over previous AHA efforts and as much as 75 percent in some donor segments.

After the card series introduction, the number of gifts per donor went up to 1.59 a year and the annual donor gift value went up to $29.21.

To-date, the card series is still being used, with four new cards being introduced each year. Response rates are still at a consistently high level of more than 8 percent with more than a $15 average gift, thus obtaining that second gift faster and putting more revenue to work for AHA.

Source: This case was kindly supplied by DMW (www.dmwdirect.com). The case and associated materials remain the copyright of DMW and the American Humane Association. Used with permission.

The most commonly used feedback vehicle is the newsletter, in which donors are provided with news, progress reports, and updates on the work they have supported. Newsletters at their best are informative and entertaining for donors as well as useful and profitable for fundraisers, as they can be used to provide information on projects and programs the donor may have supported, to introduce and promote new projects, and to encourage other methods of giving, such as bequests.

Although most donors want to receive feedback communications, some prefer not to, and they should be offered the opportunity to indicate this preference early in their relationship with the organization. Many donors want to receive just one communication a year, and (if asked) specify that this should be a brief report on the financial position of the charity and its achievements in the preceding twelve months. Organizations satisfy this request by mailing donors a copy of their annual reports, although some generate a simpler and cheaper version specifically for these individuals. We expect that donors will opt increasingly to receive their updates and feedback by e-mail and through the charity's website rather than on paper.

Oxfam GB provides excellent feedback to its donors. The issue of *Oxfam Reports* in Exhibit 10.2 was mailed to donors in December 2002. The cover letter (from the director of Oxfam) thanks the donor for his or her support, provides a brief assessment of progress in the previous year, and looks forward to the next. As well as containing newsletter-style reports, the brochure folds out to provide a calendar with images that reflect the full range of the charity's work. The package also describes an opportunity to take part in a lobbying action and in addition gently prompts donors to consider other ways of supporting the organization, such as through using an Oxfam credit card, taking part in a challenge event (for instance, a trek or other sporting or endurance challenge to raise sponsorship funds for a nonprofit cause), or leaving a legacy gift. The information is presented in a clear, succinct way, and the contact details for the supporter relations/donor care team and the address of the Oxfam website are displayed prominently.

EXHIBIT 10.2. OXFAM THANK-YOU LETTER AND NEWSLETTER.

Source: Reproduced with the permission of Oxfam GB.

The Red Cloud Indian School in Pine Ridge, South Dakota, uses a regular newsletter, *Red Cloud Country,* to provide feedback to supporters. The private, Lakota, Catholic institution in the Jesuit tradition comprises two elementary schools and a high school. It was founded in 1888 by the Jesuits at the request of Chief Red Cloud. The newsletters are written in a personal and distinct style that successfully creates the impression of a sincere and direct relationship between the donor and the charity; each issue, for instance, includes a letter from the Jesuit father who is director of the mission.

The issue of *Red Cloud Country* in Exhibit 10.3 features the results of a donor survey the charity had undertaken. Often when donors are asked to provide information or to take part in lobbying activities, they are subsequently given little information on the outcomes of the exercise they have been a part of. In this case, the feedback from the survey lets donors know that their efforts were useful and also reinforces some fundamental facts about the organization, its activities, and what it stands for.

This issue of the newsletter also promotes several other giving options so that donors can become engaged with the charity in multiple ways. A matching-gift program through a corporate sponsor, a monthly-giving Friends of Red Cloud club, and legacy gifts are all described, alongside updates on the progress of some of the children at the school. The Red Cloud materials are inexpensively produced and are personal, warm, and genuine while also being effective fundraising communications.

Labeling Donors

Many organizations provide labels for their donors, such as *supporter, advocate, partner,* depending on the level of their gifts. Labeling works only when there are concrete behaviors to be labeled. Giving donors labels for unspecified "valuable support" is thus far less effective than giving them labels for a specific form of donation and amount. The label chosen should also be consistent with the uniqueness and impact of the donor's contribution. Labels enhance giving best when they reinforce donors' own views of their giving. Fundraisers need to avoid the temptation to use inappropriate language that is overly flattering to the donor. Labels must be credible. Thus in drafting labels fundraisers need to think about how giving like a particular donor would make them feel. Reinforcing self-labeling can be an effective way of developing donors' existing motives for giving. We know from research that donors believe the labels they are given if they are repeated over time (Tybout and Yalch, 1980).

Tangible Rewards

Most donors require the basic recognition and feedback that thank-you letters and newsletters provide, but some are eager to receive tangible rewards. Because the desire to receive rewards is based on individual preference and motivation, it is

EXHIBIT 10.3. RED CLOUD INDIAN SCHOOL
NEWSLETTER AND REPLY CARD.

Source: Reproduced with the permission of Red Cloud Indian School, www.redcloudschool.org.

impossible to predict with accuracy which donors want rewards. For every donor who gives at least partly to receive a reward or who is encouraged to give higher amounts and to keep giving for longer if a tangible benefit is attached, another insists on anonymity or feels it is inappropriate for a nonprofit to spend money sending gifts to its supporters or entertaining them at special events. Fundraisers therefore have to be sensitive to individual preference and ready to manage the expectations of those donors who like to receive as well as to give.

One of the clearest findings of our research (as explained in Chapter Two) was that individuals seeking a personal benefit or reward for their giving are significantly more likely to lapse than those who do not seek such a reward. This is not to say that rewards and recognition devices are not suitable fundraising tools or to deny that they can be used profitably in a fundraising program. But fundraisers should recognize that when the reward is central to the giving decision, the giving may cease as soon as the reward does or when a competitor charity offers a better "deal."

We saw in Chapter Two that the rewards offered to donors can be categorized as either intrinsic (that is, inherently related to the core work and mission of the organization) or extrinsic (unrelated). For example, donors to an art gallery who receive invitations to special showings of exhibitions are receiving intrinsic rewards. Donors who support a hospital and are sent two theater tickets as a thank-you are receiving a reward that is extrinsic, unconnected to the cause they have supported. The art-gallery supporters who attend the special showing are likely to feel close to the organization and to be loyal as a result, while the hospital donors may switch their allegiance if they find a nonprofit that offers a reward with a greater value than their theater tickets. In order to increase donor loyalty any rewards program therefore has to be centered on the cause, and the incentives offered should be inextricably linked in the donor's mind to the specific organization and what it does.

When using recognition schemes, fundraisers should let donors choose whether they want a reward and should then adhere to their wishes. In addition, donor rewards should be both appropriate to the donor's level of giving and effective in encouraging the donor to give for longer, to give more, and to feel more engaged with the cause. Rewards for givers of significant gifts should be negotiated as part of their personal cultivation and stewardship program, and policy guidelines should clearly state what such individual recognition can and should consist of.

The Museum of Modern Art (MoMA) in New York City offers a comprehensive tiered range of membership programs featuring intrinsic rewards at different price levels, as outlined in Exhibit 10.4.

EXHIBIT 10.4. MUSEUM OF MODERN ART MEMBERSHIP PROGRAMS.

MoMA (the Museum of Modern Art) in New York offers a tiered range of membership programs at different price levels:

Individual

$75 (100% tax-deductible)

- Admission for one to the Museum's galleries, gallery talks, and regular film programs
- Permanent red membership card
- Admission and invitations to selected programs at P.S.1 Contemporary Art Center
- Discounted admission to view many of MoMA's most beloved sculptures, temporarily relocated to the New York Botanical Garden
- Building Project and membership updates
- Invitations for two to exclusive members-only programs and events
- Invitations to members-only exhibition previews
- 10% discount in the MoMA Online Store, through MoMA mail order, and at the MoMA Stores, including our new location in Soho, NYC
- Members-only sales and special events at the MoMA Stores
- Discounted guest admission tickets
- Discounts at a variety of restaurants in Queens and Manhattan
- Discounts on parking, hotels, and exhibition audio tours

Family or Dual

$120 (Family: 100% tax-deductible, Dual: $115 tax-deductible)
All of the above benefits, plus:

- Admission for two to the Museum's galleries, gallery talks, and regular film programs
- Admission cards for members' children ages 12–18
- Parent/child workshops, films, and family gallery programs
- Opportunities to attend the annual MoMA Family Festival and the annual MoMA Family Picnic

Fellow

$275 ($210 tax-deductible)
All of the above benefits, plus:

- Permanent silver membership card
- Invitations for two to special exhibition previews and evening receptions
- The MoMA Appointment Calendar
- Admission for up to four guests when accompanied by member
- Two complimentary admission passes for unaccompanied guests
- Priority reservation privileges for all member programs and events
- Invitations for two to our Exclusive Designer Series; meet today's leading designers and enjoy an elegant reception

EXHIBIT 10.4. MUSEUM OF MODERN ART
MEMBERSHIP PROGRAMS, Cont'd.

Supporting

$400 ($250 tax-deductible)
All of the above benefits, plus:
- Invitations for two to previews of major films
- Invitations for two to private film screenings
- Listing in and copy of MoMA's Member/Donor report
- Two additional (four total) complimentary admission passes for unaccompanied guests
- One Museum-selected major exhibition catalogue

Sustaining

$750 ($523 tax-deductible)
All of the above benefits, plus:
- Invitations for two to the opening-night previews of all major exhibitions
- Invitations to behind-the-scenes curatorial talks and receptions
- 15% discount at the MoMA Stores
- A beautiful assortment of MoMA exhibition catalogues
- Opportunities to attend study tours, courses, and selected special events
- Invitations for two to additional private film screenings

Patron

$1,500 ($1,161 tax-deductible)
All of the above benefits, plus:
- Permanent gold membership card
- Invitation to one additional reception
- Special viewing hours for major exhibitions, held while the Museum is closed to the public
- Invitations for two to opening-night screenings of Museum film programs
- Additional MoMA exhibition catalogues

Benefactor

$2,500 ($2,058 tax-deductible)
All of the above benefits, plus:
- Invitation for two to the Annual Benefactor Luncheon
- 20% discount at the MoMA Stores, through MoMA mail order, and in the MoMA Online Store
- Invitations for two to the opening preview of all exhibitions
- Invitations for two to Breakfast with the Director
- Complimentary audio tour for all major exhibitions

Student

$35 (100% tax deductible)
A Student membership is available for full-time students enrolled at an accredited high school, college, university, or art school, and includes all the benefits of an individual membership except special mailings and invitations.
Must present a valid student I.D. or bursar's receipt when joining.

EXHIBIT 10.4. MUSEUM OF MODERN ART
MEMBERSHIP PROGRAMS, Cont'd.

National/International

$60 (100% tax-deductible)

If you live beyond a 150-mile radius of New York City, this special membership category gives you all the benefits of Individual membership except for special mailings and invitations.

Increased Involvement:

The MoMA Family Council

$1,500 ($1,023 tax-deductible)

The MoMA Family Council is a special membership group created for parents and their children ages three to fourteen. Exclusive programs and events introduce children to MoMA's collection of modern and contemporary art, allowing them to develop their appreciation of the visual arts in an exciting, engaging way.

All year long, children enjoy art workshops, behind-the-scenes tours, visits to artists' studios, gallery walks in Soho and Chelsea, special film programs, trips to sculpture parks in the New York City area, fantastic annual events like the MoMA Family Festival, and much more.

Parents receive the special privileges of Patron membership, which include black-tie exhibitions previews, Museum publications, private collection visits, private film screenings, curatorial talks, special viewing hours, and other exclusive programs.

Family Council members may also attend all MoMA family programs free, as a benefit of their membership.

Members at $5,000 and Above

Members at $5,000 and above enjoy increased access to MoMA and closer involvement with curators and trustees at annual receptions including the Director's Dinner, President's Reception, Curatorial Luncheon, and other exclusive events.

For additional information about all levels of membership, please call (212) 708–9687.

Source: Reproduced with the permission of the Museum of Modern Art in New York from its website.

Recognition Clubs and Societies

Many organizations invite donors to join a club or society, and by doing so donors receive rewards according to their giving status. A typical system might feature Diamond, Gold, Silver, and Bronze member levels for gifts of $5,000, $2,500, $1,000, and $500, respectively. Members at the Diamond level receive two tickets to a gala event, a recognition plaque, and a lapel pin; members subscribing at the Bronze level receive only the lapel pin; and members at the two intermediate levels receive commensurate combinations of these rewards.

The idea behind such schemes is that they will be attractive to donors who are able to give more than the average donor and who are attracted (or at least not averse) to the idea of receiving some benefit in return for their gifts. Donors who join these clubs feel increased loyalty because they are receiving a tangible benefit (that is intrinsic to the cause) and a reminder of their commitment. Once donors have bought into this sort of structured scheme, they can subsequently be encouraged to upgrade their support to the next level. In addition, a "community" of club members can be established and developed through events and functions.

As with other fundraising products, recognition clubs should be introduced with care, tested thoroughly, costed out fully, and monitored over time to assess donor lifetime value and return on investment. In many cases memberships will be taken up by only a minority of donors. If the numbers subscribing are big enough to make the club profitable and if, over time, it has a positive impact on the value and loyalty of the relevant donor group, it is worth continuing. If it attracts too few donors to be profitable or if the members exhibit levels of loyalty and value similar to or lower than those of average donors over time, the scheme should be reconsidered. The most common mistakes made with recognition clubs are to value donors in them more highly than others, when in fact other donors may be more valuable to the organization, and to continue them out of inertia rather than reviewing and retesting them regularly.

Recognition Tools

An entire industry provides donor-recognition tools. Donors can be sent plaques, certificates, badges, or pins that are personalized with their names and their contributions. They can be named at an organization's offices on donor walls, honor rolls, and books of remembrance. They can have their names featured in newsletters and annual reports. Major donors can have rooms, buildings, chairs, staff positions, events, programs, and performances named in their honor, or they can have plaques attached to trees, benches, books, or works of art.

We have stressed that in order to be effective in promoting donor loyalty any rewards or recognition vehicles offered to donors should be intrinsic to the cause. They should be unique and distinctive rather than off-the shelf products available under slightly different guises to every nonprofit in the donor-recognition marketplace. They should also be personalized. This is a challenge in such a developed fundraising field, but organizations should invest time and resources into researching creative and distinctive ways to thank and recognize donors rather than purchasing standard products that are unlikely to inspire donors to separate your organization from others or to feel closer to and more involved with your work. Many donors prize the recognition gifts they have received and display them with great pride.

Recognition devices are often most powerful when they are unsolicited by the donor. The mailing in Exhibit 10.5 is sent by the National Foundation for Cancer

**EXHIBIT 10.5. NATIONAL FOUNDATION
FOR CANCER RESEARCH HONOR-ROLL MAILING.**

 NATIONAL FOUNDATION FOR CANCER RESEARCH

HONOR ROLL ACCEPTANCE
FOR INSCRIPTION

Dear Lastname,

     I am pleased to acknowledge my election to the Annual Honor Roll of the National Foundation for Cancer Research. Please inscribe my name as follows on this National Register to be kept on view at NFCR headquarters.

_____
(PLEASE PRINT)

FROM: Mr. John Q. Sample
          1234 Main Street
          Anytown, USA 12345

☑ CHECK ONE:

☐   I do indeed agree that the costs of those advances made against cancer this year by NFCR's researchers must not be allowed to slow the work of these master scientists.

     I am therefore responding to your plea for a final 2004 tax-deductible gift by including my check for the amount specified.

     Enclosed is my contribution of:

     ( ) $100.00   ( ) $150.00   ( ) $200.00

     ( ) Other $_____
                    (Please Specify)

        NOTE: Please make checks payable to
       National Foundation for Cancer Research
       (ALL CONTRIBUTIONS ARE TAX-DEDUCTIBLE)

☐   I regret that I am unable to respond to your special plea. However, proceed with my inclusion in the NFCR Annual Honor Roll as indicated.

Commonwealth of Virginia residents may obtain a financial statement from the Commonwealth of Virginia, Department of Agriculture and Consumer Services, Division of Consumer Affairs, P. O. Box 1163, Richmond, VA 23209.

Research to repeat donors asking their permission to include their names on an honor roll that will be kept on view at the headquarters of the organization. Although the mailing also asks for a further gift, the donor does not have to make a contribution to be included on the roll. The mailing involves donors by asking them to check and correct their names for entry on the register. It also includes a deadline, as an accompanying letter states that the honor roll "will be inscribed within the next week or so."

The Internet is currently inspiring some of the most creative donor-recognition schemes with virtual walls of honor, tributes, and books of remembrance. Many libraries now feature virtual bookplates in their electronic libraries, and donors for many causes are routinely named on organizations' websites. The Internet also offers many opportunities to create instant feedback and to visibly demonstrate the impact a gift is having. On-line giving is recognized by some nonprofits through visual devices in which the gift counts against a total or through tallies in which the gift is immediately deducted from the total amount required.

The World Wildlife Fund's Panda Passport is an interactive web-based fundraising program. The site lists environmental campaigns from all over the world. Passport holders can visit these campaigns on-line and take action. Each action is recognized by the placing of a stamp into a virtual passport. Each stamp has a point value, and these are added up and used to calculate a "campaigning level" for each person. Passport holders can see immediately what they have achieved, and any action they take is immediately recognized and rewarded in an interactive and engaging way. They can print out a certificate displaying this status and can also register to receive a series of rewards as they progress through the various campaigning levels. As this program is entirely e-based, the rewards are also related to web use, such as screensavers and desktop pictures, patterns, and buttons (see Exhibit 10.6).

Linking the Donor to the Beneficiary

As we saw in Chapter Eight, one of the most effective ways to draw donors closer to an organization and to provide recognition and feedback is to link them directly to the beneficiaries their donations are helping. For low-value donors organizations can offer sponsorship or adoption products and can provide testimonials from and reports about the beneficiaries in newsletters and appeal communications. For major donors organizations can offer face-to-face contact with beneficiaries or the staff members who work directly with them; they can meet staff in the field or at events, conferences, or functions. Even donors giving lower amounts can be invited to events with program staff; invitations to such events increase involvement and engagement, even if the donor is unable to attend.

EXHIBIT 10.6. WORLD WILDLIFE FUND'S WEB PAGE
EXPLAINING MEMBERSHIP BENEFITS.

Welcome to YOUR Passport Rewards!

Click on any of the section links below and right to download your choice/s of dramatic screensavers, desktop pictures, patterns and official Passport member banners and buttons to add to your site and show you work for a Living Planet.

Thank you, and enjoy!

Screensavers

Desktop Pictures

Desktop Patterns

Banners and Buttons

The Importance of Service Quality

As we have explained, most donors judge the efficiency of the organization through the service they receive. Our research proved the connection between service quality and donor loyalty. Given this connection, recognition ideally starts the moment donors call an organization to change their address or to offer a gift, and they should be rewarded for their commitment and generosity with special

EXHIBIT 10.7. AFP DONOR BILL OF RIGHTS.

A Donor Bill of Rights

PHILANTHROPY is based on voluntary action for the common good. It is a tradition of giving and sharing that is primary to the quality of life. To assure that philanthropy merits the respect and trust of the general public, and that donors and prospective donors can have full confidence in the not-for-profit organizations and causes they are asked to support, we declare that all donors have these rights:

I.

To be informed of the organization's mission, of the way the organization intends to use donated resources, and of its capacity to use donations effectively for their intended purposes.

II.

To be informed of the identity of those serving on the organization's governing board, and to expect the board to exercise prudent judgement in its stewardship responsibilities.

III.

To have access to the organization's most recent financial statements.

IV.

To be assured their gifts will be used for the purposes for which they were given.

V.

To receive appropriate acknowledgement and recognition.

VI.

To be assured that information about their donations is handled with respect and with confidentiality to the extent provided by law.

VII.

To expect that all relationships with individuals representing organizations of interest to the donor will be professional in nature.

VIII.

To be informed whether those seeking donations are volunteers, employees of the organization or hired solicitors.

IX.

To have the opportunity for their names to be deleted from mailing lists that an organization may intend to share.

X.

To feel free to ask questions when making a donation and to receive prompt, truthful and forthright answers.

DEVELOPED BY
AMERICAN ASSOCIATION OF FUND RAISING COUNSEL (AAFRC)
ASSOCIATION FOR HEALTHCARE PHILANTHROPY (AHP)
COUNCIL FOR ADVANCEMENT AND SUPPORT OF EDUCATION (CASE)
ASSOCIATION OF FUNDRAISING PROFESSIONALS (AFP)

ENDORSED BY
(IN FORMATION)
INDEPENDENT SECTOR
NATIONAL CATHOLIC DEVELOPMENT CONFERENCE (NCDC)
NATIONAL COMMITTEE ON PLANNED GIVING (NCPG)
COUNCIL FOR RESOURCE DEVELOPMENT (CRD)
UNITED WAY OF AMERICA

Please help us distribute this widely.

Source: Reproduced with the permission of Association of Fundraising Professionals (AFP).

treatment from every member of staff. High standards of care can be promoted by providing donors with "charters," such as the AFP Donor Bill of Rights (Exhibit 10.7), in which the organization pledges to treat donors in a particular way. Such care includes securing record systems to ensure that donors are not approached or solicited for gifts or programs that are inappropriate, that donors' wishes regarding the frequency and type of communications they receive are respected, and that information about them is used sensitively.

Summary

In this chapter we have provided an overview of donor recognition. We have highlighted the need to offer donors choices about the rewards or recognition they receive. Some individuals expect to be thanked and rewarded for their gift, while others prefer to receive the minimum possible from the nonprofit as a way to cut down on what they regard as needless expenditures. Nonprofits are thus well advised to ask donors whether they want to opt-out of recognition opportunities.

When an organization considers rewards to be desirable and appropriate, it needs to tie them as tightly as possible to the cause. Here tangible rewards can be invaluable because they not only say thank you but also remind donors of their association with the cause. As we learned in Chapter Two, many donors simply forget the organizations they have supported, particularly with the passage of time. We also stressed the importance of being memorable, of providing feedback and rewards that are unique or distinctive. Many recognition tools are boring, predictable, and add little value. Creative approaches stand out, make the donor feel special, and reinforce the donor's link to the cause. Donors typically give to many different organizations, each of which offers some form of recognition. Receipt of three or four plaques in the space of a year is unlikely to stimulate loyalty.

CHAPTER ELEVEN

USING LIFETIME VALUE TO INFORM RETENTION STRATEGY

In previous chapters we have highlighted the role that calculating donor lifetime value can play in developing effective retention strategies. So far we have deliberately avoided technical complexities and in particular a discussion of some of the more difficult issues surrounding the calculation of lifetime value figures. In this chapter we provide a definition of lifetime value and explore how it can be calculated for both individual givers and for segments of donors in a typical fundraising database. We also explain why it is worth taking the time to make these calculations and suggest the benefits that this analysis can deliver for all aspects of professional fundraising practice and for donor retention in particular.

Lifetime value (LTV) is essentially a measure of how much a donor will be worth to an organization over the duration of the relationship. Bitran and Mondschein (1997, p. 109) define it as "the total net contribution that a customer generates during his/her lifetime on a house-list."

Calculating the LTVs of Individual Donors

To calculate LTV for a donor you have to estimate the costs and revenues that will be associated with managing communications with that donor during each year of his or her relationship with your organization. If, for example, the relationship is predicted to extend over four years, you subtract the projected costs of servicing the relationship with that donor each year from the revenue that will be generated. In essence the donor's contribution each year to the organization's overheads and programs can be calculated. A certain amount of crystal-ball gazing is involved because it becomes increasingly more difficult to predict costs and revenues the further you look into the future. To take account of this uncertainty and to reflect the fact that a $100 donation in four years will be worth much less in real terms than it is today, it is also important to discount the value of the future revenue that will be generated. After all, instead of investing the money in its fundraising programs your charity could simply place it in an interest-bearing account. Unless the return from the fundraising activity can be expected to match or exceed the return on an interest-bearing account, it will clearly not be worthwhile. If this analysis is conducted across your database, a key advantage accrues: you can increase your organization's overall profitability by getting rid of donors who will never be profitable and concentrating resources on recruiting and retaining those who will.

The formula for calculating LTV for an individual donor is as follows:

$$LTV = \sum_{i=1}^{n} C_i (1 + d)^{-i}$$

where

C = net annual contribution (revenue minus costs of each year's fundraising activities)
d = discount rate
n = expected duration of the relationship (in years)

This somewhat complex-looking equation merely indicates that it is necessary to calculate the likely future contribution (revenue minus costs) by a donor to each year's fundraising activities, discount these future contributions, and then add them all together. The grand total is the LTV of a given donor.

In calculating contributions, an organization should subtract all the relevant costs of servicing the relationship with a given donor from all the revenues generated from that donor. The determination of what constitutes revenues and costs is driven by the purposes for which the analysis is being conducted. The LTV calculation could, for example, take into consideration much more than just the revenue from direct donations. Donors often purchase goods from catalogues, sell raffle tickets, donate their time to fundraising events, recruit others, and so on. Each of these contributions can be accounted for in the equation. As an example, the net contribution figure for each year could include the costs of the following items: newsletters, appeal letters, acknowledgement and thank-you letters, promotional merchandise, donor gifts, and telemarketing activity. Revenues could include cash donations, the cash value of donations in kind, the cash value of any volunteering undertaken, the cash value of referrals (the introduction of other donors), and revenue from the sale of promotional merchandise.

Table 11.1 is a simple example. A donor has started a relationship with the charity as an occasional giver. This person is female, aged forty-five, lives in a certain type of accommodation (identifiable from her zip code information), and responded to a specific type of appeal (on famine relief) conveyed through an equally specific recruitment media—a list-swap mailing. On the basis of a historical analysis of the database, the fundraiser understands that donors matching this profile typically upgrade to monthly giving in the third year of their relationship with the charity and tend to be regular purchasers of raffle tickets. Indeed it is not unusual for this type of person to persuade friends or relatives to sell raffle tickets on the charity's behalf. On the basis of this information, coupled with projected costs, it is possible to produce the forecast given in Table 11.1 of the contributions that this donor will make to the organization over the duration of her predicted five-year relationship. As previously indicated, the value of future contributions must be discounted, and on this basis the predicted lifetime value of the donor is calculated

TABLE 11.1. SAMPLE LTV ANALYSIS FOR AN INDIVIDUAL DONOR.

	Year 1	Year 2	Year 3	Year 4	Year 5	Total
Revenue						
Cash	$50	$50	$0	$0	$0	$100
Raffles	10	20	30	30	40	130
Covenants and tax refunded	0	0	100	100	100	300
Referrals	0	0	0	10	10	20
Total income	60	70	130	140	150	550
Costs						
Newsletters	2	2	2	2	3	11
Appeals	4	4	5	5	5	23
Thank-you letters	1	1	1	2	2	7
Raffles	2	2	2	3	3	12
Incentives	0	0	0	5	5	10
Total costs	9	9	10	17	18	63
Contribution	51	61	120	123	132	487
Discounted value	51	55	99	92	90	387

Note: Discount rate is 10 percent per year.

to be $387. This information can then be used to assign the donor to an appropriate pattern of contact and quality of care.

Although planned and bequest giving is the key source of income for many voluntary organizations, it is extremely difficult to predict such income, and organizations thus tend to exclude it from LTV calculations. If your organization is able to predict these gifts with any degree of accuracy, they should be included in your calculations.

Some Common Mistakes

Many organizations make two key mistakes in calculating LTV: they misallocate recruitment costs, and they misallocate overheads.

Misallocation of Recruitment Costs

Initial acquisition costs should be included in an LTV analysis only if an organization wants either to decide on an appropriate allocation of recruitment expenditures (among the different media options available) or to predict the returns that will ultimately be generated by a given recruitment campaign. Generally speaking, there is no justification for including the costs of acquisition in LTV calculations because this cost reflects merely the quality of an organization's fundraising, not the value of its donors. To take a simple example, suppose that the net contribution generated by a donor recruited by direct mail is $250. If this direct-mail campaign was poorly targeted, with a creative strategy that did not complement the nature of the appeal, comparatively few donors may have been recruited, and the cost of acquiring each new donor could have been as high as $245. Subtracting this value from the donor's gift would leave a contribution of only $5 for the first year, which would place the donor in a low-value segment and make him or her a good candidate for deletion from the charity's database. Yet this person is a high-value donor! Recruitment costs are a past measure of the efficiency of an organization's fundraising strategy, nothing more. They should not be used in any way to determine the standard of care a given donor receives.

Misallocation of Overheads

The other mistake organizations make in calculating LTV is to include indirect costs in the equation. Many organizations set off a percentage of future fundraising overheads (fixed costs like database maintenance and administration) against donor revenues. But this strategy is wrong for a simple reason. LTV calculations can be employed to deselect donors who will never be profitable in order to concentrate resources on those who will. Many organizations simply delete or reciprocate (swap) those donors with a negative LTV. But if overhead costs are included in LTV calculations, this procedure can result in an unfortunate cycle of events.

For example, suppose a very small charity has a donor base of only one hundred individuals, each of whom has an LTV varying between $50 and $500 when only the direct costs or revenues are taken into consideration. By adding a proportion of fundraising overhead to the costs, LTV figures are reduced to a range of −$50 to $400. Suddenly, it appears to be unprofitable to deal with a number of donors, namely, those with a negative LTV value. Assuming that there were ten such individuals, the prevailing logic would be to delete them from the active portion of the database. Many organizations in this situation fail to understand, however, the marginal contribution each donor makes. If the organization in this example deletes the ten donors with negative LTVs and then runs a second LTV analysis, it will find (probably to its surprise) that it again has ten donors in the negative range, perhaps this time from −$61 to −$389. This situation occurs because although the organization's overhead costs have not changed, it now has only ninety donors to allocate these costs among. Each donor therefore bears a larger percentage of the overhead, and some previously profitable donors now appear unprofitable. If the decision is made to delete these ten donors, the organization will be left with only eighty donors. Following this strategy through to a logical conclusion, a charity could continue to delete negative donors until it appears sensible to abandon its fundraising activities altogether.

For this reason LTV was earlier defined as the total net contribution from a donor. As long as the revenue generated by a given donor is more than it costs directly to service that donor, she or he is making some form of contribution to general fundraising overheads. So although such donors may be, in an accounting sense, unprofitable, it would be folly to stop communicating with them. Only when the direct costs of fundraising are likely to exceed the revenues generated should a donor be deleted from the active portion of the database.

Calculating the LTV of Particular Donor Segments

In the example above we were concerned with how lifetime value might be calculated for an individual donor. More usually, nonprofits want to understand whether specific segments of their database exhibit higher lifetime values than others. This calculation calls for a more sophisticated analysis. To measure the LTV of a particular donor segment, the following process is recommended.

Process

First, decide what the purpose of the analysis will be. Fundraisers often want to determine whether certain segments of the database have a higher or lower value than others so that they can target their appeals accordingly. Thus if female donors appear to be worth more than male donors or if donors recruited by direct mail have a higher LTV than those recruited by press advertising, fundraising resources can be allocated accordingly. Alternatively, strategies for providing appropriate degrees of care can be developed to ensure loyalty among those segments with the highest lifetime values.

Second, determine how many years in the future you want the analysis to cover. It is not essential here that the time period selected be based on the longest-standing donors (Carpenter, 1995). Because predicting behavior becomes progressively more difficult the further one looks into the future and because contributions in the medium to long term will be heavily discounted, it is important only that the time period selected captures the majority of the contributions for a given segment of donors. Previous research in the commercial sector suggests that a time frame of five years might be most appropriate in the fundraising context (Sargeant and West, 2001). The value of contributions beyond this time frame will be difficult to predict, as will the rates of donor attrition. In a sense, therefore, the term *lifetime* value is something of a misnomer. The organization sets a suitable time frame for the analysis and projects the LTV of its donors over this specific period.

Third, divide, or segment, the donor database into a manageable but distinct group of cells on the basis of the primary variable to be explored. If you wish to obtain the LTVs of donors who offer their first donation at different gift levels, divide the database into a number of cells based on the level of the initial gift. In theory, the greater the number of cells, the more accurate the predictive capability of the eventual model. But in practice, there is a trade-off between accuracy and simplicity; increasing the number of cells adds greatly to the complexity of the model. As a general rule, in the fundraising context, between ten and thirty cells are optimal. You might therefore allocate donors to cells based on their initial donations of $1 to $5, $6 to $10, $11 to $15, and so on.

Fourth, establish the attrition rates and giving history of donors in each of the cells identified. Attrition rates will almost certainly vary from year to year. For example, comparatively few single-gift givers will give a second donation. Those who do will probably exhibit a steady pattern of attrition. This information can be used to calculate the percentage of donors within the cell who are likely to be active in year 2, year 3, and so forth. By looking at giving histories, you should be able to calculate typical response rates for members of each cell according to, say, the type of donor-development activity employed or the actual amount donated in response to each campaign. A number of donors will typically migrate from one cell to another as they decide to give more (or less) or to upgrade, for example, to monthly giving.

Fifth, determine costs. If you are planning a new development strategy, calculate, for example, the projected costs of all mailings including those that a donor would typically receive even though the communication (a newsletter, say) is not specifically aimed at raising funds.

Sixth, use all these data to predict future value. With information about likely attrition rates, the future costs of servicing donors, the predicted revenue streams, and an appropriate discount rate, you can make predictions about the projected LTV of each cell, or category of donor.

An Example

An LTV analysis using the method we presented above was conducted on behalf of a large international aid organization. The charity is involved in a number of development projects worldwide. The aim was to determine which acquisition media generated the highest LTVs. Only single-gift (rather than monthly) giving was considered. A random sample of one thousand donors was chosen from people recruited through each of five primary media. The researcher was then able to build a model that predicted the LTVs of donors who might be acquired through each medium in a forthcoming acquisition campaign. The results of the analysis were used to allocate funds among the media available and to forecast the likely (lifetime) return on investment (ROI) of the campaign. A 10 percent discount rate was used, and a donor lifetime was assumed to be five years. As the organization was concerned here with the relative performance of each acquisition medium, the costs of acquisition were included in the LTV calculation. The results are presented in Table 11.2 and are similar to those reported by Sargeant (1998) for the fundraising sector as a whole.

TABLE 11.2. LIFETIME VALUE BY RECRUITMENT MEDIUM.

Medium	Mean LTV	Standard Deviation
Direct mail (cold mailing)	$196.17	103.24
Direct mail (list swap)	185.25	104.45
Unaddressed mail	156.85	56.22
Direct-response press advertising	154.82	53.84
Press/magazine inserts	194.21	126.93

The Benefits of LTV Analysis

At this stage you could be forgiven for thinking that calculating LTV is so complex that it's not worth the effort. For many organizations it's sufficient to stick with the simple historic value of donors and to make decisions on that basis. Such a procedure would work for small nonprofits with relatively small donor databases. Some medium-sized and larger organizations, however, may find that calculating future LTV is helpful because LTV can be used to drive four key management decisions: establishing acquisition budgets, choosing media for initial donor acquisition, determining development strategies, and investing in the reactivation of lapsed donors.

Establishing Acquisition Budgets

An understanding of the LTVs of a nonprofit's donors can guide decisions about how much the organization should spend to acquire each new donor. Many nonprofits strive to achieve a break-even position at the end of each of their acquisition campaigns. Although commendable, meeting this goal is not necessary as long as the future contributions of the donors recruited are positive. Nonprofits employing LTV therefore tend to establish somewhat higher acquisition budgets than those that do not. In financial terms, this is simply because a fundraiser employing a transaction-based approach will calculate campaign ROI as

$$ROI = \frac{\text{immediate revenue generated}}{\text{cost of acquisition campaign}}$$

A fundraiser adopting LTV would calculate campaign ROI as

$$ROI = \frac{\text{initial revenue} + (\text{sum of all future contributions} - \text{discount})}{\text{cost of acquisition campaign}}$$

where

ROI = return on donor-acquisition investment
future contribution = estimated annual contribution to profit
discount = reduction in value of future dollars to today's rate
(discounted cash flow)

As Peppers and Rogers (1995, p. 49) note, "Instead of measuring the effectiveness of a marketing program by how many sales transactions occur across an entire market during a particular period, the . . . marketer [should] gauge success by the projected increase or decrease in a customer's expected future value to the company."

Choosing Media for Initial Donor Acquisition

Fundraisers engaged in donor acquisition constantly ask questions like, Which media should I be using for my acquisition activity? and How should I balance media options? The traditional approach to answering these questions is to calculate the immediate ROI for each medium based on previous response rates. Some fundraisers may go further and calculate the cost per new donor attracted (that is, the cost of the campaign divided by the number of new donors), the level of the average gift, and so on. Such analyses ignore certain known donor behaviors however. Donors recruited through one medium may never give again, while donors recruited through another medium may be much more loyal. LTV calculations take this kind of behavior into account and so give fundraisers a far better idea than traditional approaches do of which recruitment media will attract loyal and higher-value donors.

Determining Development Strategies

LTV calculations can be useful for more than just recruitment planning. The information can guide contact strategies for ongoing donor development. Initially, fundraisers may simply recognize the differences in contributions and offer particularly high-value donors a pattern of care that reflects their status. As they become more experienced in the use of LTV analysis, they can calculate the impact of differentiated standards of care or forms of contact on LTV. In a sense, they begin to model optimal lifetime value.

A simple example illustrates this point. Suppose a charity with projects in the Third World has divided donors into segments on the basis of projected LTV and has decided to do an expensive mailing to the highest-value segments in order to raise funds to support Third World families. On the basis of the projected LTV the organization has calculated that it can include in the mailing a detailed case history of one family that warrants support, photographs of each of the family members, and a promotional video highlighting the work the organization could do with that family. Although the LTV calculations suggest this is a viable form of contact and that it will generate an acceptable rate of return, the charity has no way of knowing initially whether this is the best it can do. With experience, however, a charity can monitor the impact on LTV of different contact strategies (such as a standard rather than an expensive mailing, a mailing that includes the photographs rather than one that does not, a mailing that includes the video rather than one that does not). Contact strategies can then be selected that maximize the LTV of a given segment of donors. In our example, it may be that including the video is not necessary, and therefore it lowers the value of subsequent donations. Or the video may increase the value of subsequent donations because it has such an emotive and tangible feel that donors' commitment to their relationship with the organization increases.

Investing in the Reactivation of Lapsed Donors

Most nonprofits now recognize the value of their databases, and few question the established wisdom that existing donors are the most cost-effective source of additional donations (Lindahl and Winship, 1992). Few would also disagree with the notion that reactivating lapsed donors can be profitable. Having been motivated to give at least once in the past, with the proper encouragement donors will do so again. The problem for many organizations is deciding which lapsed donors should be selected for contact. Although you could do this easily on the basis of the total amount donated, the level of the last gift, or the length of time since the last donation, it can be more effective to use projected LTV. Targeting donors with a high forecast LTV is likely to be the most efficient use of resources. An appropriate amount for reactivation activities can also be built into the budget by using projected LTV.

Summary

Lifetime value can play a pivotal role in the development of a relationship fundraising strategy. It can help identify appropriate donors with whom to develop a relationship and can help an organization calculate the amount of money it should be prepared to invest in them. LTV can also be used to inform the nature and quality of the relationship an organization has with its donors. Higher-value donors, for example, can be assigned to a standard of care that adequately reflects their worth. Similarly, an organization can choose acquisition media that tend to recruit donors worth more to the organization over time. Indeed, one of the central themes of this chapter has been that by using LTV analyses an organization can target valuable fundraising resources at the areas of activity where they are likely to have the greatest impact. As this benefit becomes increasingly evident to charity fundraisers, the LTV bandwagon will begin to roll.

CHAPTER TWELVE

PLANNING FOR RETENTION

In this chapter we draw together all our thinking on donor loyalty by presenting a framework that can be used for effective retention planning. We revisit all the key themes from the preceding chapters and show how they can inform fundraising planning at every stage. As you read this chapter it is important to bear in mind that nonprofits vary widely in size, available resources, and structure. There is therefore no one "correct" structure for a retention plan and no single "right way" of organizing fundraising activity. However, if an organization is to succeed at donor retention, it needs to plan for it, and such planning involves far more than simply devising the communications that donors will receive. An organization needs to think about the relationships that will be developed with each group of donors and how the organization will deliver and deepen these relationships over time.

As with all frameworks, the benefit of following the one we introduce here lies in ensuring that you do not forget any of the relevant factors. The framework provides a logical structure for planning, and the resulting plan is easy to put into operation. Figure 12.1 is the framework for developing a retention plan. It contains objectives, the general fundraising strategy, and an overview of the tactics the organization will use. We discuss each component of the plan in turn in this chapter.

FIGURE 12.1. FRAMEWORK FOR DEVELOPING A RETENTION PLAN.

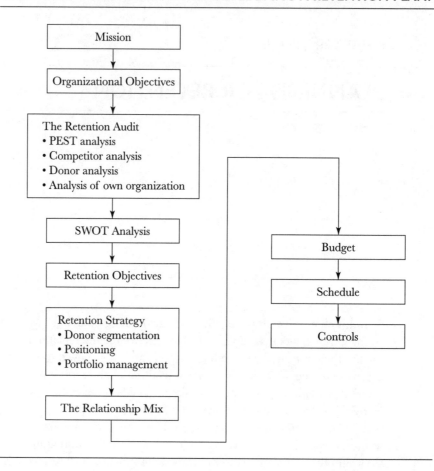

Mission

A nonprofit's mission should be stated at the beginning of every plan the organization produces. In the context of donor retention, restating the mission reminds fundraisers of the central purpose of their organization and helps focus their minds on the impact their work has on the beneficiaries. Unless fundraisers have a firm grasp of the aspirations of their organization, they will be in no position to communicate these goals to donors or to communicate a consistent message about the progress that has been made toward those goals. A number of nonprofits still resist developing a mission statement, feeling perhaps that it is yet another business practice they have to adopt, and they resent doing so. These people believe that mission statements are little more than promotional hype and that they have no useful managerial purpose. Such views are shortsighted. A good mission statement can act as a reference point so that board members, managers, staff, volunteers, donors, and beneficiaries all understand exactly what the nonprofit is trying to achieve.

Good mission statements specify the beneficiaries who will be served, the specific needs that will be met, and how these needs will be met. A glance through a selection of nonprofit publicity material reveals that many nonprofits have been intuitively writing mission statements for years, even if they prefer to use other terms such as *aims, purpose,* or *philosophy.* The terminology is unimportant. But an organization must be able to summarize in a few words its reason for being and reflect this purpose in its communications, its attitudes, and its behaviors.

Sample mission statements are provided here:

The American Cancer Society is the nationwide community-based voluntary health organization dedicated to eliminating cancer as a major health problem by preventing cancer, saving lives, and diminishing suffering from cancer, through research, education, advocacy, and service.

The mission of the American Diabetes organization is to prevent and cure diabetes and to improve the lives of all people affected by diabetes.

MADD's (Mother's Against Drunk Driving) mission is to stop drunk driving, support the victims of this violent crime, and prevent underage drinking.

The mission of Planned Parenthood is:

- To provide comprehensive reproductive and complementary health care services in settings which preserve and protect the essential privacy and rights of each individual;
- To advocate public policies that guarantee these rights and ensure access to such services;
- To provide educational programs which enhance understanding of individual and societal implications of human sexuality;
- To promote research and the advancement of technology in reproductive health care and encourage understanding of their inherent bioethical, behavioral, and social implications.

These diverse materials all exhibit a strong sense of purpose. Communicating these messages to donors makes it crystal clear exactly why they are giving and what their support will be likely to achieve. These statements also deliberately contain no statistics. Mission statements should reflect general and long-term aspirations, so that they can be used as guidelines over time. It should not be necessary to rewrite mission statements on an annual basis as doing so would hamper consistency in communications and confuse donors and other stakeholder groups.

Organizational Objectives

The specific goals that an organization hopes to reach within the planning period are usually mapped out separately. Although fundraisers may have little input into the operational plans of an organization, it is useful to restate the organizational objectives at the start of a fundraising plan because they help fundraisers concentrate on exactly what their organization hopes to achieve in the short term, and they clearly signal to staff and volunteers the impact the successful implementation of their fundraising plan will have.

For an animal-welfare nonprofit, for example, organizational objectives might look something like the following:

1. To treat 120,000 sick or injured animals each year
2. To re-home 60 percent of the animals that are brought to our centers
3. To visit 10 percent of the schools in the state each year to educate young people about animal welfare and care
4. To provide a twenty-four-hour help and advice line

The Retention Audit

Next, fundraising planners move beyond the mere restatement of existing material and begin to develop the retention plan itself. Any retention plan answers three key questions: Where are we now? Where do we want to be? How will we get there? The retention audit addresses the first of these elements. It is the most crucial stage of the whole process, as without a thorough understanding of the organization's current position planners cannot determine what they can realistically accomplish in the future. The retention audit is essentially a detailed review of any factors that are likely to affect the organization's ability to be able to retain donors, including factors generated internally and those originating in the external environment.

PEST Factors

The audit process usually begins with an examination of the wider environment in which the nonprofit is operating. The factors identified here are usually beyond the control of the nonprofit, but they will nevertheless have an impact on the organization at some stage in the future. This analysis is typically referred to by its acronym, PEST, for the types of elements it comprises: political, economic, sociocultural, and technological.

The aim here is to list factors that could affect donor retention and to outline how these are expected to change over the duration of the plan. At this point in the process it is best not to spend too much time assessing the impact that these factors might have. Other clues to the impact of PEST factors will emerge as the audit process progresses. It is therefore better to consider potential impacts all together when the audit is complete. A sample PEST analysis is presented in Exhibit 12.1.

Competitor Analysis

Although the work that many nonprofits do is distinctive, they still face considerable competition for funds. This competition typically takes one of three forms. First, competition comes from nonprofits with similar missions. Many donors identify with a cause rather than with an organization involved with that cause. Some

EXHIBIT 12.1. SAMPLE PEST ANALYSIS.

Political Factors	**Sociocultural Factors**
Federal legislative changes State legislative changes Attitude of government toward the cause Federal/state policy Implementation of do-not-call registry	Demographic patterns and trends Societal concern for the cause Levels of public trust and confidence Trends in social participation Perceived unacceptability of certain media (e-mail, telephone)
Economic Factors	**Technological Factors**
Federal/state fiscal changes Inflation Interest rates Growth or decline in economy Level of unemployment Trends in disposable income	Development of new digital media Trends in Internet usage and penetration Introduction of digital television and radio Falling database costs Falling costs of analytical database software

nonprofits therefore face competition for funds from organizations working in a related field.

Second, competition comes from large nonprofits. Large organizations such as the United Way and national organizations such as the American Cancer Society have communication budgets that deliver strong brand awareness in most states and communities. Smaller organizations can have difficulty making their voices heard above this promotional "noise," and thus the activities of large nonprofits can pose a significant threat to the retention of donors and fundraising in general.

Third, donors may support nonprofits, or they may spend their money on other lifestyle choices. This type of competition is a particular threat to retention; as we saw in Chapter Two, many donors stop giving because they think they can no longer afford it. They may have had a genuine change in their financial circumstances, or they may have other spending priorities. Nonprofits need to understand this type of competition.

When a nonprofit is in competition for funds with other organizations, it needs to develop a sense of who the primary competitors are. This knowledge can be gained quite easily by just talking to donors about the other organizations they support or have an interest in. More often than not, some pattern will emerge, and competitors can then be identified.

Every nonprofit needs to have the following information about its competitors:

Who its competitors are

Their activities and interests (i.e., their program provision)

Their fundraising performance

The fundraising strategies and tactics they have adopted and intend to adopt in the future

The alliances they have formed

Their major fundraising strengths and weaknesses

Obtaining such data is not usually difficult. Accounting data can be captured from www.guidestar.org or annual reports. Details of fundraising strategy and performance can sometimes be found in the trade or local press or simply by chatting with individuals working for the organization at fundraising conferences and events. Some nonprofits also make "dummy" donations: members of their team offer a competitor a gift so that they can sample the communication programs designed to solicit gifts from particular categories of donors.

Information about competitors can be used to obtain good fundraising ideas that have been developed elsewhere or to design a strategy to counter activities that appear to pose a threat and that may encourage donors to switch their support as a consequence.

Donor Analysis

Perhaps the most critical aspect of the audit is the gathering of data about how donors perceive the organization and their own giving behavior and preferences. Because this is a retention plan, it is useful to conduct even a small ongoing program of research to track various kinds of information:

> Who supports the organization
>
> Why they support the organization
>
> What drives their commitment to the organization
>
> What they like and dislike about the organization and its fundraising activities
>
> How they perceive the quality of the service offered
>
> What their interests are
>
> Whether their current needs for information are met
>
> Why they elect to support or not to support the organization in particular ways (single gifts, regular gifts, planned gifts)
>
> What other nonprofits they support and why
>
> What factors drive their decisions about the proportion of their charitable pot that is donated to the organization
>
> How they decide how much to give
>
> How they make charitable-gift decisions in general

This list includes many of the factors we identified as being of relevance to retention in Chapters Two and Three. Obtaining answers to these questions will help you develop a detailed understanding of all the factors that affect donor behavior. We cannot stress too highly just how crucial these data will be. It is impossible to develop a meaningful retention strategy without first understanding donors' perceptions of the organization and their own charitable-giving behavior.

Analysis of Own Organization

Having analyzed the components of the external environment, you now need to examine the capabilities of your organization. A detailed audit should be undertaken of the organization's current retention strategy and tactics. The following checklist indicates the information that might typically be regarded as relevant. In each case the researcher needs to establish the performance achieved and trends over time.

Fundraising income by donor segment

Retention rates by donor segment

Response rates to particular forms of communication

Response rates to upgrade opportunities (for example, attempts to switch single-gift donors to a regular gift)

Trends in donor interests

Trends in the volume and nature of inquiries

Trends in the volume and nature of complaints

Trends in the quality of service the organization provides

Conducting such an audit can be a time-consuming process, and given that it is good practice to conduct an audit each year, it can place considerable demands on organizational resources. Nevertheless, the benefits that the audit can offer in improving management decision making far outweigh the costs. Indeed, if the auditing process is instituted on an annual basis, most of the necessary mechanisms for the gathering of data are put in place in the first year, and so the costs in both time and effort should subsequently fall substantially.

SWOT Analysis

At this stage the output from the retention audit is not much more than a collection of data, and in this format it is of little value for planning purposes. The next stage in the planning process is to reflect on all the data that have been gathered and to consider whether each piece represents a strength, a weakness, an opportunity, or a threat. This form of analysis is usually referred to by its mnemonic—SWOT. Strengths and weaknesses are derived from an analysis of the own-organization data, while opportunities and threats are external and thus are derived from the PEST analysis and the competitor and donor analyses.

In performing a SWOT analysis it is important to look at each factor objectively. All too often organizations write out long lists of strengths without reflecting on them. A strength is a strength only if an organization is better at it than any other organization and, in particular, is better at it than its major competitors. It is also important to look at strengths from the donor's perspective. A strength is a strength only if the donor believes it is or if it delivers something that the donor believes is a strength.

Exhibit 12.2 is a sample SWOT analysis. . Here the impact of each factor has been carefully assessed, and within each general heading the relative importance of each factor has been highlighted by listing them in order of importance. The organization is therefore now in a position to develop a plan that mitigates the major weaknesses, capitalizes on the strengths, takes full advantage of the opportunities, and minimizes the environmental threats. In short the audit data are now in a format that can be used to inform planning.

EXHIBIT 12.2. SAMPLE SWOT ANALYSIS.

Strengths	Opportunities
1. High loyalty among high-value givers 2. Trusted brand name 3. Substantial growth in income from donors 4. Good size of donor database 5. Availability of economies of scale 6. High number of well-established fundraising products 7. High name recognition throughout state 8. Depth of experience in fundraising team 9. Regular press coverage of activities undertaken 10. Strong telephone fundraising team	1. Development of monthly giving 2. Development of planned giving 3. Development of Internet giving 4. Use of new e-media 5. Development of fundraising partnerships 6. Development of workplace giving 7. Use of fundraising intermediaries
Weaknesses	**Threats**
1. High attrition rate 2. Poor fundraising ratios 3. Aging profile of donors 4. Rising number of complaints 5. Poor perception of service quality 6. Planned giving department under-performing 7. Recent loss of two major corporate donors 8. Inability to attract younger donors 9. Low percentage of volunteers who become donors 10. Fulfillment times rising	1. Strong competition from local United Way 2. Growth in national do-not-call registry 3. Public perception of the cause is that it is now less of an issue 4. Increasing public concern over fundraising costs 5. Additional data-protection legislation

Some nonprofits can take this analysis one step further. When a strength for one donor segment is a weakness for another, it may make sense to develop a separate SWOT analysis for each donor segment. This procedure may make the analysis more meaningful and can make a big difference in the quality of the eventual retention plan for each segment.

Retention Objectives

Having identified where your organization is now, you can decide what it should try to achieve in the future; this is the second component of a retention plan: Where do we want to be? Objectives should be achievable and should flow logically from the SWOT analysis. Objectives are important because they are the only mechanism by which the plan's success can be measured. If a plan achieves its stated objectives, you can reasonably conclude that it has been a success. Without them, you can only speculate as to the planner's original intent and the effectiveness of the activities undertaken. Valuable resources (donated by donors!) could be being wasted, but your organization would have no mechanism for identifying that this was the case.

As a minimum, retention objectives should include the following information:

The amount of funds that will be raised

The donor segments that will supply these funds

The acceptable costs of raising these funds

The acceptable attrition level for each donor segment

Objectives can also address changes in the lifetime value of donors (see Chapter Eleven), donor perceptions of service quality, and metrics such as average gift, response rate, and return on investment. For many organizations it may be appropriate to write separate objectives for each donor segment.

Several characteristics of objectives are significant. To be managerially useful, good objectives should be specific, measurable, achievable, relevant, and time-scaled—in a word, SMART!

Specific objectives each cover one particular aspect of fundraising activity or one particular category of donors. Objectives that relate simultaneously to diverse aspects of fundraising are difficult to assess because they may require the organization to use different techniques of measurement and different planning horizons. Combining activities leads to confusion or, at least, to a lack of focus.

Measurable objectives specify quantifiable values. Words such as *maximize* and *increase* are not helpful in assessing the effectiveness of fundraising activity. To be useful, objectives should be able to be measured—for example, "to achieve a 10 percent increase in bequest income."

Achievable objectives are derived from a thorough analysis of the retention audit, not from creative thinking on the part of managers. Objectives that cannot be accomplished demoralize those responsible for their achievement and deplete resources that could potentially have a greater impact elsewhere.

Relevant objectives are consistent with the objectives of the organization as a whole. They should merely supply a greater level of detail than the organizational objectives do, identifying specifically what the fundraising team will have to achieve to provide the nonprofit with the resources it needs to continue to offer the desired services.

Time-scaled objectives clearly specify when they are to be achieved. Not only does knowing this time frame help you plan strategies and tactics, but it also enables the organization to put control procedures in place to ensure that the stated targets will be met. Thus monthly subtargets for each segment of donors can be set, and corrective action can be initiated early, as soon as a variance is detected.

Here are some typical retention objectives that follow these rules.

- To attract $250,000 from existing individual donors by the end of the financial year
- To lower the annual attrition rate to 15 percent by the end of December 2006
- To increase the number of donors "very satisfied" with the quality of service provided by 10 percent by the end of December 2005

Retention Strategy

Having specified the objectives of the plan, you can now address the means by which they will be accomplished. This is the final stage of retention planning: How are we going to get where we want to be? The broad approach is the fundraising strategy, while the fine details are usually referred to as tactics. In the retention context, when fundraisers devise strategies, they need to consider (as a core) three elements: donor segmentation, positioning, and portfolio management.

Donor Segmentation

This section of the plan describes the organization's approach to segmenting its donor base. We described in Chapter Six the form that segmentation might take, and we mapped out a number of alternatives. In writing a retention plan, an organization needs to explain the basis for the form of segmentation that will be used and the number of segments that will be generated.

It is possible for an organization to develop a wide range of quite diverse segments, each with a particular set of needs. But a large number of segments are
likely to become so unwieldy that they are impossible to manage, and all economies of scale in delivery are lost. In short, oversegmentation can cost the organization money. Most organizations find it appropriate to develop somewhere
between eight and twenty segments depending on the size of the giving base.
Small organizations tend to opt for the lower end of this scale, perhaps teasing
out only different donor value categories, different forms of giving, and different
categories of donor interest.

The key lies in selecting enough segments to enable you to meet the needs of
most donors while at the same time keeping the number of segments low enough
to be manageable and profitable. Consider Figure 12.2. When the number of
donor segments is low (point (a)), the return on investment is far below the opti-
mum. Individual donor needs are probably not being met, and donors are being
asked for inappropriate amounts and in inappropriate ways. As the number of
segments rises, individuals find their needs for communication more adequately

FIGURE 12.2. RELATIONSHIP BETWEEN
RETURN ON INVESTMENT AND NUMBER OF DONOR SEGMENTS.

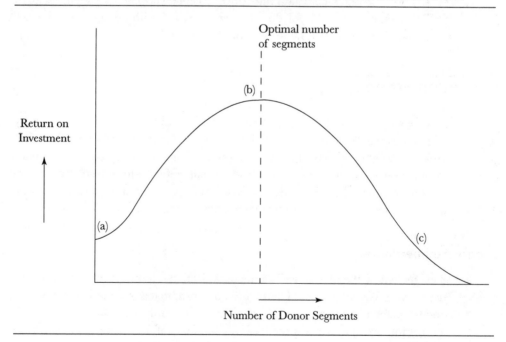

met by the organization, and their levels of satisfaction increase. Individuals can be asked for sums that reflect their interests, their level of wealth, or their previous giving. At this point, the organization is maximizing its return on investment. Finally, as the number of segments increases still further, donors find that the marginal improvement in the quality of service provided doesn't make a big difference to them. The reflection of their needs and interests at point (c) is not much better than it was at point (b), and they are not motivated to exhibit higher degrees of loyalty or to give higher sums. At point (c) also the additional number of segments has added substantially to the cost of communication, and the return on investment has therefore fallen.

Aside from managing this trade-off, the key to retention at this stage is to develop a profile of each donor segment; the profile should include not only giving behavior but also the kind of people the segment contains. Some fundraisers develop word sketches of a typical person in each segment and perhaps even have a photograph of a typical individual to help them think about how best to serve the needs of each segment. These visual representations can be quite powerful.

Positioning Strategy

Having decided how best to segment its donor base, a nonprofit next has to decide how it wishes its donors to view the organization. This step involves much more than building a case for support. The case for support tends to differ from appeal to appeal as the fundraising team develops a detailed explanation of how particular funds will be used. But these cases for support have an underlying theme that reflects the unique nature of the organization's mission. And this generic distinctiveness is at the core of positioning.

Positioning is the act of defining in the minds of the target audience what a particular organization stands for and can offer in comparison with other nonprofits. Positioning indicates to donors the distinctive nature of the work that is being undertaken or the distinctive nature of the benefits that might accrue from being a member or donor. Donors need to know from the outset the nature of the work the organization undertakes and how it is different from the work of other nonprofits they could support. Positioning is a general statement about the organization as a whole; it will later drive the specific cases for support that are created for each segment of donors or, in the case of major donors, for each individual donor. The positioning statement should be reflected in all the communications of the organization.

As an example, consider Figure 12.3. Organizations often represent positioning graphically after conducting research to identify how donors (and other stakeholders) perceive them relative to other organizations. In this hypothetical

FIGURE 12.3. SAMPLE POSITIONING
OF ANIMAL-WELFARE ORGANIZATIONS.

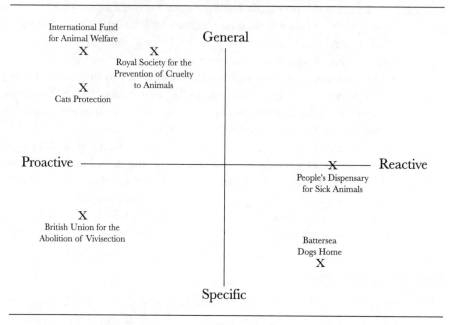

case donors have been asked to indicate the extent to which they view a selection of animal-welfare organizations as being reactive or proactive and general (that is, dealing with all animals) or specific (that is, dealing with a specific animal or group of animals). An average score is calculated for each organization based on the responses; when the scores are plotted on the graph, it is possible to see at a glance how each of the organizations is perceived.

Portfolio Strategy

The final aspect of devising a retention strategy is consideration of both the current portfolio of the organization's fundraising methods and products and the portfolio the organization is prepared to offer in the future. Throughout the audit and the process of segmenting individual donors and devising a positioning strategy, the focus has been on determining donor needs and preferences. This stage of the plan deals with how these needs will be met and the fundraising methods that will be used.

Exhibit 12.3 is a list of fundraising products and methods commonly used in the United States and the United Kingdom. Each product is matched with the

EXHIBIT 12.3. FUNDRAISING PRODUCTS AND AUDIENCES FOR THEM.

Product	Potential Supporter Audience
Adoption schemes (e.g., adopt a dog)	Low-value donors
Sponsorship schemes (e.g., sponsor a child)	Low- and high-value donors
Membership	Service users, low-value donors
Events	Service users, high- and low-value donors, volunteers, activists, lobbyists
Planned-giving rewards	High-value donors
Legacy/bequest clubs	Service users, high- and low-value donors, volunteers, activists, and lobbyers
Friends schemes	Low- and high-value donors
Recognition societies	High-value donors
Monthly-giving clubs	Low-value donors
Activist community	Service users, high- and low-value donors, volunteers, activists, lobbyers
Lobbying community	Service users, high- and low-value donors, volunteers, activists, lobbyers
Research updates	Service users, high- and low-value donors, volunteers, activists, and lobbyers
Newsletters	Service users, high- and low-value donors, volunteers, activists, lobbyers
Service-user group	Service users, high- and low-value donors, volunteers, activists, lobbyers
Merchandise for sale	Service users, low-value donors, volunteers, activists, and lobbyers

supporters who might want it. As can be seen, supporters in each donor segment can be interested in engaging with the organization in many ways. The significance for fundraising, as we established in Chapter Nine, is that donors who can be persuaded to offer their support to the organization in a variety of different ways show higher degrees of loyalty than those who offer their support in only one way. By considering the range of products in the portfolio, the fundraiser can spot opportunities to "sell" donors other methods of engagement and, from their perspective, other benefits.

Organizations need to take a holistic perspective on fundraising products. Donors may be able to interact with the organization in nonfundraising ways, such as through lobbying or volunteering. Although these activities have no direct impact on the bottom line for fundraisers, they can enhance commitment and loyalty, and therefore they offer considerable benefits in the long term.

How should an organization manage its portfolio so that it maintains and develops an appropriate mix of fundraising offers? Here it can be helpful to determine whether each product is internally appropriate and also whether it is attractive to donors. Successful products are both.

In regard to external attractiveness, not all an organization's fundraising products will be equally attractive to donors. Those that are more appealing are more worthy of investment. The degree of attractiveness can also change over time. Although the specific factors that drive how attractive a product might be to donors vary from one organization to another, external attractiveness might depend on some combination of these factors:

The number of potential donors with an interest in the product

The level of general public concern about the issues raised by the product

The perceived impact giving in this particular way will have on the beneficiary group

The uniqueness or novelty of the product

The ease of participation in the product

This list is not exhaustive; organizations can include whatever factors they see as relevant to their own environment and circumstances.

Internal appropriateness is the extent to which the product fits the needs and profile of the organization. In other words, is it appropriate to provide this product given the skills, expertise, organizational structure, and resources available? Relevant factors here might include the following:

The extent of relevant staff expertise

The extent of the organization's past experience with the product

The fundraising returns generated by the product

The availability of volunteers

Once again this list can vary from context to context; an organization should identify those factors that are most pertinent to its particular circumstances.

Having identified the relevant external and internal factors, an organization will not consider them all to have equal importance. For this reason it should weight the factors according to their relative importance. To make this process clear, consider a fictional child-sponsorship product that we will call product A. The method for weighting the factors relevant to external attractiveness is presented in Table 12.1. The weights for the factors should add up to 1. In the example, the key factor driving external attractiveness is the perceived impact on the beneficiary group. This factor therefore receives a relatively high weighting. The issues of novelty and ease of participation are less important and therefore warrant a low weighting.

The next step is to give each product a score from 1 (very poor) to 10 (excellent) based on how it measures up against each of the factors listed. Product A offers a clear benefit to the beneficiary group, so we rate it 10 out of 10 for this factor. The product also scores highly against the level of public concern. But it is available from many other nonprofits and so cannot be considered unique. The rating against this factor is therefore only 2 out of 10. The number of potential donors for the product is not high, and it is not easy to participate in the child-sponsorship activity. The product thus rates only 5 out of 10 against these factors. Multiplying the weights by the ratings produces a value for each factor. Summing these values gives product A an overall score for external attractiveness of 7.3.

The process is identical for internal appropriateness. Each factor is assigned a weight, and each product is given a rating according to its performance in respect to each factor. Once again the ratings range from 1 (very poor) to 10 (excellent). Returning to our analysis of product A, you can see in Table 12.2 that internal appropriateness for this organization is driven largely by staff expertise and the

TABLE 12.1. SAMPLE WEIGHTING OF FACTORS RELEVANT TO EXTERNAL ATTRACTIVENESS.

Factor	Weight	Rating	Value
Level of general public concern about the content of the product	0.2	8	1.6
Number of potential donors	0.2	5	1.0
Perceived impact on the beneficiary group	0.4	10	4.0
Uniqueness or novelty of the product	0.1	2	0.2
Ease of participation in the product	0.1	5	0.5
Total	1.0		7.3

TABLE 12.2. SAMPLE WEIGHTING OF
FACTORS RELEVANT TO INTERNAL APPROPRIATENESS.

Factor	Weight	Rating	Value
Extent of relevant staff expertise	0.4	8	3.2
Extent of the organization's past experience with this product	0.1	5	0.5
Fundraising returns generated by the product	0.4	10	4.0
Availability of volunteers	0.1	7	0.7
Total	1.0		8.4

returns generated. These factors have relatively high weightings. The returns from product A are obviously excellent, and the level of staff/volunteer expertise is also good. Multiplying the weights by the ratings gives us a value for each factor and summing these values generates an overall score of 8.4 for internal appropriateness.

These figures are plotted in Figure 12.4, where the position of product A is clearly indicated. If it is conceptually useful some organizations choose to take the analysis one stage further and draw a circle around the plotted position, the diameter of which is directly proportional to the percentage of fundraising income it generates. Once all the products that the organization provides have been plotted, as in Figure 12.4, managers can see at a glance the relative significance and position of each of the products in their portfolios. Only then can an analysis be undertaken of the health and balance of the portfolio as a whole. Depending on the location of each product in the matrix, the organization can then either invest further in its development, divest itself of the product and use the resources elsewhere, or subject the product to further evaluation if its status is unclear.

Activities falling in the top left-hand corner of the matrix are highly attractive to their respective audiences, and the organization is well placed to deliver them. These are clear candidates for continuing development. Activities falling in the bottom right-hand corner, however, can be causing an unnecessary drain on resources. They are not seen as attractive by the target donors, and the organization has no particular skill in delivering them. Activities in this area of the matrix should be scrutinized with a view to termination or divestment. In this case, the analysis has yielded considerable insight into the potential for valuable resources to be conserved and perhaps put to other, more appropriate, uses. Activities falling elsewhere in the matrix should be carefully evaluated as they are only moderately appropriate for the organization to provide and they have only limited external attractiveness.

FIGURE 12.4. SAMPLE PORTFOLIO MATRIX.

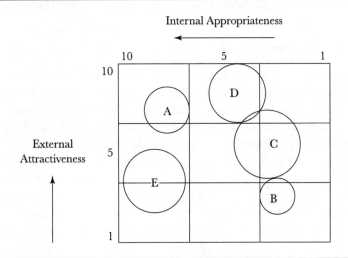

The Relationship Mix

Next, you need to take each segment of donors in turn and determine the nature of the relationship your organization wishes to have with each. This relationship mix has several elements: consideration of donor choices, donor development, service quality provided, the case for support presented, media selected, and donor feedback and recognition.

Choice

Development of the relationship mix begins by defining the range of choices that will be offered to each donor segment. The choices have to be realistic and (as we noted previously) should not add inappropriately to the cost of managing a particular group of individuals. Choice therefore has to be carefully managed. A nonprofit needs to be sure from the beginning that sufficient donors will prefer a particular option to make offering it viable and sustainable; few developments will antagonize a body of donors as much as having a favored option removed. For most nonprofits it will be appropriate to offer donors some choice of the timing, content, and nature of the communications they receive. They may also be given choices of the form that their support might take and (in keeping with the portfolio strategy we described above) be given opportunities to engage with the organization in a variety of different ways. At this point in the plan a description of the choices available to a particular segment should be outlined.

Donor Development: The Journey

A further major ingredient in a relationship fundraising strategy is consideration of how each relationship will develop over time, what the journey that the donor and the organization take together will be like. Nonprofits need to understand the starting point for each segment of donors: the level of knowledge or interest they have when they are recruited. The fundraising team then needs to determine how they intend to shape that knowledge or interest over time. It is essential that donor development reflect donor preferences, but it should also reflect the nature of the cause and the mission of the organization. Any messages that the organization wishes the donor to receive can be integrated into communications as the relationship develops. During the journey donors may also switch to (or add) other forms of giving and other forms of engagement with the nonprofit. Indeed, the ultimate goal for the organization may be to have the donor offer a bequest. Whatever the case, the organization needs to plan the journey that it intends to take each segment of donors on as they develop their relationship with the organization. This should not be allowed to happen by default as appeal after appeal is produced. The journey should be coherent and carefully planned from the start.

Once the nature of the journey has been defined, a discrete set of communications should be drafted for each segment of donors. This set should contain all the communications every department within the nonprofit intends to send over the duration of the plan. A schedule for sending them should also be included. This schedule often takes the form of a Gantt chart (an example is provided in Exhibit 12.4). The point is to manage the volume, timing, and nature of the communications that the organization as a whole sends to each donor. This pattern of communication should represent a coherent whole. It should also re-

EXHIBIT 12.4. SAMPLE GANTT CHART: COMMUNICATIONS PLAN FOR MONTHLY GIVERS.

	Jan.	Feb.	Mar.	Apr.	May	June	July	Aug.	Sept.	Oct.	Nov.	Dec.
Newsletter	X			X			X					X
Additional Appeals					X							X
Telephone Upgrade								X				
Trading Catalogue									X			

semble an ongoing dialogue with a friend that develops genuinely over time, not a disparate set of unrelated materials.

Service Quality

Donors differ in their value and potential value to an organization, and thus a primary decision for fundraisers is determining the appropriate level of investment to make in each donor segment. The team should also try to reflect the value of donors in the pattern and form of communications donors receive, and they should also ensure that they provide the highest possible quality of service to the highest-value supporters. Planning the quality of service, using the techniques we outlined in Chapter Nine, therefore also needs to be undertaken by segment.

Case for Support

You also need to develop an appropriate case for support for each segment. This case will vary to some degree with the nature of each appeal. And because segments include distinctive kinds of people with distinctive interests, the case for support may also vary from segment to segment.

Media

Decisions also need to be made about the media that will be used to contact each group. Most segments have a favored medium that they like and are comfortable responding to. Media strategy should therefore be based on donor choice. It will increasingly involve the use of e-mail as organizations use new technology to cut the costs associated with printing and postage.

Feedback and Recognition

Finally, you need to devise a process for feedback and choose any rewards or incentives that will be offered. As we discussed in Chapter Ten, recognition should reflect donor needs and interests but also should be based on gift levels and ideally should offer some incentive for donors to upgrade either their giving or their commitment to the organization (for example, by pledging a bequest).

Budget

Having detailed the steps that will be necessary to achieve the fundraising objectives, you should then be in a position to cost out the various proposals and to set up an overall fundraising budget for the planning period. This is the optimal approach. In reality costs will have been on the minds of fundraising planners even before they commenced the audit. At the least the development of a budget is likely in practice to be an iterative process, with proposals constantly being reevaluated in the light of budgetary constraints.

A fundraising budget can be constructed in a variety of ways. The ideal is to specify the strategy and tactics that are necessary to achieve the fundraising objectives and then to cost these out. This is often referred to as the task method. In practice this method is seldom employed because financial pressures from senior management, the budget and accounting practices of the organization, and uncertainty all hamper the process. Therefore, budgets tend to be set by the following methods:

A percentage of the previous year's donations can be set aside to fund the following year's fundraising activity. Although easy to calculate, this approach has two drawbacks. First, the amount allocated may bear no resemblance to the cost of raising the funds needed for the coming year's operations. Second, setting the budget in this way can lower fundraising spending when income levels fall, but in these circumstances one can argue that organizations should be investing in new forms of income generation to secure their long-term future.

A percentage of projected donations can be allotted to fundraising. This approach eliminates the weaknesses mentioned above but requires great care in the calculation of an appropriate percentage. Different fundraising techniques vary widely in the returns they are capable of generating, and an aggregate percentage allocation can therefore be too simplistic.

The fundraising budget can match that of a competitor. A nonprofit that carefully chooses a competitor against which to benchmark can often come up with a ballpark figure, but this approach again fails to take account of the nonprofit's own objectives and need for funds, which can be quite different from those of the competitor.

The fundraising allocation can be the amount the senior management thinks it can afford. This is perhaps the least rational of all the methods of budgeting. Once again, little or no reference is made to the fundraising objectives.

For organizations serious about donor retention, spending an amount appropriate to the stated objectives is the best and only approach. Fundraisers also need to achieve an effective balance between acquisition and development spending. In many nonprofits expenditures are split 60–40 or even 70–30 in favor of acquisition. This amount is far too high. Although some donor-acquisition activities are necessary to increase the donor base and to replace those who die or move away, it is cheaper and easier to focus on the retention of existing givers than to seek additional new donors. The balance of these two activities in the fundraising budget should thus reflect this fact.

Scheduling

At this point, a large number of tactics will have been specified in the main body of the plan. To ensure that these are executed in a coordinated fashion over the duration of the plan, a schedule should be established that specifies when each activity will take place. If the responsibilities for various fundraising activities are split among different groups of staff, the schedule is an important coordination mechanism. Indeed, if tasks are split in this way, the schedule should specify the individual or group responsible for each activity.

Monitoring and Control

As soon as the plan has been agreed on, fundraising management takes responsibility for monitoring the progress of the organization toward the goals specified. Managers also concern themselves with the costs incurred at each stage of implementation and monitor these against budget. Control mechanisms should be put in place to monitor:

The donations collected against the budget

The costs incurred against the budget

The performance of specific fundraising activities

The appropriateness of the strategies and tactics adopted

The reported attrition rates against the targets set

For financial objectives, such as revenue and cost projections, the aggregate target for a given year can be broken down into monthly targets, perhaps for each form of fundraising undertaken, each donor segment, and so on. These objectives should also stipulate how much variation from these monthly subtargets will be tolerated before an alarm is raised. When performance falls below the permissible level, the matter can be brought to the attention of the fundraising managers, who then have the opportunity to instigate some form of corrective action.

Summary

In this chapter we have described a process that can be used by fundraisers to plan donor-retention activities. In so doing we have provided a framework for drawing together many of the strategies and tactics that we have proposed in this book for enhancing donor loyalty. A retention plan, like other plans, answers three key questions: Where are we now? Where do we want to be? How will we get there? We hope that you will find many of the tools and models we describe to be of value in enhancing donor retention in your own organization. Blank versions of the sample forms in this chapter are available for your use on this book's website in the Wiley on-line catalogue. Above all, we hope that this framework will help you to develop high-quality, memorable, and effective fundraising strategies that will keep donors loyal to your organization for many years.

CONCLUSION

A Call to Action

If you have read this book from cover to cover, you will appreciate the many ways in which fundraisers can build donor loyalty to their organizations. Because control over many of these methods is not vested in one individual, to achieve marked increases in loyalty the fundraising department and the organization as a whole must be involved in and committed to making changes.

The starting point usually is making a strong case for achieving change. Few organizations invest in the development of the fundraising function unless a good argument is presented for the time and funds needed. In setting out why your organization should develop a focus on retention, you need to do the calculations we outlined in Chapter One. What would the impact be for your nonprofit of achieving a 1, 2, 5, or 10 percent increase in donor loyalty? In running these calculations, be sure to factor in all the advantages of having loyal donors (such as additional gifts and engagement with the organization in multiple ways). Ask for help from the whole communications team in developing estimates of how donors exhibiting greater loyalty might behave. If the team has been involved in developing the assumptions, they are unlikely to disagree with the results you produce. It is important to explain in detail how the figures have been reached because they will initially make for shocking reading, and many people will be skeptical. To make your presentation easy to follow, start with the current amount of the donations to your nonprofit; next calculate the amounts that would result from retaining an increased number of donors; then add in the reduced costs of acquisition and all the additional value that increasingly loyal donors might generate.

In the commercial sector many organizations now run these calculations routinely, and staff at all levels, no matter what their role in the organization, know just what difference a 1 or a 5 percent increase in loyalty (in their case, customer loyalty) can make. In a nonprofit all staff and volunteers should also know the impact that small increases in loyalty can have on the bottom line and understand the role that they might play, however small, in achieving those increases.

Making the case for enhancing loyalty is always easiest when talking to fellow fundraisers. It is often more difficult to secure the buy-in of the board or the trustees who run the organization. It costs money to achieve increases in loyalty, and because the benefits are evident only in the medium term, many nonprofits prefer to invest in fundraising techniques they know will deliver—now. They are also under pressure to focus on program expenditures, and in the present climate, where costs are increasingly subject to external scrutiny, they feel a need to achieve "acceptable" fundraising cost ratios. To make the case at the board level requires the support of senior fundraising management and almost always a champion on the board prepared to argue the case.

We have stressed throughout this book the diverse methods by which loyalty can be enhanced; many of these methods fall under the umbrella term *service quality*. Making changes to the service provided to donors requires the whole organization to accept the need for change, not just the board. All staff and volunteers need to understand the difference they can make in enhancing loyalty. Front-line staff are best placed to identify a concrete series of procedural and even attitudinal changes that can be made. After changes are implemented, it is important to provide ongoing feedback so that everyone involved is aware of the difference she or he has made and is motivated to do even better in the future.

Our experience with this process suggests that it is important to begin with changes that produce quick, easy wins. Of the many ways that donor loyalty could be enhanced, the fundraising team should place the highest priority on those likely to have the greatest impact. If staff members can be persuaded to adopt a few changes and can see tangible results, they will be much more likely to accept the need for the more pervasive changes that perhaps will yield results only in the long term.

We have suggested a number of new fundraising programs, aside from enhancing service quality, that can improve donor loyalty. Fundraising products and monthly-giving programs are both ideas that are worth considering. Developing such programs may involve a step change in how the organization conducts its fundraising and some lessening of expectations about initial profitability. The benefits may become obvious only in the second and subsequent years. In addition, these products and programs cannot be designed overnight. It is necessary to talk to existing and potential donors about how their needs might be met through these programs and to consider many of the issues we referred to in Chapter Three. In general, the planning framework we present in Chapter Twelve should be of value to fundraisers who want to increase the loyalty of their donors; it discusses and summarizes many of the issues raised in other parts of the book.

Throughout the book we have deliberately looked at retention from the perspective of the fundraiser and have concentrated on the benefits and advantages to nonprofit organizations of increasing donor loyalty. But there is another perspective. We hope that the donors who give to us enjoy their philanthropy and take pleasure in the contact they have with the organizations they support. We know that the sense of enjoyment and personal fulfillment that comes through giving is greatly enhanced in committed and long-term relationships. Encouraging donors to stay loyal to a cause, to learn about what is accomplished over time, and to share in a developing mission is important for the finances of the organizations we work for, and it is also the kind of relationship the donors themselves would choose.

REFERENCES

Adler, A. B., Wright, B. A., and Ulicny, G. R. "Fundraising Portrayals of People with Disabilities: Donations and Attitudes." *Rehabilitation Psychology,* 1991, *36*(4), 231–240.

American Association of Fundraising Counsel (AAFRC) Trust. *Giving USA.* Indianapolis, In.: AAFRC Trust for Philanthropy, 2003.

Auten, G. E., Sieg, H., and Clotfelter, C. T. "Charitable Giving, Income and Taxes: An Analysis of Panel Data." *American Economic Review,* 2002, *92*(1), 371–382.

Batson, C. D. "How Social an Animal? The Human Capacity for Caring." *American Psychologist,* 1990, *45*, 336–346.

Bendapudi, N., and Singh, S. N. "Enhancing Helping Behavior: An Integrative Framework for Promotion Planning." *Journal of Marketing,* 1996, *60*(3), 33–54.

Bitran, G., and Mondschein, S. "A Comparative Analysis of Decision Making Procedures in the Catalog Sales Industry." *European Management Journal,* 1997, *15*(2), 105–116.

Braus, P. "Will Boomers Give Generously?" American Demographics, 1994, *16*(7), 48–52, 57.

Brehm, J. W. *A Theory of Psychological Reactance.* Orlando, Fla.: Academic Press, 1966.

Brolley, D. Y., and Anderson, S. C. "Advertising and Attitudes." *Rehabilitation Digest,* 1986, *17*, 15–17.

Burnett, K. *Relationship Fundraising.* San Francisco: Jossey-Bass, 2002.

Carpenter, P. "Customer Lifetime Value: Do the Math." *Marketing Computers,* Jan. 1995, pp. 18–19.

Chierco, S., Rosa, C., and Kayson, W. A. "Effects of Location Appearance and Monetary Value on Altruistic Behaviour." *Psychological Reports,* 1982, *51*, 199–202.

Chisnall, P. M. *Marketing Research.* New York: McGraw-Hill, 1996.

Churchill, G. A. *Basic Marketing Research.* New York: Thomson Learning, 2000.

Clark, R. D., and Word, L. E. "Why Don't Bystanders Help? Because of Ambiguity?" *Journal of Personality and Social Psychology,* 1972, *24*, 392–400.

Clary, E. G., and Snyder, M. "A Functional Analysis of Altruism and Prosocial Behaviour: The Case of Volunteerism." In *Review of Personality and Social Psychology*, Vol. 12. Thousand Oaks, Calif.: Sage,1991.

Clotfelter, C. T. *Federal Tax Policy and Charitabe Giving.* Chicago, Chicago University Press, 1985.

Darby, M. R., and Karni, E. "Free Competition and the Optimal Amount of Fraud." *Journal of Law and Economics,* Apr. 1973, pp. 67–86.

Davis, M. H., Hull, J. G., Young, R. D., and Warren, G. G. "Emotional Reactions to Dramatic Film Stimuli: The Influence of Cognitive and Emotional Empathy." *Journal of Personality and Social Psychology,* 1987, *52*(1), 126–133.

Dowd, J. J. *Stratification of the Aged.* Pacific Grove, Calif.: Brooks/Cole, 1975.

Eayrs, C. B., and Ellis, N. "Charity Advertising: For or Against People with a Mental Handicap?" *British Journal of Social Psychology,* 1990, *29*, 349–360.

Eisenberg, N., and Miller, P. A. "The Relation of Empathy to Prosocial and Related Behaviours." *Psychological Bulletin,* 1987, *101*, 91–119.

Elliot, T. R., and Byrd, E. K. "Media and Disability." *Rehabilitation Literature,* 1982, *43*, 348–355.

Feinman, S. "When Does Sex Affect Altruistic Behaviour?" *Psychological Reports,* 1978, *43*, 12–18.

Feldman, D., and Feldman, B. "The Effect of a Telethon on Attitudes Toward Disabled People and Financial Contributions." *Journal of Rehabilitation,* 1985, *51*, 42–45.

Festinger, L. "A Theory of Social Comparison Processes." *Human Relations,* 1954, *7*, 117–140.

Fultz, J. C., and others. "Social Evaluation and the Empathy Altruism Hypothesis." *Journal of Personality and Social Psychology,* 1986, *50*, 761–769.

Geer, J. H., and Jermecky, L. "The Effect of Being Responsible for Reducing Others' Pain on Subjects' Response and Arousal." *Journal of Personality and Social Psychology,* 1973, *27*, 100–108.

Glaser, J. S. *The United Way Scandal—An Insider's Account of What Went Wrong and Why.* New York: Wiley, 1994.

Gruder, C. L., and Cook, T. D. "Sex, Dependency and Helping." *Journal of Personality and Social Psychology,* 1971, *19*, 290–294.

Harris, R. M. "The Effect of Perspective Taking, Similarity and Dependency on Raising Funds for Persons with Disabilities." Unpublished master's thesis, University of Kansas, 1975.

Harvey, J. W., and McCrohan, K. F. "Fundraising Costs—Societal Implications for Philanthropies and Their Supporters." *Business and Society,* 1988, *27*(1), 15–22.

Harvey, T. "Service Quality: The Culprit and the Cure." *Bank Marketing,* June 1995, pp. 24–28.

Hogg, M. A., and Abrams, D. *Special Identifications: A Social Psychology of Intergroup Relations and Group Processes.* New York: Routledge, 1988.

Jay, E. "The Rise (and Fall?) of Face to Face Fundraising in the United Kingdom." *New Directions for Philanthropic Fundraising,* 2002, *33*(Fall), 83–94.

Jones, T. O., and Sasser, W. E. "Why Satisfied Customers Defect." *Harvard Business Review,* Nov./Dec. 1995, pp. 88–99.

Kotler, P. *Marketing Management: Analysis, Planning, Implementation and Control.* (8th ed.) Upper Saddle River, N.J.: Prentice Hall, 1991.

Kotler, P., and Andreasen, A. *Strategic Marketing for Nonprofit Organizations.* Upper Saddle River, N.J.: Prentice Hall, 1996.

Latane, B., and Nida, S. "Ten Years of Research on Group Size and Helping." *Psychological Bulletin*, 1981, *89*(2), 308–324.

Levitt, T. "Marketing Intangible Products and Product Intangibles." *Harvard Business Review*, May-June 1981, 94–102.

Lewis, B. "Quality in the Service Sector: A Review." *International Journal of Bank Marketing*, 1989, *7*(5), 4–12.

Lindahl, W. E., and Winship, C. "Predictive Models for Annual Fundraising and Major Gift Fundraising." *Nonprofit Management and Leadership*, 1992, *3*(1), 43–64.

Marx, J. D. "Women and Human Services Giving." *Social Work*, 2000, *45*(1), 22–34.

McKinnon, H. *Hidden Gold: How Monthly Giving Will Build Donor Loyalty, Boost Your Organization's Income, and Increase Financial Stability.* Chicago: Bonus Books, 1999.

Miller, D. T. "Altruism and Threat to a Belief in a Just World." *Journal of Experimental Psychology*, 1977, *13*, 113–124.

Mount, J., and Quirion, F. "A Study of Donors to a University Campaign." *The Philanthropist*, 1988, *8*(1), 56–64.

Nelson, P. "Advertising as Information." *Journal of Political Economy*, 1974, *81*, 729–754.

Ovretveit, J. A. "Towards Market Focused Measures of Customer/Purchaser Perceptions of Service." *Quality Forum*, 1992, *18*(1), 21–24.

Parasuraman, A., Zeithaml, V. A., and Berry, L. L. "SERVQUAL: A Multiple Item Scale for Measuring Customer Perceptions of Service Quality." *Journal of Retailing*, 1988, *64*(1), 12–40.

Peppers, D., and Rogers, M. "A New Marketing Paradigm: Share of Customer, Not Market Share." *Managing Service Quality*, 1995, *5*(3), 48–51.

Peters, T. J. *Thriving on Chaos: Handbook for a Management Revolution.* New York: HarperCollins, 1987.

Pharoah, C., and Tanner, S. "Trends in Charitable Giving." *Fiscal Studies*, 1997, *18*(4), 427–443.

Piliavin, I. M., Piliavin, J. A., and Rodin, J. "Costs of Diffusion and the Stigmatised Victim." *Journal of Personality and Social Psychology*, 1975, *32*, 429–438.

Reichheld, F. F. *The Loyalty Effect.* Boston: Harvard Business School Press, 1994.

Reichheld, F. F. *The Loyalty Effect: The Hidden Force Behind Growth, Profits and Lasting Value.* Boston: Harvard Business School Press, 2000.

Reichheld, F. F., and Sasser, W. E. "Zero Defections: Quality Comes to Services." *Harvard Business Review*, Sept.–Oct. 1990, pp. 105–111.

Reingen, P. H. "On Inducing Compliance with Requests." *Journal of Consumer Research*, 1978, *5*, 96–102.

Sargeant, A. "Donor Lifetime Value: An Empirical Analysis." *Journal of Nonprofit and Voluntary Sector Marketing*, 1998, *3*(4), 283–297.

Sargeant, A. "Charity Giving: Towards a Model of Donor Behaviour." *Journal of Marketing Management*, 1999, *15*, 215–238.

Sargeant, A. "How to Keep Donors Loyal." Presentation to the National Society of Fundraising Executives annual conference, New Orleans, Mar. 2000.

Sargeant, A. "Relationship Fundraising: How to Keep Donors Loyal." *Nonprofit Management and Leadership*, 2001, *12*(2), 177–192.

Sargeant, A. *Marketing Management for Nonprofit Organizations.* (2nd ed.) Oxford: Oxford University Press, 2004.

Sargeant, A., and Lee, S. "Benchmarking the Performance of UK Charities." Benchmarking Conference, Horwarth Clark Whitehill, London, June 2003.

Sargeant, A., and McKenzie, J. *A Lifetime of Giving: An Analysis of Donor Lifetime Value.* West Malling, U.K.: Charities Aid Foundation, 1998.

Sargeant, A., and West, D. *Direct and Interactive Marketing.* Oxford: Oxford University Press, 2001.

Sargeant, A., and Wymer, W. "Understanding Giving: a New Framework for Conceptualizing Donor Behaviour." Working paper, February 2004, University of the West of England.

Schervish, P. G., and Havens, J. J. "Social Participation and Charitable Giving: A Multivariate Analysis." *Voluntas,* 1997, *8*(3), 235–260.

Schwartz, B. "The Social Psychology of the Gift." *American Journal of Sociology,* 1967, *73*(1), 1–11.

Shelton, M. L., and Rogers, R. W. "Fear Arousing and Empathy Arousing Appeals to Help: The Pathos of Persuasion." *Journal of Applied Psychology,* 1981, *11*(4), 366–378.

Shurka, E., Siller, J., and Dvonch, P. "Coping Behaviour and Personal Responsibility as Factors in the Perception of Disabled Persons by the Non Disabled." *Rehabilitation Psychology,* 1982, *27*, 225–233.

Thompson, G. "Charities Disappoint." *Third Sector,* May 1998, p. 4.

Tybout, A. M., and Yalch, R. F. "The Effect of Experience: A Matter of Salience?" *Journal of Consumer Research,* 1980, *6*, 406–413.

Wagner, C., and Wheeler, L. "Model Need and Cost Effects in Helping Behaviour." *Journal of Personality and Social Psychology,* 1969, *12*, 111–116.

Warwick, M. *Raising Money by Mail: Strategies for Growth and Financial Stability.* Berkeley, Calif.: Strathmoor Press, 1994.

Wilson, R.M.S., Gilligan, C., and Pearson, D. J. *Strategic Marketing Management.* Oxford, U.K.: Butterworth-Heinemann, 1992.

Zeithaml, V. A., and Bitner, M. J. *Services Marketing.* New York: McGraw-Hill, 1996.

INDEX